Make Me One with Everything

BUDDHIST MEDITATIONS
TO AWAKEN FROM THE ILLUSION
OF SEPARATION

Lama Surya Das

SOUNDS TRUE
BOULDER, COLORADO

Sounds True
Boulder, CO 80306

Cover design by Rachael Murray
Book design by Beth Skelley

Printed in the United States of America

Library of Congress Cataloging-in-Publication Data
Surya Das, Lama, 1950- author.
Make me one with everything : Buddhist meditations to awaken
from the illusion of separation / Lama Surya Das.
        pages cm
Includes bibliographical references.
ISBN 978-1-62203-412-3
1. Buddhist meditations. 2. Meditation—Buddhism. I. Title.
BQ5572.S87 2015
294.3'4435—dc23
                          2014046084

Ebook ISBN 978-1-62203-454-3

10 9 8 7 6 5 4 3 2 1

The whole universe is my body, all beings my mind.

From *The Vajrayogini Tantra*

Contents

Make Me One with Everything

What did the Dalai Lama say to the hot dog vendor?
"Make me one with everything."

It's a joke—and a pretty good one—but there's more to it than that. Becoming one with everything by seeing through separateness and solidity is the heart of what I call *inter-meditation*. Inter-meditation means meditating *with*—the practice and art of intimacy and union with whatever is, just as it is. It is the yoga of convergence, connection, co-meditation, and spontaneous oneness. It's a path we can take to overcome our illusions of duality.

A recent encounter with a Tibetan Buddhist teacher illustrated to me the incredible value of inter-meditation in our disconnected, plugged in yet tuned-out times. I was at a retreat in Carmel, California, with Tibetan master Anam Thubten Rinpoche. During one of his talks, a woman in the audience asked him a searing question: What should I do with the great fear I experience? For several months, she had noticed that the medication for her bipolar disorder was no longer effective. Her doctors confirmed that this was the case and that Western medicine likely had nothing more to offer her. She had been in therapy on and off for many years, and more recently had tried all manner of alternative approaches, but her mood swings were increasing in frequency as well as becoming more intense.

The woman spoke to Rinpoche about her terrible uncertainty for her sanity, and after a few words he invited her to come close and sit facing him. By the time she had shared all she needed to, her eyes were full of tears. Rinpoche remained silent for a minute or two, and then he quietly said, "Your suffering is mine. Your fear is mine." Many of us gasped at the exquisite beauty of his response. And there were tears in his eyes as well as he added, "You are not alone."

The woman and Rinpoche meditated together for a few more minutes and then he asked, "What do you feel?"

"Love. Great love, but after all, it's *you*."

He replied, "No, the love is *you*—your seeing and knowing what's inside of you."

For me, their exchange beautifully represents what it means to be in the present moment, connecting to another and allowing all-encompassing compassion and surrender to flow back and forth with no boundaries—inter-meditation. My Buddhist Dzogchen lineage would call this the Natural Great Perfection in action. It is a living example of healing and awakening together, and shows us that love does not come from outside of us, not really. Love comes from *loving*. Love is self-perpetuating. Love is a verb. Infinite love is both enlightenment and our birthright.

One of my most powerful encounters with inter-meditation occurred during the 1980s, when I lived for three and a half years in cloistered retreat at the Nyingmapa Tibetan center in the forest of Dordogne, France. My fellow students and I spent most of our days in individual monastic cells, where we meditated and maintained silence at all times except when we gathered for chanting, liturgical rituals, and teachings before breakfast and at dusk. One afternoon, our beloved teacher, Lama Nyoshul Khenpo Rinpoche, summoned all twenty-three of us to the hermitage's meditation hall for a lesson.

Typically we sat on cushions in parallel rows like warm-hearted ice cubes lined up in a tray, but on this occasion Khenpo Rinpoche asked us to sit knee-to-knee, very close together, almost overlapping as we chanted in unison.

"See how that is . . . and feels . . . Notice intently how it goes," he instructed.

This was no small challenge. Imagine, after months of celibacy and solitude, a group of monks and nuns—all friends and comrades—suddenly sitting in such intimate proximity, with nowhere to run and hide, no opportunity to employ personality tricks or defense mechanisms or holier-than-thou airs, no way to avoid the presence of the people in front of and around us. Any and all of our movements were exposed, as if we were naked and vulnerable, in kinship with all.

Time passed in a far more agonizing fashion than when I'd sat in solitude waiting for the gong to signal the end of the meditation period, and far more slowly than any time I'd watched a teakettle and waited for the water to boil, or looked forward to a holiday that was months away. The seconds and minutes ticked by in pure, clear silence. I could only hear the sound of breathing and my pulse beating so thunderously that I was convinced that everyone else could hear it, too.

I have no idea how much time went by. Time is plastic, malleable, subject to the vagaries of mind and body, energy, and space. At last our venerable meditation master said, "Now close your eyes, and tune in. Pay attention. Listen. Feel. Intuit.

Observe sensations in the body and whatever momentarily arises in the field of consciousness. Let go and relax, and let be. As it is. Nothing more to do, understand, or accomplish. Not meditating, not manipulating or altering, not interfering or fabricating anything. Just breathing and awareness, open, spacious, relaxed, and clear."

We sat like that for a while. Stillness reigned, except of course in my head. I fretted about *samsara*—the ordinary worldly realm of conditioned existence, suffering, and confusion. What was causing my feelings of existential angst and imprisonment when I was merely sitting still and had no other problems or responsibilities? *My wild, untamed, distracted monkey-mind!*

Then Khenpo Rinpoche asked us to open our eyes and continue to meditate. I became intensely aware that a wonderful woman was touching one of my knees, or should I say that I was touching hers? (With my consciousness, that is, as well as my knee.) This contact inspired further thoughts and fantasies—I just couldn't silence that monkey-mind.

Khenpo Rinpoche broke my reverie by saying, "Now close your eyes again, and start breathing together, in sync. In-breath . . . out-breath. Inhaling slowly, exhaling slowly. Not deep breathing or breath retention, just natural, normal in-breath . . . out-breath." He didn't want us to give the in-breath any more attention or weight than the out-breath—they were the same. "In-breath . . . out-breath. Observe the gentle wind, the settling tides of ordinary breath. Observe, vigilantly. Pay attention with careful alert presence of mind. Allow clarity to emerge from within."

So I inhaled and exhaled and inhaled and my breath took on a lovely rhythm, like a gentle waltz. In-breath, out-breath, with nothing in between—*flow*. Gradually I noticed we were all breathing together effortlessly, naturally, as a group and almost in unison. Palpable energy emanated from my solar plexus, out and in, radially, as if expanding and contracting on the subtle *pranic,* or energetic, level. It felt as if I were a cosmic balloon or bellows operated by powers beyond myself, perhaps Higher Powers, perhaps deeper. I felt infinitely large and full, then infinitely small and deflated. My bifurcating mind and discursive conceptual thinking blended into what was, just as it was.

Everything, including time and mind, seemed to stop. *I was limitless.* The sacred space of the meditation room seemed far greater inside than outside. Was this the legendary crystal cathedral of the shining Void? The divine candle in a hidden niche of the pearl mosque of which the mystics sing?

At some point, with a few pithy instructions, Khenpo Rinpoche guided us deeper and further into contemplation, incandescent presence, bliss, and spacious clarity. All separate parts merged—like mother and child—in the light of reality, groundless and boundless. He urged, "Enjoy the natural state of pure being, incandescence, now-ness—or whatever state you think you're in. This will have to do. *Emaho!* Be here! Wondrous!"

After that moment, nothing was as it had been before. There were no longer beings in the room, or a human being sitting in my seat, but simply naked *being* itself. I experienced what was meant by the Surangama Sutra: *Things are not what they seem; nor are they otherwise.* It felt as if I'd entered a dream, a mirage, or maybe a movie directed from Above. This was genuine inter-meditation: *shared spirituality beyond the polarities and dichotomies of self and other.*

I wanted to continue in that blessed state of utter transcendence. However, every experience, just like every dream or song or childhood, has its end. The bronze gong rang, signaling the completion of the session. I noticed that the habitual framework of forms and sights—of others and myself as separate and distinct entities—began to re-emerge, coalesce, and eventually make sense. I realized that I was still just sitting there. Questions came to mind: What should I do now that the meditation had been completed . . . *or had it?* Why should it ever end, this primordial purity beyond the contrariety of perfect and imperfect? Could I inter-meditate with everything? Why not?

I was almost back where I'd begun, but not quite. Somehow "I" was actually able to breathe, smile, appreciate my friends and fellows in front of and around me, and even stand up and walk out of the meditation hall on my own two feet. Could I speak? We continued our silent retreat, so I would not find out for days.

Outside, the sun shined on. I heard the wind in the beech trees. I strolled around the courtyard a couple of times to get my land legs, and then returned to my little bare monk's cell with its three-year growth of grapevine curling up and over and around the door, and wooden latticework overhead to keep out the rain. Everything seemed just as I'd left it, although I couldn't be entirely sure. *Once upon a time "I" was no more.* Now I had to live as if it were true.

Some weeks later, when I told Khenpo Rinpoche about my realization, he laughed and laughed. "Good dream!" was all he would say. In response to my quizzical expression and obvious wish for more, he added, kindly, "American boy, very nice, good. Now drink tea."

You don't have to spend years in silent retreat or even give up your day job to inter-meditate. I no longer lead a very monastic life, but every hour of every day I apply and live what I learned at that glorious monastery where just listening to rain on the roof in that sylvan glade was meditatively delightful.

Now drink tea. Order a hot dog, and make it one with everything. Because if we can't find enlightenment, freedom, autonomy, divinity, and bliss amid every nitty-gritty detail of life, then all the rituals, sacraments, prayers, chants, yoga *asanas,* gurus, and pilgrimages in the world are useless.

Breathing in: relaxing, letting go, centering.
Breathing out: calm and clear,
feeling is healing, opening.

Introduction

Awakening Together through Inter-Meditation

I f you've ever felt truly "one" with something—your beloved in the throes of intimacy, nature as you inhaled the perfume and silence of a pine forest after a snowstorm, your child as you watched her sleep, or victims of an earthquake in a country you've never visited—you've experienced inter-meditation. If you've ever looked into the eyes of your dying father and known the exact moment his spirit departed, wept because a friend was grieving, or felt overwhelmed with love for a pet—you've experienced inter-meditation. Inter-meditating means meditating with "other"; it's an intentional connection in order to realize non-duality. This subtle transpersonal intimacy and integrity are the Two I's of our best life, far beyond the small i of egotism and selfishness. How we can sustain both this connection and intent is the subject of this book. Once you do it, it's like learning how to swim—you won't know how to *not* do it.

Through inter-meditation, we ultimately go beyond the experience of separation; we realize that there is no essential difference between inward and outward, us and them, yin and yang. It takes two complementary parts to make a whole—like bowing down and rising up, or breathing in and out.

We're used to thinking of meditation as turning inward and intentionally applying ourselves to *achieving* something with our minds: mindfulness and introspection, the dissolution of obstacles through self-inquiry, or moments of peace through concentration, contemplation, and self-emptying. But inter-meditation is the other half of meditation—it's inclusive, *not* just letting go, but letting come *and* go. As it is. Letting be. Not trying to get rid of stuff, but recognizing that stuff and being at ease and even intimate with it.

Inter-meditation provides many methods for closing the gaps between self and others, allowing us to see through the illusory veils of separation. It transports us beyond the individual—the "small self"—into the universal—the "Big Self"—obliterating the borders between the two. This boundary-less, shared spirituality takes us into the infinite space and buoyancy of the transpersonal—what my old friend, the Venerable Thich Nhat Hanh, has termed *interbeing*.

To understand both the Big Self and the small self simultaneously is to see beyond the limits of our egos and recognize that there is no separation between us and the rest of the cosmos—the entire population of the earth, the microbes in our digestive systems, the stars in galaxies we can't even imagine. In the Indian epic the Ramayana, Hanuman, the monkey god embodying selfless devotion to a higher purpose, says, "When I forget who I am, I serve God. When I remember who I am, I am God." This is how our small selves are part of our Big Selves. And it's the essence of the spiritual path, the ongoing dialogue between our human and Divine nature.

When we learn to mindfully practice inter-meditation, employing techniques and exercises like the ones in this book, we deepen our relationships and connections to one another in a microcosmic and macrocosmic, subatomic and universal way. Although inter-meditation can happen spontaneously and does indeed occur naturally throughout our lives, it is extraordinarily beneficial to be aware of it. Conscious inter-meditation has helped me more than almost any other spiritual exercise. The day-to-day effects of breaking through the imagined walls between our small self and Big Self—outer and inner, I and Thou, here and there, the wanted and unwanted—vanquish fear and anxiety as they arise and allow us to embrace life genuinely, unhesitatingly, with fervor and delight. Inter-meditation helps heal not only psychological and spiritual afflictions, but also physical ailments. Anyone can practice it in any situation: from a school to a corporation, from a military base to a cemetery.

You can learn to inter-meditate in myriad ways, not just on a cushion, or a pew, or a green mat at a yoga studio. You don't need to close your eyes, cross your legs, and hope to reach Nirvana or Heaven someday. When practiced with meditative intent, activities like hikes become pilgrimages, thoughts of gratitude and hope become prayers, shared silence becomes sacred dialogue, and family dinner becomes communion. Inter-meditation is authentic lovemaking—spirits connecting on multiple levels at once, both conscious and unconscious.

We Buddhists call the result of overcoming the duality of self and other *Bodhichitta*, the awakened heart/mind that has empathic compassion for all beings—our best Selves. This is the state from which St. Paul urges Christians to "pray without ceasing." Psychologist Mihály Csíkszentmihályi calls it "flow." South African civil rights activist and retired bishop Desmond Tutu describes it as *ubuntu*—the idea that a single person thrives only when the community thrives. My teacher, the late master Dilgo Khyentse Rinpoche, called it "the luminous heart of the Dharma, a wheel of virtuous good karma which turns day and night."

These descriptions might seem esoteric, but they're not when you experience them for yourself. I have a friend named Amelia whose favorite inter-meditation practice is on the New York City subway. When she feels tired, anxious, or angry, wishing she could be as far from her fellow passengers as possible, Amelia stops, takes a breath, and *really* looks at one person. She pictures him or her as a baby—pure, innocent, nothing other than hope and joy—and she holds that image until she feels truly connected, breathing and inter-meditating with that pure, innocent soul. Then Amelia moves on to the next passenger. A commute that could have been just another stressor is elevated to something meaningful, even holy. Who knew that a sacred subway runs right beneath the sidewalks?

You don't ride the subway? Another adaptive inter-meditator I know practices when he's stuck in Chicago traffic by making compassionate eye contact with fellow drivers. He calls up empathy for what they are feeling behind the wheel, pondering where they may be rushing to and why, and wishing them well in whatever they may be doing, rather than dwelling on his own frustration.

Irritated with someone? In this book I'll show you a way to overcome conflict by entraining small self with Big Self, sweeping it into its flow like a glass of water poured into a river. Inter-meditation dissolves comparison and judgment through an inner listening that encourages you to be fully, attentively present and accountable.

Suffering from an illness? I introduce healing inter-meditations that help you work with your disease instead of against it. Our illusion of separation feeds anxiety, and as countless scientists and doctors have discovered, freeing ourselves from it can facilitate wellness. Stress (or dis-ease) contributes to disease.

Tending to a dying relative? I share how I inter-meditated with my mother as she was dying, and how she and I continue to meditate together to this day. This isn't some simple fantasy or helicopter-parent-from-beyond story.

Devastated by moment-to-moment tragedies in the news? In these pages, you'll learn to breathe, summon Bodhisattva intent, and meditate with *the world* using newspapers, television, and handheld devices—rather than remaining distracted by their insistent interruptions. Co-meditation is how we're *with it* rather than *against it*—whatever *it* is or momentarily happens to be. What I call *webitation* can help us turn social media into spiritual media and the Internet into Indra's Cosmic Web.

When I hear my Christian friends talk about the communion of the Holy Spirit, I remember that the Greek root word for communion, *koinonia*, may just as easily be rendered as "transformation" or "communication" or "companionship." It could apply to a business partnership, a union of lives in marriage, a spiritual relationship with any interpretation of God, a fellowship between friends—all of which suggest joint or joined spirituality. *Koinonia* is inter-meditation at its best.

My old friend Baba Ram Dass, a.k.a. Richard Alpert—who likes to call me LSD, so my mother cleverly nicknamed him "Baba Rum Raisin" in return—recently reminded me of a story told by our beloved late guru, Neem Karoli Baba (Maharajji). It's about the metaphorical nature of the entire Hindu pantheon and the need to go beyond seeking God outside ourselves. Maharajji said, "We look for God in all the wrong places. He's hiding in the last place we ever look, within our own hearts and souls. We think we're chasing after and following Him, but it's more like He's trying to catch us and we're running away!"

Inter-meditation is inclusive; it's not about getting rid of anything—people, feelings, or events. It's not about meditating *on* or separate *from*, but *with*, always with. Remember the lines from the Beatles song: "And the time will come when you see we're all one. And life flows on within you and without you." No separation here—so why unravel ourselves from the exquisite fabric we're woven into? Why should we disengage from the whole and then struggle and yearn for reunion?

There are everyday "real world" consequences when we genuinely begin to inter-meditate. We find that we're better friends, better parents, better lovers, and better workers. We're better listeners—more tuned in. The mundane becomes co-emergent with the sacred. Inter-meditation brings genuine peace and tranquility, regardless of the high-decibel chaos surrounding us. And it's not just the lamas and priests and gurus that are attesting to this—neuroscientists like Richard Davidson and Dan Siegel are in the news because they're proving in their laboratories and research centers things that the Buddha discovered under a fig tree over two thousand years ago.

Our world is increasingly interconnected, interdependent. We regularly see vivid examples in the news of the butterfly effect—the phenomenon in which a tiny localized change in a complex system can have momentous consequences elsewhere. Though people generally think of Buddhism as an introspective and meditating religion, His Holiness the Dalai Lama himself often says—humbly yet with genuine authority—that we need each other to become enlightened. After a lifetime of apprenticeship with extraordinary teachers, I have been astonished to learn of the profundity of ordinary people of all kinds, and that true transformation—if it is authentic, meaningful, and enduring—must include collective awakening as well as effect systemic change.

The Buddha spent forty-five years meditating with the multitudes. He famously proclaimed, "Good spiritual friends are the whole of the holy life. Find refuge in the Sangha, in kindred spirits, and in community." Jesus told his followers, "For where two or three come together in my name, there am I with them." Martin Luther King Jr. said his goal was to "create a beloved community and this will require a qualitative change in our souls as well as a quantitative change in our lives." Here is the heart and soul of inter-meditation via interbeing. The Jewish wisdom-book the Talmud teaches, "And whoever saves a life, it is considered as if he saved an entire world." The great Persian poet Rumi sings, "Every prophet sought out companions. A wall standing alone is useless, but put three or four walls together, and they'll support a roof and keep the grain dry and safe."[1] Nobody can do it alone. Believe me, I've tried!

In this book I draw on the universal wisdom of the ages and combine it with my own realizations to help upend assumptions about meditation and spirituality. The more we practice inter-meditation, the more we'll want to practice it. I share new techniques as well as interpret traditional Buddhist wisdom, particularly Tonglen (giving and receiving) and Lojong (attitude transformation and spiritual refinement) in ways new and old for the modern seeker. These practices dovetail with teachings involving yoga, meditation, scripture study, mind training and attitude transformation, and the sacred ritual and tantric energy in which Tibetan Buddhism is grounded. Co-meditation is a potent path of merging, unity consciousness, and backyard spirituality—not mere withdrawal, quietism, narcissism, or solipsism—which helps us integrate every aspect of our lives into our sacred journeys and every aspect of our sacred journeys into our lives.

We're all engaged in relationships—with others, with ourselves, with animals, nature, and the Divine—with something beyond ourselves. How we relate to people and things defines us and informs all of our actions. Human beings hunger for deeper and more authentic connection within those relationships. Not even a hermit in a cave is in isolation; weather, animals, microbes, food and drink, and memories involving other people exist with and within him or her. Our interwoven connections are essential for spiritual growth and evolutionary development. They help us find meaning and purpose, feel joy and love—human as well as divine. They provide the pigment that stands out from the almost-neutral palette of consciousness. By practicing inter-meditation we can delight in a state of true interbeing beyond words and concepts, names and forms, while realizing the very best in others and ourselves. Practice is perfect, and we just do it—just as practice *does* us, in the tides of spiritual activity. We are surfing the cresting wave of evolution, which is really just the froth and bubbling effulgence of nowness-awareness, the sparkles in God's eye.

Let's dive into the flow.

Ten Keys to Inter-Meditation:
What Oneness Feels Like

1. **Authenticity**—which arises from attention, honesty, and pure presence (of mind and heart)

2. **Selflessness**—a Big-Self-interest that goes beyond selfish, with a little bit of healthy individuation so we can take care of and be responsible for ourselves

3. **Generosity**—giving of ourselves and sharing things, emotions, energy, time, and wisdom

4. **Patience**—our commitment to forbearance, tolerance, acceptance, flexibility, and resilience

5. **Trust**—seeing who or what we're inter-meditating with as a gateway to the Divine, as the mutual respect this encourages is necessary for love

6. **Genuine love**—empathic compassion, benevolence, and caring

7. **Delight, joy, pleasure, play, fun**—we don't need to take all of this (or ourselves) so seriously

8. **Passion, enchantment, ardor, interest in *other*—** this inquiring mind-state is one of wonderment and goes deeper, is more empathically connected and altruistic, than mere curiosity or fascination

9. **Openness**—to the mystery, to not knowing, to not having it all worked out, and to life that is larger than our individual minds and wills

10. **A meaningful, mutual purpose and direction—** we're doing this for the benefit of both ourselves and others, always remembering that there is no real difference in the bigger picture

What is the name
of the deep breath I would take
over and over
for all of us?

From "Sunrise" by **MARY OLIVER**

1

Seeing the World
through Another's Eyes

An Ancient Lens for Contemporary Wisdom

I'll be candid. In our Tibetan Buddhist tradition, we are usually exhorted not to share our inner and mystical epiphanies, especially in public, although an exception might be with one's teacher. I have kept quiet about most if not all of my esoteric meditation adventures for almost forty-five years, and even some of my own heartfelt opinions, although I have certainly published and spoken about plenty of them. However, I believe these teachings will now be of use and interest if I make them accessible to others. It's far too late to turn back now!

Fools seek from afar; the wise find truth beneath their feet. Here we have an opportunity to explore, exploit, and develop our own inner natural resources: innate wisdom, silence and stillness, luminous awareness and goodhearted devotion to humanistic higher principles—what Buddha himself called "the heart's sure release." I hope that unlocking the treasury of my own spiritual experiences and non-dualistic tantric practice will help give birth to some recognition and familiarity, as well as mutual benefit—for we are all living spirit, radiant energy, learning how to exist together in this human form and embodiment. By sharing my stories, as well as the stories of my students, teachers, and contemporaries, you will more easily be able to understand how you can awaken today by seeing the world through someone else's eyes.

I believe that esoteric sects, highly ritualized initiations, and secret teachings from pre-industrial societies have mostly outlasted their usefulness in our post-modern times. While these shamanic currents may offer their own particular power and relevance to preserve and nourish the timeless wisdom traditions, we need an intellectually rigorous era of openness and sharing, marked by inquiry, mutual exploration, respect, and transparence on all levels. We must strive to accomplish this together on our increasingly interconnected, interdependent, and endangered planet, if we are to survive and even flourish. As the nineteenth-century Romantic poet Lord Byron wrote: "All who joy would win/Must share it,—happiness was born a twin."

I have had grand times: powerful teaching and learning experiences, breakthroughs and even breakdowns, mystical epiphanies and enlightenment experiences at pilgrimage places and retreat centers, in ashrams, caves, deserts, and on mountaintops around the world over the years. But I have also learned that there's another, very different side to meditation and spirituality—the Dharma teaching of daily life, and the wisdom secreted within experiencing the dark shadows as well as the most brilliant spiritual light. This is the secular sacred, street Dharma—everyday Dharma without excess drama. It's often better to open our eyes rather than close them, relate to the environment beyond our selves, and awaken in the midst of activity. God, Buddha, the

Divine, and ultimate reality are nowhere if not in one's own backyard, and more significantly, within our hearts, bodies, and souls. This truth cannot be emphasized often enough.

It is all *within,* by which I mean available when sought more deeply. This does not mean only within oneself, or within special or trusted people. Over the years, I have observed that closed-eye solitary meditation might not be best for everyone, as much as it often helps to redress our extreme outward focus, materialistic seeking, and coyote-like desire systems. In fact, in some cases closed-eyed introspective meditation might even be contraindicated, such as for extreme introverts or those suffering from paranoia or other pathological symptoms where solitude and separation could cause more harm than benefit. When I shared with some psychiatrist friends this unexpected conclusion based on my own observations, they replied as in one voice: "*Duh.* Of course. Thank you, lama! Very insightful." For some people, other forms of inter- and co-meditation practices, such as yoga, hymn singing, tai chi and qigong, sacred chanting, Sufi dancing, devotional prayers, and the like, are more helpful and healthy than just sitting.

Inter-meditation is the antithesis of navel-gazing and narcissism, or the religion-as-escape, yoga-as-commodity, spirituality-as-a-vacation, "How can I make *me* happy and permanently feel better?" trends that seem so in vogue. For some, mindfulness has become mere mental calisthenics and concentrative exercises. When we apply mindfulness as mental floss, a routine of daily mental hygiene to maintain physical and mental health and well-being, we miss at least half of its most profound spiritual benefits. These practical, secular, rational approaches to awareness practice are just the vestibule leading to the harmony, spiritual freedom, transformation, and ultimate enlightenment that the great wisdom traditions promise and to which their practical instructions guide us.

Inter-meditating offers a counter-practice to the prevailing tendency to separate ourselves from others and from things. It provides a skillful means for reconditioning and deconditioning habitual patterns and reactions. Inter-meditating produces the cure to the fractured, discordant communications and multiplicity of superficial encounters which afflict us today. I call this *communicatus interruptus*. Our communication is regularly filtered through handheld devices and punctuated by constant interruptions, disturbances, and distractions.

Inter-meditation offers us the antidote to distraction and feelings of overwhelm and powerlessness. It moves us away from self-involvement—which at its extreme can become solipsism and narcissism—and toward a mutually beneficial genuine connection through which we can arrive at a synergistic relational understanding much larger than the mere individual. It's how we get with it rather than always pushing and struggling *against* the grain of separation. This brand of co-meditation is convergent, all-inclusive, intimate, and connected. When me, myself, and I get together in inter-meditation, no one and no thing is excluded. We understand each other, transcending language, almost like mother and fetus breathing and metabolizing together.

Here is the secret: we can enter into and organically enjoy a state of inter-meditation in any and every situation. We can aspire to co-meditate without ceasing, with our partners, our friends, teachers, students, critics and antagonists, all creatures great and small, the shining Higher Power, the Big Self, and the cosmos. Everyone is going to die one day, but who among us shall choose to truly *live*? Thus the eminent British wit Jonathan Swift prayed: "May you live all the days of your life." This is precisely where mind-fullness cultivation comes in. What is the alternative—*mindlessness* perhaps? Do we really want to sleepwalk through our lives?

This delightful way of interbeing opens up new vistas for us. Letting go doesn't mean throwing things away or suppressing and repressing them. As I said earlier, it means letting come *and* letting go—letting *be*. I cannot stress this too often—it helps us distinguish between active cultivation of awareness and harmony on the one hand, and merely falling into quietude, indifference, or somnolence on the other. Facing truth and reality with *acceptance* has its own transformative magic. It has become obvious to me over the years that closing my eyes and attempting to shut everything out, trying not to think about anything—as most of us try to do when we first start meditating—is heading in the wrong direction. If I want to be totally present, I have to *be there* fully and wholeheartedly, here and now—open and aware, vulnerable, and undefended, transparent even—and let it all spontaneously happen without me and within me—as it does anyway, whether or not we fervid brainiacs recognize what is actually taking place. One moment of brilliant illumination dispels the darkness of centuries.

Introducing Heart/Mind Training

Throughout this book, I share with you a profound, ancient, and yet extraordinarily timely series of inter-meditation and co-meditation practices, including Lojong (attitude transformation and spiritual refinement) in the Tibetan Mahayana tradition of Buddhism. These insights, practical tips, awareness practices, and reflections show us how to relate fully with our own experience in order to open to and love others, both human and otherwise, by removing the hard shell of defenses and delusions which habitually separate us. Let me relate a story that demonstrates the power of timeless wisdom and its practice; it's a true tale of someone actually walking the talk and practicing what we preach. A few years ago I attended a very interesting ecumenical meeting in Boston with rabbis, priests and pastors, imams, roshis, swamis, and spiritual leaders from multiple traditions, and I met a minister from Texas. I think she was a Methodist. During a break we started chatting over coffee and she told me this story: One night after Bible class, she was robbed at gunpoint in the church parking lot. A man stuck a revolver in this gentle lady's face and demanded her wallet. The minister spontaneously opened her purse, handed the man her money, and said, "I wish I had more to give you. I love you." The minister told me this in the most un-self-conscious way. It was no big deal to her, because her heart/mind had been so well trained and steadied over years, if not lifetimes.

> Join whatever you meet with awareness practice, so even the unexpected becomes the path.

I think you have to love first and see second. The minister must have developed that capacity to love and then see, through her own path. That's heart/mind training. She applied the mind-training slogan, "I love you." The right practice led to the right response at precisely the right moment.

How would you react if you were alone in a parking lot at night and a masked man stuck a gun in your face? Would you pass the Bodhisattva test: *What would the Dalai Lama do?* The minister's mind was trained and purified—open, pliable, undefended—so she was able to connect to something greater than and far more profound than the momentary robbery. She saw herself and Jesus and the Buddha in the robber, and intuitively felt their commonality. That's the level of connection through inter-meditation I want to impart. It is crucial for our times—far more important than simply meditating and trying to be peaceful, or even merely mindful, without insightful and empathic compassion. I'm tired of fiddling while Rome burns.

After I'd thought about the minister's story for a while, I asked her how she managed to be like that—not in theory, but in reality. She said, "I just saw the fearful, lovable child beneath the dark Halloween mask." (Just like seeing the inner babies beneath the hardened masks of people in the subway.) That's both an inter-meditation—a moment of intentional connection—and an argument for having Lojong in our toolkit as a portal and precipitant to genuinely transformative practice.

The Origin of Heart/Mind Training

In Tibet in the year 1042, there lived an Indian holy man named Atisha (also called the "Lamp Master"). I think of him as a superhero, a major player on Team Buddha. Atisha studied with the renowned enlightened guru of Indonesia, the Mahayana master known to posterity only as Serlingpa or "The Man from the Golden Island" (now known as Sumatra). In Atisha's teachings on attaining Bodhichitta—the noble heart/mind that aspires to wisdom, awakening, and emphatic compassion for all beings—he systematized and compiled a revolutionary method of training called Lojong. Lojong means "taming" or "mastering"—you might even say retooling and refining—our attitude, awareness, and habitual ways of thinking. Tibetan

Buddhists consider Lojong to be the most powerful agent for sacred transformation and daily-life character development. It's like a contemplative enactment of the adage "virtue is its own reward." The Dalai Lama himself stresses it above all other public teachings. Within Lojong is the unique breath-centered Tonglen practice, which is a way of vacuuming up all the dark stuff in life and turning it into light and directing it outward, ending up with no separation between self and other or among the various parts of one's own inner psyche. Tonglen is the ultimate co-meditation, with or without other people involved.

Atisha was practical, too. He distilled Serlingpa's principles into fifty-nine slogans or tenets later recorded by his disciple Geshe Chekawa. Here are some examples:

> Join whatever you meet with awareness practice,
> so even the unexpected becomes the path.

> Don't be a spiritual competitor.

And my favorite:

> Only a joyful, open mind and
> attitude, always sustaining you.

Many of these tenets embody and apply to the way of inter-meditation. Throughout this book I've included a selection of those that help enhance our understanding along with my own guided inter-meditations and exercises, as well as wisdom from tried-and-true sources both ancient and contemporary. The beauty of studying the Lojong slogans is that we can draw on them whenever we need them. They're conducive to writing on sticky notes and posting on a refrigerator door, over our desks, on our dashboards, or even on our Twitter feeds. Atisha's ancient gift to us is one that continues to give.

Bringing Out the Heart and Soul of Meditation

Lojong is often described as *mind training*. Translators and scholars seem to love the term; lots of people want to learn about mind training nowadays! "Mind training" sounds a little too mental to me, so modern and intellectual; there's too much mind in Buddhism these days, at least for my taste. In the retreats and workshops I lead, I like to explain Lojong as a practice that effects genuine change of heart. Baba Ram Dass has been nagging us Western Buddhist teachers for years: *How about a little more heart and a dollop of soul, too?* How about unselfishness? Forgiveness? Joy and creativity? How about tamping down greed and selfish desire while cultivating generosity and expansiveness? Not just with a donation to charity for a nice tax deduction, but having a generous, loving spirit, giving it all up to God, including our attachment to the outcome. I find this extraordinarily useful, a panacea even. The Master's heart has many mansions.

> Don't be a spiritual competitor.

You don't need a Buddhist lama from Long Island like me to tune in to the people around you, to take a walk in the other guy's shoes, or give your coat to someone who is shivering. The Lojong teachings don't just say you *should* do it—everybody with the least bit of spiritual curiosity and experience knows that. Lojong shows us *how* to do it, by reconditioning and deconditioning our habitual patterns and self-centered tendencies. The practice also gives us an incredibly effective tool for this transformation: Tonglen, the co-meditation practice described as "exchanging self and others."

A Way to Put the Slogans into Practice

The literal translation of Tonglen from Tibetan means "giving and receiving," and the practice evolved from one of Atisha's core slogans: drive all blames into one(self) [and give to others your profit and victory]. Tonglen is a heart/mind training or attitude transformation practice meant to help us erode our egotism, dualism, and self-clinging. It is a way of exchanging self and other, of *really* putting ourselves in someone else's skin, of giving and receiving to help us feel and identify with the suffering of others, thereby challenging the perceived separation between me and you and we.

Only a joyful, open mind and attitude, always sustaining you.

I first encountered Tonglen a few years before my intermeditation epiphany in France. It was in 1975 when I was Kalu Rinpoche's disciple at his monastery near Darjeeling. He taught me to begin Tonglen by breathing in and out, collecting our scattered thoughts and energies while concentrating on our breath as our main object of focused attention, gradually equalizing the external and internal energy and reversing our tendency to be attracted to the things we want and averse to the things we don't. We are in the habit of rating our lives in real time—a sad day, a nice visit, a terrible commute, a good meditation—qualifying and quantifying everything. There are actually neither unequivocally good nor bad events, things, or people—only the wanted and the unwanted—and everything is subjective. This is strong medicine; think about it. It's a matter of perspective.

Like Lojong, Tonglen is applicable to our 21st-century lives and has helped me greatly during some rough times. It allows us to realize, among other things, that we are not alone, that others suffer similarly, and that no feelings are forever. This humble training in the form of pithy instructions always reminds me of what Jesus taught in the book of Matthew: "So the last will be first and the first will be last" and "Blessed are the meek, for they shall inherit the Earth." This universal truth is the thread upon which I've chosen to string the beads of inter-meditation in this book. Tonglen isn't the only form of inter-meditation we'll work with—far from it. Inter-meditation opens up worlds of spiritual practice available for integrating into every facet of daily life. I incorporate everything from Tantra to mantra to meditating with nature, animals, and music, too. But I'm stressing Tonglen because I have found this attitude-transforming practice crucial to my own sanity and well-being, to my pilgrim's progress, and cannot recommend it highly enough. Seeing through illusions of separation and reaching a place (which of course isn't a place at all) of true connection is the crux of every kind of inter-meditation—with our friends, families, lovers, teachers, nations, enemies, and the universe. Let's start right where we are, with ourselves—because if we befriend ourselves we can befriend and love the world.

Tonglen

Train in giving and taking alternately
(sending and receiving).

Breathe out the giving; breathe in
the taking. Ride the breath.

This is the essential instruction on how to practice Tonglen,
which can be broken down like this:

- Still your mind, relax, and center yourself. Find a
  heart-space of compassion and love. Meditate for a
  moment on who is suffering—you, your friend, your
  enemy, the world. This will make room internally for
  softening and heart opening.

- Begin with yourself—right where you are. Ride the
  breath—as you inhale, concentrate on the good in your life,
  and as you exhale let go of your challenges, conflicts, the
  things that separate you from others and from everything. As
  you inhale, it might be helpful to offer these words: May all
  the difficulties, doubts, and fears in the world be absorbed
  into the empty nature of my mind. And as you exhale: May
  all beings have all my happiness, conviction, and fearlessness.

- Continue to inhale and exhale, equalizing the outside and
  the inside and reversing the tendency to be attracted to
  the wanted and averse to the unwanted, past the illusions

of our own satisfaction or
self-interest. Don't just let go,
let come and go: let be. Be
as you are, resting naturally in
unfabricated awareness, nowness.

Breathe out the giving;
breathe in the taking.
Ride the breath.

• Breathe—visualize and imagine inhaling the
difficulties of those close to your heart, exhaling the
goodness. Open the circle outward until it encompasses
all beings throughout space and time.

• Whatever you meet, bring it into your breath, your
heart, your path. Face it. Don't try to get around it,
hope it isn't there, or ignore it. This moment, this
obstacle, this illness, this delight is the meditation
opportunity. Pleasures and highs can be as distracting as
lows and difficulties, which is why we talk about sending
and receiving both wanted and unwanted circumstances.

Inter-meditative awareness,
nowness, incandescent presence of mind
is like kryptonite
to the super-criminal named Delusion & Confusion,
which is dualistic vision and the illusion of separateness.

Seeing through separateness,
seeing through the bubble confines of my ego-self,
everything is clear, open, and free.

All is possible. All good, Bodhisattva.

Me,

We.[1]

A spontaneous poem delivered by MUHAMMAD ALI

2

Befriending Ourselves, Befriending the World

Self-Acceptance, Forgiveness, and Authentic Connection

There are three elements to befriending ourselves: attention, self-compassion, and authentic connection. Once we've learned to practice these, we've built the groundwork for inter-meditation. It's that simple, though not necessarily easy. How can we love and accept others if we don't learn to love and accept ourselves?

> Train in giving and taking alternately (sending and receiving). [And start with yourself.]

Attention and Nowness-Awareness

One day a man of the people said to Zen master Ikkyu:

"Master, will you please write for me some maxims of the highest wisdom?"

Ikkyu immediately took his brush and wrote the word "Attention."

> Train in giving and taking alternately (sending and receiving). [And start with yourself.]

"Is that all?" asked the man. "Will you add something more?"

Ikkyu then wrote twice running, "Attention. Attention."

"Well," remarked the man rather irritably, "I really don't see much depth or subtlety in what you have just written."

Then Ikkyu wrote the same word three times running: "Attention. Attention. Attention."

Half-angered, the man demanded, "What does that word 'Attention' mean anyway?"

And Ikkyu answered gently, "Attention means attention."[2]

Pay attention, friends. It pays off. Attention is the essence of any contemplative practice, whether it's prayer, chanting, seated meditation, or movement practices such as tai chi, yoga, or sacred dance. In fact, attention makes the sphere of relationships go round. We can't live well without it, and focusing our attention is a key to inter-meditation. I find it's easier to start with ourselves and then direct our meditation outward in widening concentric circles of inclusive embrace, first to one or two others, and eventually to the universe. The size of our heart directly correlates to the scope of our attention, receptivity, and intentions. Moreover, expanding our conscious heart is the best tool—perhaps the only tool—that can ultimately iron out our differences.

I have met plenty of people who attend meditation retreats, read a spiritual book, listen to a compelling podcast, go to a lecture, and tell me they've been transformed. The effect may linger for a day or two, but then the "real" world kicks in and they go back to the cranky selves they were before, losing perspective, becoming distracted and entangled, sweating the small stuff, reacting angrily to slights, harboring resentment, and sleepwalking through their lives. So how can we manifest the incandescent presence of natural wakefulness and innocent openness that supports meaningful connection? Not by discussing it or unthinkingly nodding our heads as we listen to a Dharma talk or sermon, parroting prayers and mantras, or sitting in pews or on meditation cushions while daydreaming and indulging in internal monologues—as we so often do! Me too—guilty as charged. This lack of interest and focus doesn't accomplish much of anything. Genuine attention, lucid moment-to-moment awareness is the armor that protects us from such mind-numbness. How do we intentionally engage with our lives? How do we pay attention, or as St. Paul said, pray without ceasing, making every breath a prayer? Every breath a mantra, a moment of awakened mindfulness?

It isn't easy. We live in psychically noisy times—technologically connected, electrifying, distracted, and complex. But whether we're in a cubicle, a cafe, a kitchen, or a classroom, our lives are our principal paths and our spiritual work. We are like the mystics and holy ones, gods and goddesses walking on this altar of the earth—we're the ones we've been waiting for, so let's not waste time. Let's usher in the Kingdom of Heaven now. Why hesitate? It's now or never, as always.

One of the best techniques, and one I've seen work time and again, is what I call nowness-awareness or *presencing*, in which awareness is a verb, attention is alive, and we become enlivened. It's an integral way of bringing Tonglen into practice by *intentionally opening our hearts to our selves while simultaneously and intentionally opening our hearts to others and to life*. If you've ever read the novel *Stranger in a Strange Land* by Robert Heinlein, you'll know what I'm talking about. He coined the term *grok*. Grok became so well used it ended up in Webster's dictionary: *to understand profoundly and intuitively*. Or to make something part of oneself. That's what we need to practice doing first with ourselves, then with each other, and ultimately with our universe. This kind of focused attention is an extraordinary spiritual remedy; it alleviates all afflictions. It's the essence of co-meditation, relational meditation—inter-meditation.

INTER-MEDITATION PRACTICE

Presencing

Here are the steps in nowness-awareness, the practice of presencing:

- Start by becoming aware of the rising and falling of your breath: breathing in, breathing out, slowly and mindfully.
- Now apply that lucid awareness to everything you perceive and experience—sight, sound, smell, taste, sensation, and, of course, thought.
- Just simply be lucidly aware, mindful rather than mindless.
- Recognize that each sensation suddenly arises and appears like a dream, a mirage, a story.
- Let it come.
- Now, let it go.

- And as you let it go, let it be.
- Become it, be it—no separation—as it is.
- Let go and let whatever your Higher (deepest) Power may be move through you.

Do this for a few minutes each day. You don't need any props—incense, the ability to sit in the lotus position, pictures of saints, stained-glass windows, or altars. Wherever you practice this will become a sacred space—in your kitchen while you're cooking dinner, in line at the bank, or on the treadmill. The intentional use of lucid attention, incandescent presence of mind, applied to and in the present moment is the very heart of Buddhist meditation in general, and relational meditation practice in particular. But you have to do it—not just read about doing it, talk about doing it, think about doing it—just do it! Let's co-meditate together.

If you are not here now you won't be there then. The Dzogchen or Innate Great Perfection meditation masters of Tibetan Buddhism describe nowness-awareness as the authentic and un-fabricated Buddha, the natural sacred or divine that's within each of us. Presencing is a way of fully accepting ourselves, befriending oneself and befriending the world. This remembering to remember, to catch yourself before things catch you, and to choose how, when, and if to respond—rather than just blindly react—is the very essence of emotional balance and equanimity. Nowness-awareness promotes meditative emotional management—the heart of mindful anger management, so needed in our agitated, violent world. This remembering to catch yourself, or *remindfulness,* helps create a zone of peace and autonomy from which we can act and respond proactively.

Nowness-awareness is freedom—the ultimate therapy. When we become totally aware and awake there is no past to bind us and no future to distract us; no selfing or self-story remembering and reification taking place. We're in the "zone" of inter-meditation.

Simply aware of the arising-falling
Of all and everything
Right before your eyes

Like a dream
Mirage
Sit-com

Letting it come and go
Letting go
Letting be

Breathing out
Into it
And in
Out of it

Grokking it all
As part of yourself

Like a film-meditation
(Who is the projector?)

Letting go totally
Letting be

Purely presencing

Being it
Inseparable
With one and all

This is the joyous co-meditation
Totally with it all

The Neuroscience of Inseparability through Empathy

You don't have to take my word for it; read the news. I love learning about the latest developments that move inter-meditation and spirituality out of the temple and into the university, the research laboratory, or the library. (If only so I can bring them all back again.) It's exciting to understand how modern methods of quantification and observation can "prove" (or perhaps catch up with) what the mystics have been teaching us about inter-meditation for millennia.

Take, for example, the recent studies of Cognitively Based Compassion Training (CBCT)—essentially a secular version of Lojong—at Emory University. Scholars assert, "When most people think of meditation, they think of a style known as 'mindfulness,' in which practitioners seek to improve their ability to concentrate and to be non-judgmentally aware of their thoughts and feelings. While CBCT includes these mindfulness elements, the practice focuses more specifically on training people to analyze and reinterpret their relationships with others."[3] There's that word—*relationships*—again.

According to researcher Charles Raison, "These findings raise the intriguing possibility that CBCT may have enhanced empathic abilities by increasing activity in parts of the brain that are of central importance for our ability to recognize the emotional states of others."[4] Raison—whether he knows it or not—presents a sterling 21st-century example of meditation going outward, not just inward—what we'd call inter-meditation or co-meditation.

Forbes magazine recently reported about similar research at the University of Virginia that teaches us about inter-meditation. In their study, "researchers had to get a bit medieval. They had participants undergo fMRI [functional magnetic resonance imaging] brain scans while threatening to give them electrical shocks, or to give shocks to a stranger or a friend. Results showed that regions of the brain responsible for threat response—the anterior insula, putamen, and supramarginal gyrus—became active under threat of shock to the self; that much was expected. When researchers threatened to shock a stranger, those same brain regions showed virtually no activity. But when they threatened to shock a friend, the brain regions showed activity nearly identical to that displayed when the participant was threatened."[5] In other words, empathizing with a person one cares for—vibrating in tune with their feelings, their plight—instinctively helps us to feel for and treat them as we would want to be treated. And we can intentionally entrain and inculcate these feelings and emotions in us for our own benefit. This is the Lojong mode of mind training and attitude transformation.

The study shows what's "gaining science-fueled momentum in recent years: the human brain is wired to connect with others so strongly that it experiences what they experience as if it's happening to us."[6] In other words, there's a neural basis for empathy, the emotion of feeling-with (another) that's at the essence of inter-meditation and the roots of compassion.

Neuroscience—or what I like to lovingly call *neuro-Dharma*—is fascinating stuff, but don't get stuck looking outside yourself for the truth in any reductionist, hyper-rational formula or quantification. This can become what my Zen Buddhist friends call eating "painted cakes"—beautiful looking, but empty spiritual calories. We can share stories of inter-meditation, present fascinating data, and prove that it's real, but just like riding a bicycle, making love, or giving birth: to understand inter-meditation you have to actually experience and do it.

This brings to mind Walt Whitman's poem, where after listening to all the learned astronomer had to say, Whitman wandered off by himself, "In the mystical moist night-air, and from time to time/Look'd up in perfect silence at the stars." We can study spiritual teachings, talk about them, even memorize them, and we can recite chants and prayers and scriptures—but it won't amount to much if we don't internalize it, grok it, live it, and do so genuinely—and with delight. I am constantly amazed at the wonders meditation brings me almost every single morning, even after all of these years.

Self-Compassion

When Zen teacher Kobun Chino Roshi's long-term students gathered in Santa Cruz, California, shortly before his death, someone asked him why we meditate. Kobun Roshi replied:

We sit . . . to make life meaningful. The significance of our life is not experienced in striving to create some perfect thing. We must simply start with accepting ourselves. Sitting brings us back to actually who and where we are. This can be very painful. Self-acceptance is the hardest thing to do. If we can't accept ourselves, we are living in ignorance, this darkest night. We may still be awake, but we don't know where we are. We cannot see. The mind has no light. Practice is this candle in our very darkest room.[7]

After attention, self-acceptance or self-compassion is the second step in inter-meditation. We like to talk about thinking globally, saving all sentient beings, and loving everyone, but we have to begin somewhere. And that somewhere is within. This is an inside job, and an insightful one too.

We can find it pretty easy to love ourselves when we're feeling generous or patient or happy, basking in positive emotions like love and altruism. The tricky part of inter-meditating comes with the more challenging places in ourselves: anxiety, fear, boredom, jealousy, impulsiveness, anger, and depression. Using the Buddhist wisdom of "the Middle Way" as a touchstone can help.

The Middle Way, or "interdependent origination," means that things don't emerge out of nothing and without causes, as if by magic. Everything is an interdependently coalescing phenomenon that morphs and subsides like waves rising and falling in the sea, the water molecules moving through them changing into other configurations, simultaneously in whirling congeries of force and energy, not just material substance. Forms seem to shift into and out of existence, although energy is neither created nor destroyed. Everything is impermanent and in flux—evolving.

Presencing as Meditation in Action

If concentrative meditation focuses our attention on a single point where we can rest our mind on an object—wherever we place it—presencing manifests as meditation in action. This means to live not just in the moment, but intentionally, consciously, *as if becoming* the moment. If the moment is about seeing, we become the essence of seeing—not a separate seer, but vivid seeing itself. If the moment is about feeling our negative qualities or conflicted emotions, we become the essence of feeling, beyond separateness and selfhood, without judging. We become the dancer and the dance, the therapist and the therapy, the teacher and the teaching, the cook and the dinner, one and the same. No separation.

Do you know what the ancient Zen master of China, known as the "Third Ancestor," said? "Make the slightest separation, and Heaven and Earth are set infinitely apart." That is one's own doing, not the natural order of things. Inter-meditation redresses that imbalance and artificial sense of duality or two-ness. Sometimes I call this *one-ing*.

This is a way to co-meditate in action, meditate with everything, and be mindfully aware and fully present as an individual. In the following chapters we'll see how that attention shifts and expands when we inter-meditate—whether with one or several other people, a teacher, nature, our beloved, or even our pet. We can achieve this by using Mary Catherine Bateson's example of "Insight," which "refers to the depth of understanding that comes by setting experiences, yours and mine, familiar and exotic, new and old, side by side, learning from letting them speak to one another."[8]

So now that we've taken the first steps toward inter-meditation, let's go further by looking somewhere else. And as we know, that somewhere is *within*. Self-compassion and breaking down the barriers between us and them, you and me, is the next step in inter-meditation.

Beginning to Connect through Self-Compassion

Because our mental attitude sets the stage in the theater of our experience, let's engage a modern three-part awareness practice based on a Tonglen meditation. As you do this, remember the slogan engraved over the arched gate to a monastery where I meditated in Sri Lanka:

> Here you will find the atmosphere
> you have in mind.

Have I mentioned yet my working hypothesis that everything is subjective? These steps are preparation for (and ultimately engagement in) inter-meditation as a way to weaken the walls between us, and ultimately to make them vanish. It's something to keep returning to as we inter-meditate, so let's break it down:

- **First of all, get comfortable.** On a cushion, in a chair, walking on the beach or a quiet street, while you're waking up in the morning—it doesn't matter where or when—try to find a regular and comfortable place with few distractions. Take a couple of deep breaths, let go of your to-do list and random thoughts as best you can, and savor the present moment. Take a breath; you deserve it.

> Here you will find the atmosphere you have in mind.

- **Be aware of the opportunities provided by the precious gift of this life, your human birth.** Make a conscious commitment to the uniqueness and potential of your existence. Consider that it's extremely rare and difficult for other creatures—insects, birds, fish, and even the higher mammals—to attain self-consciousness and the prefrontal cortex reasoning of the developed human brain as well as the physical, linguistic, and social capabilities that come with it. We have a remarkable chance to cultivate and develop what we have been given—a gift that poet Mary Oliver calls "your one rare and precious life."

I can't stress enough what an opportunity this lifetime we share is. Think about it: Trillions of beings (creatures great, small, and unseen) cohabit this planet with us. More than three hundred thousand species of beetles alone exist on the earth. So as you meditate, begin by contemplating the miracle of your birth and chart your course through mortality—to death and beyond. Billions of humans have lived and died here, and we too shall go the way of all things, so together let's make this lifetime count. The meaning of your existence is what you put into it; your purpose is to find fulfillment and help others achieve the same.

• **Be aware of the fragile and impermanent nature of all lives, including your own.** Focus on your mortality—we're here today and gone tomorrow—like a dream, hallucination, or movie. While we're here, each of us fights a great battle—the existential battle of human existence, unremittingly striving for understanding, meaning, freedom, happiness, and fulfillment. We are joined at the core, at the heart, in this great soulful endeavor, and we're all on the same team, undergoing similar if not ultimately identical struggles, travails, and achievements. This reflection helps me empathize and identify with each and all of our brothers and sisters on this spaceship Earth, all seeking, needing, and wanting pretty much the same for themselves and their loved ones, and being limited by their own understanding and illusions, conditioning, and beliefs. It also helps me give myself a break—if I make a mistake, a wrong turn, I don't dwell on it—and there's no time to waste on self-recrimination and brooding! I look at the problem, work with it, accept life as it is even while striving to contribute and improve things, and move on. Time moves on nevertheless; I might as well get with it.

One of the Buddhist tantric commitments or vows is to look at everyone and everything as Buddhas, as being inseparable from the Higher Power or deepest innermost subtle beingness. As we practice meditation and inter-meditation, we develop our ability for sacred outlook and learn to perceive the light *in* people and events, not *in spite of* them. This is embodied wisdom, like a rising sun in our hearts, spontaneously radiating warm rays of loving actions and compassionate service.

Before we go out into the world as inter-meditators, let's try practicing within our own lives by using the compassion we'd give others to refrain from criticizing ourselves too harshly. Laundered your red sweatshirt with your white undies, and now it looks tie-dyed pink? No problem. Burnt the dinner? No problem—we'll call for takeout. Slipped on the ice? Don't hate the ice or yourself. Forgive and remember; learn the lessons, let go, and move on. In the beginning you have to carry your spiritual practice—through mindfulness, perseverance, and patience. Later, your practice will carry you.

- **Be aware of the implications of your motivations and the consequences of your actions.** They radiate outward. Actions are exponential. These steps in awareness prepare us to engage in inter-meditation, learning to treat everyone as well as we treat our loved ones and ourselves. We're all in the same boat, through choppy waters and smooth seas, and we sink or sail together—all facing the enormity of the existential questions and ultimate mystery, surprises, and losses of this tenuous life. We all seek some kind of reliable mooring in this evanescent and unstable reality. We all suffer at the hands of our own unknowing and all of the things we feel are beyond our control. Empathizing with the plight of all my numberless co-congregants here on this altar of Earth naturally spurs my innate goodness of heart and little inner Buddha to feelings of compassion, empathy, acceptance, and well-wishing, and sets helpfulness, altruism, love, and generosity in motion. I have a particular soft spot for the little ones, underdogs, and disenfranchised: may they all be sheltered and lifted up in my maroon lama robe.

As you breathe in and out, remember to think of breathing as just a metaphor for welcoming it—whatever *it* may be. This is the great co-meditation: greet those parts of ourselves and those aspects of our experiences that annoy us, rather than pushing them away. To ultimately engage in inter-meditation, we need to intentionally manifest compassion for ourselves and acceptance of others. For to commune and commingle with another—and with the world—trust and acceptance is a sine qua non.

Our Authentic Selves

Tibet's first Dalai Lama wrote, "Self-cherishing is said to be the source of all conflicts of the world." On the surface, those words might seem to contradict what Kobun Roshi said about the incredible importance of self-acceptance. But there's a subtle distinction to be made here, and it's in the letting go—of the cherished and clingy parts of the whole messy egocentric package. Then we can reach a place of authenticity and flow—of befriending ourselves and embracing the world and its flaws, joyfully.

We live in an era of full disclosure and TMI—*Too Much Information*—yet insufficient understanding and wisdom. Meanwhile, we hurry and strive to become someone and something, to get ahead of others, to stand up and stand out from the crowd and shine. People concoct personae on social media presenting their best image, but image is rooted in fantasy, illusion, and imitation; we need to go beyond that, to open up in a genuine radiant way. This relates to the Lojong slogan:

> So, of the two witnesses, hold to the principal
> one—your conscience, your authentic self.

The two witnesses refer to others and yourself, meaning your own conscience. Follow the main one—it's your own conscience, because only you can decide for *you*. That doesn't mean you don't listen to others' input or advice, but it's really up to oneself after all, isn't it? So, of the two witnesses, hold to the principal one—your authentic self. Don't cherish the illusion that others' opinions matter more than yours, or that someone has real power over you. If you don't practice healthy self-care, who will take care of you? Authentic power is sacred energy stemming from within the higher self of our best nature.

Nyoshul Khenpo Rinpoche, my last Dzogchen teacher, died in 1999. He was one of the great experts on Longchen Nyingthig, the heart-essence of vastness—the most essential meditation, yoga, and naked awareness practice of Tibetan Buddhism. Khenpo and I were very close, and being Old World Tibetan through and through, he did not hesitate to pass on stories of miracles. All religions and spiritual traditions use stories and miracles to convey essential teachings—Jesus's loaves and fishes, Hanukkah's one-day supply of oil lasting eight days, countless myths of the Hindu pantheon, fabulous tales from the lives of the Buddha, and various accounts of saints and sages around the world.

Khenpo liked to talk about things from his own life, including tales from Kathok, his monastery in eastern Tibet. He shared lots of teaching stories, which were true even if not necessarily always factual. One story Khenpo loved to tell claimed that so many people had reached enlightenment at Kathok that "Thus have I heard, the sky was golden with the yellow robes of all these monk master *jalupas* (rainbow bodies) flying from their mountain caves on one side of the valley in the morning across to the other side from east to west, soaring on the sun's rays, and at sunset soaring back from the western mountains to the east. The sky glowed with all the robes of these jalupas enjoying the freedom of *transrealescence,* of being interpenetrating and non-localized."

With modern advances in science we're starting to appreciate how things can be in two places at once, like the Higgs Boson, or God particle. What's important in Khenpo's story of lamas commuting on the sun's rays is that they were authentic to my master and the other faithful in the valley who purportedly saw them every day. This teaching story raised hearts and elevated minds—spirits soared, whether the monks could literally do so or not. That's the relational communion, the inter-meditation. It's magical, fantastic, beyond the mind's ken—and yet it's real, real enough. The spirit *can* actually soar far beyond the mortal mind; this we all know. Neuroscientists and philosophers persist in their efforts to define the spirit, but what spirit actually is has yet to be satisfactorily quantified. Nor will it be—at least, not very easily, nor soon.

As our attention, self-acceptance, practice of inter-meditation, and familiarity with our authentic selves develops we begin to realize that the skin that separates us from other people is just a veil, a permeable garment as magical and as true as the flying lamas. Go visit one of those science museum exhibits that show the human musculature, organs, and skeletons stripped bare; scrutinize what our human skin-bag is all about. No one can realize this for us, no one can take it away from us, and no one needs to agree or confirm it—it's like knowing when you're in love. Unzip your skin-sack and remove it (at least metaphorically) for a moment or two and recognize the tenuous, impermanent, and fragile nature of our corporeal form. This exercise will help you tune in to what might be more reliable and less subject to loss and decay—our inner being, our Buddha or Divine nature.

So, of the two witnesses, hold to the principal one—your conscience, your authentic self.

But really, it has nothing to do with Buddha or God or an otherworldly being; these are mainly concepts, as we currently conceive of them. It's our own authentic nature no matter where you spend your Sunday mornings or go to contemplate or sing hymns. It's *everybody's* spiritual nature. We all have it. As English teacher David McCullough Jr. admonished graduates in his much-buzzed-about Wellesley High School commencement address, "The sweetest joys of life, then, come only with the recognition that you're not special. Because everyone is." Or as eighth-century Indian Buddhist monk-scholar Shantideva (known as the "Peace Master") said, "All the happiness of this world comes from thinking of the welfare of others. All the suffering of this world comes from thinking only of oneself." This is one of the Dalai Lama's top-three favorite sayings. (The other two are "My religion is kindness" and "We are all part of the human race; we need to develop a genuine sense of universal responsibility and heartfelt compassion.")

This is also the message of Tonglen and the purpose of inter-meditation. This is the very heart of the Bodhisattva's compassionate vow to deliver all beings across the ocean of *samsara*—suffering and confusion—and to the continent of Nirvana, liberation, and enlightenment. It's the way to reverse the tendency to dualistic, self-centered clinging, craving, and aversion, making that magnificent journey from head to heart, Earth to Heaven, separation to unity. We can span such gaps and dichotomies—moving from the ordinary places of You and I to the blissful country of *We*, the promised land of oneness far beyond joining and parting.

"I'll show you my we-ness if you'll show me yours," as the cartoon in my mind quips. Once we accept *we* as our authentic self, our larger and inclusive sphere of being, we can finally crack the eggshell of ego. We may begin by meditating alone and cultivating inner calm and personal peace, but integrating relational life is the advanced practice—far more challenging and rewarding.

Now that we've decided to play on "Team We," let's meet our coaches, cheerleaders, and teammates, for we are never apart from them. They're the invisible array of everyone who holds our welfare dear to their hearts, just as we hold theirs to ours.

My religion is kindness.

Homage
to the Gurus. Guru om! Thanks to the teachers
Who taught us to breathe . . .

ALLEN GINSBERG

3

I/Thou Implies Infinite Love

How to Co-Meditate with the Dalai Lama
and Our Spiritual Teachers

After twelve years teaching and transmitting selfless wisdom in Tibet, Atisha the Lamp Master found his way back to India where he became renowned as a teacher of Bodhichitta, the heart/mind awakening training. Whenever he mentioned Dharmakirti—his own venerable teacher—he'd clasp his hands together in devotion as he intoned, *"And I learned this teaching through my teacher, Dharmakirti."* Atisha always said his teacher's name with some form of grateful, laudatory epithet. This reminds me of how my father would always say his father's name and add, "May he rest in peace." Always. I used to think that was funny, but now that my father—*May he rest in peace*—is gone, I'm getting the point. This feeling of gratitude and devotion informs our entire practice. Without him, no me, none of this. I get it!

It has often been said that every meditation, every act of mental prayer, even if it may have some immediate practical purpose like alleviating stress, heartache, or sending peace into the world, can also bring us into direct communion with the sacred holiness, deepest power, or God (if we prefer that word). People of all spiritual traditions learn how to pray, meditate, discriminate, and ultimately reach that elevated state of communion and illumination from a teacher, preceptor, guide, or mentor. It's a path I call "Teacher Practice." The little guys—nuns, lamas, rabbis, abbesses, swamis, and priests—are all models for our relationships with the big ones—prophets, saints, and founders like Jesus, Buddha, Abraham, and Mohammed—and, ultimately, they show us how to relate to the biggest one—the Divine, the most profound power or sublime energy, beyond all imagining. We all have spiritual teachers and guiding benefactors. They may take the form of a holy person, therapist, mentor, or even soccer coach or piano teacher. Someone served as our guide when we first tied our shoes, rode a bicycle, drove a car, wrote our names, made love, and so on. We can't learn these things just from books or hearsay.

Our teachers give us the tools and the environment to intermeditate, to enter into the spirit of the thing they're imparting as well as the nitty-gritty practical details. That's why we feel so much gratitude and devotion to our teachers. A Lojong slogan puts it like this:

> Cleave close to three essentials: your teachers,
> their instruction, and the requisites for
> practice: the enlightened Buddha, liberating
> Dharma, and supportive Sangha.

I can't tell you how important it is to make the spiritual journey today—in this distracted, conflicted, and agitated age—and endeavor authentically, in whatever form you might undertake it. By working with our teachers we can learn to synthesize the two parts of inter-meditation—us and them, inner and outer—in an arena where we're allowed to take chances, make mistakes, grasp important lessons, and appreciate the virtue of adversity. Teacher Practice allows us to combine "self power" (striving and self-actualization) and "other power" (help, predecessors, grace, and blessings). Zen master Dogen labeled this *gyoji*—pure or continuous practice, or a state of constant inter-meditation. Here we find flow—the right balance between doing and being, willful effort and humble surrender. It's a potent recipe for radiant awakefulness.

> Cleave close to three essentials: your teachers, their instruction, and the requisites for practice: the enlightened Buddha, liberating Dharma, and supportive Sangha.

Religions around the world stress devotion, faith, adherence to various codes, and unquestioning loyalty to a guru or spiritual master, but inter-meditation goes beyond belief and compliance. It provides us with a clear mirroring of our own higher, deeper, and best selves via our spiritual friends, lovers, and companions, paving a way to exquisite awakefulness. What we admire in inspiring teachers and role models exists in us as well, even if latent or not yet fully apparent. A master teacher resembles a mirror to our best, highest self, in which we glimpse who and what we are and can be. A guru is like the doorway to God. But, as it says in the ancient Vedic scriptures, the holy Upanishads: don't get stuck in the doorway! God, guru, and practitioner are one and inseparable.

When we remember our teacher's kindness, generosity, patience, and the trouble he or she took with us, we feel almost overwhelmed with a gratitude that goes beyond words. If I combine that with contemplating the kindness of my parents and grandparents, aunts and uncles—all who loved me and treated me very well for decades, always there when I needed them the most—it warms my heart and softens my defensive shell of separateness. This kind of vulnerable thankfulness is a good way to begin and end every day, or every practice session, to enter into the permeable, transrealescent luminous state of inter-meditation. Each of us has someone we'd like to thank.

Moreover, contemplating the real possibility of paying that forward to those who are similarly in need—in our own family, community, and country—sets the highest intention for things to proceed in an extraordinarily positive way today, and every day. Pass it on. If you want to keep it alive and make the most of this inheritance of care and loving-kindness, pass it on. We gratify our forebears by sharing what they have garnered. In some cases, it involved tremendous sacrifice, and they unstintingly bequeathed everything to us—just as the best teachers and parents revel in the success and good fortunes of their mentees, without an iota of jealousy, envy, or competition. In fact, the Buddha taught that rejoicing in the virtues, accomplishments, and meritorious deeds of others includes one in a full share of the benefits of such goodness and virtue. This is the traditional heart-practice of sympathetic joy, or *Mudita*, reveling in the progress and success of others, an inter-meditation which we'll delve into more deeply in chapter 6.

However, we should exercise great care. Without letting the blind lead the blind and falling into all kinds of possible pitfalls and potholes along the path, we must investigate our teachers thoroughly—to the best of our ability, at least—before we put our full trust in them. Doing otherwise has caused all sorts of problems, and many a larger-than-life human has slipped from their pedestal due to feet of clay. Trust is tremendously important, and it works both ways. Moreover, trust wants and deserves to be earned and not just freely, frivolously given.

Lineages

We Buddhists revere our various intertwined lineages, all descending from the historical Buddha and even further/deeper in the ultimate sphere. We believe in direct, mind-to-mind, heart-to-heart transmission of the living, breathing teachings, their palpable energies and related aspects. So it's important to question who taught our teachers, and to whom they are accountable. It's not unlike knowing where the food on your plate came from. Who is preparing dinner in your spiritual kitchen? Who wrote the cookbook? Did they test the recipes or are they just making them up?

If you've read my other books or heard one of my talks, you probably know that I've studied with more than several of the great spiritual teachers of our time. I spent over twenty-three years in Asia living in their monasteries and ashrams, translating for them, serving and travelling with them in both the East and West. I lived with them my entire adult life in their communities and as part of the sangha (Buddhist fellowship). Just the day before writing this, I had lunch alone with His Holiness the Twelfth Gyalwang Drukpa, head of the Drukpa Kagyu Dragon sect of Tibetan Buddhism, in his hotel room in New York. This happened not because I'm a spiritual social climber, but because I taught him English at his Darjeeling refugee monastery in the 1970s, when he was a ten-year-old boy, and we have been close ever since, just like family.

Although my parents named me Jeffrey Allen Miller, I received the name Surya Das in February of 1973 from the venerated old Hindu saint Neem Karoli Baba, known as Maharajji, whom Baba Ram Dass made famous with books like *Be Here Now*. I was empowered and authorized by my teachers Kyabje Dudjom Rinpoche and Dilgo Khyentse Rinpoche to become a lama after my three-year retreat in 1984. Nyoshul Khenpo Rinpoche was my personal Dzogchen master, and I also learned from pioneering Tibetan Buddhist lamas Thubten Yeshe, Kalu Rinpoche, His Holiness the Sixteenth Gyalwa Karmapa, Tulku Urgyen, Thrangu Rinpoche, Dezhung Rinpoche, and Kangyur Rinpoche—my Tibetan root lamas. In 1974 and 1975 I studied and meditated in *sesshins* for one year with Zen Buddhist master Uchiyama Roshi, in Kyoto, Japan. I sat in silent retreats in Rangoon and in Thai monasteries after studying under Vipassana masters S. N. Goenka and Anagarika Munindra in India during the early and mid-seventies. I knew Chögyam Trungpa Rinpoche personally, as well as J. Krishnamurti. I'm well acquainted with the Dalai Lama, Thich Nhat Hanh, Sulak Sivaraksha of Thailand, Tai Situ Rinpoche, Chökyi Nyima Rinpoche and Tulku Thondup of India, and other such contemporary masters. I'm also close to a few younger generation masters, such as Anam Thubten Rinpoche, Kilung Rinpoche, Khandro Rinpoche, and the Nyingma Khenpo brothers. I spent time with Indian saints Anandamayi Ma, Swami Muktananda, Kunur Lama, and Sai Baba. I just recently saw, almost by chance,

Sri Ravi Shankar and heard him teach at his ashram outside Bangalore, in South India. I sometimes study with a realized American rishi in Vermont.

I revere each and every one of these, my gracious teachers, and they have all informed my inter-meditation practice in one manner or another. I've had other kinds of teachers as well—baseball coaches, music and poetry instructors, intimate partners, friends, critics, and enemies. But my first real mentor in this life—besides my parents—wasn't a priest or a saint or a living incarnation of the Buddha (then again . . . maybe he was). He was a pretty regular guy. His name was Jon Ray Hamann, a professor at the University of Buffalo in the late 1960s who totally lit my lamp. I was a teenage jock from Long Island with idealistic Woodstock-generation peace-and-love aspirations, and Jon was exceedingly empowering to me. I have never forgotten him, and we've maintained occasional contact over the years. A prodigious intellect as well as a stellar individual, he was a dedicated teacher, and he eventually became a good friend. A Dakota farm boy from a Lutheran family who could fix anything and worked on his own car and motorcycle, Jon had studied theology first, then chemistry, math, and philosophy, and had an appointment at the Center for Theoretical Biology at SUNY at Buffalo, a prestigious institute which was at the time doing groundbreaking research into the origins of life. Jon was a genuine polymath. My roommate David Schneider introduced me to him, as Jon was tutoring David's independent study in poetry and journal writing. I too began to bring my poetry, short stories, and songs to Jon's office. Later we met at his home or the all-night diner and pizza parlor, where beer and wine flowed as freely as the constant current of fine talk and stellar camaraderie. Even my brother—now a brain scientist and bio-medical engineering professor—came up to study informally with Jon during one of his high school summers.

Like all truly great teachers, Jon understood that education was meant to educe the best in us, to bring out all that we were and could become. He believed in me, and saw my potential. Jon made me feel like his special protégé, like the sky was the limit when it came to learning and creativity. (David told me later that Jon helped him to feel the exact same way, and who knows how many others?) Jon also showed me how to navigate the byways of academia, craft my curriculum and courses, and how to learn *how to learn* so that my schooling could and would eventually continue far beyond the walls of the university and into my life.

Jon taught me that teaching was a unique responsibility and a sacred profession, holding the power to influence young hearts and minds, and thus entire lives. True teachers (unlike cult leaders) intend for their students to outgrow and outstrip them. They see sparks in their students, have faith in that potential, and work toward facilitating and midwifing exponential growth. It is a mutually beneficial project not unlike inter-meditation. The culmination is a grand achievement on both sides, and the fruit of the education-job well done. (Although I am certain that Jon, being somewhat of a scientist and anarchist-Marxist-agnostic, never used terms such as sacred or midwifing.)

Qualities of a Teacher

When I was looking through some of my little red Dharma notebooks from the 1970s when I studied under Kalu Rinpoche and Khenpo Thrangu Rinpoche in Darjeeling, Sikkim, and

Kathmandu, I found this little psalm, or *doha,* on the Six Mahayana Buddhist Paramitas, or perfections: *generosity, moral self-discipline, patience, enthusiastic effort, mindful awareness,* and *transcendental wisdom.* It sums up my essential thinking on the matter of a good teacher:

> Generosity is the ultimate gift and career.
>
> Moral self-discipline is the ultimate
> virtue of life.
>
> Patient forbearance and acceptance is the
> hardest practice.
>
> Constant enthusiastic effort and inspiration
> is the greatest challenge to maintain.
>
> Mindful awareness and alert presence of
> mind is the main thing to be cultivated.
>
> Discriminating wisdom and selfless love
> are the ultimate fruits.
>
> These are like six spokes of Buddha's ever-
> rolling Dharma wheel.

I aspire to these perfections. They're the characteristics we should look for as we pick guides for inter-meditation. Generosity, kindness, patience, and unselfishness are a true teacher's salient characteristics.

Good Teaching

I don't remember the first moment I realized I was a teacher. It came gradually—in my late teens when I gave poetry readings at and around college, and in my twenties as I translated for lamas and helped people in answering their questions if the lama wasn't conversant with cross-cultural issues and dilemmas. Gradually, over more than a decade of assisting my teachers in various ways, I apprenticed and grew into the teacher role by helping others. But teaching, like inter-meditation, is permeable; the boundaries are not fixed. People chronologically or spiritually younger than you might become more adept. The Buddha considered a teacher—spiritual friend, or *kalyanamitra*—as someone who can help us along the path. It's not really a quantitative judgment—it implies wiser but not necessarily older. And our roles can change over the years; no one need be stuck in any place forever. We learn this the hard but tried-and-true way—through personal experience.

Teaching takes work, character, fortitude, and a strong foundation—so buyer beware, window shop before you try things on and acquire them. Before you trust someone as your spiritual guide in a formal inter-meditation situation—before you entertain the real possibility of putting your spiritual life in their hands—be sure that they are qualified, that the selfless intent and altruistic Bodhichitta is there. When I teach, I always start by setting my intentions and remembering why I'm in that role—for the benefit of the people I'm teaching. I'm there to serve and to transmit what was taught and transmitted to me, from antiquity or from Above, through the entire lineage of enlightenment. I'm reminded to act more for the students' good than for my own; although, as an inter-meditation, the feelings are mutual and certainly work both ways. Again, it's like Tonglen: *Give the profit and victory to others; take the blame and loss for oneself.* Teaching is reciprocal, like parent and child—you're not there only for them, of course, but those who are smaller or weaker come first. As a teacher, you need to be there more for others than yourself. The power and knowledge imbalance, the different roles, and the essential contract require it. Similarly, your contract with your higher self tips the balance in inter-meditation toward the greater good—as the German philosopher Immanuel Kant urged: "Live your life as though your every act were to become a universal law." It's a venerable categorical imperative writ large on the Mahayana canvas of universal deliverance.

Inter-meditating with students and empowering them never weakens or disempowers the teacher. It's about seeing the best in others as well as in yourself and trying to bring it out. I love the Italian Renaissance art in Florence, Michelangelo's sculptures above all. He said: "In every block of marble I see a statue as plain as though it stood before me, shaped and perfect in attitude and action. I have only to hew away the rough walls that imprison the lovely apparition to reveal it to the other eyes as mine see it."[1] There's a beautiful form in there; the David or the Pietà emerges from within it. Teachers see that perfection in people, just like we see our best selves in others. The greatest teachers are like mirrors; they reflect the student's higher self, not the teacher's egotism or even greatness. This mutually beneficial reflection and interpenetration is inter-meditation and co-meditation, mutually elevating us together onto the farther reaches of the illumined life.

Forgive me for being so bold, but here it is: I can wholeheartedly state today that, after many years as a truth-seeker, I have found and accomplished what I want and need in life; for me now it's all about the young'uns—of whatever age they may be.

I want to be the Bodhisattva of Children of All Ages. I genuinely wish only to lift them up in my maroon lama's robe, and into the light. Won't you join me?

According to the Kalama Sutta (the Buddha's "charter of free inquiry"), "An authentic teacher, like the Buddha himself, welcomes questioning and helps to put his spiritual charges in touch with their own internal spiritual center—with the Buddhaness within." The best teachers don't follow the limited "It's my way or the highway" approach, but have the chops to help facilitate the next steps on whatever path their students are meant to be on, according to the British dictum "Different courses for different horses." Imitation simply will not do. A Bodhisattva teacher resembles a midwife who helps souls take rebirth into a life far beyond their wildest imaginings—Nirvana. But it's closer than we think; it's in this very life, not somewhere far away or some magical place after we die. This is the promise of sages throughout the ages.

Bad Teachers

Not all teachers have their students' best interests at heart. You should be careful whom you trust, whom you inter-meditate with, until you have a little experience—unless you want to risk catching something you might not appreciate. Having spent a significant amount of my life training in silent Buddhist meditation retreats, cloisters, mountain forests, caves, and the like, I have seen what can sometimes happen. Isolation, the monastic hierarchy, autocratic teachers, rigid systems, extended silence, chastity, poverty, and obedience can—for some seekers—have dangerous repercussions, and therefore may be contraindicated in some cases. A wise, objective, and experienced teacher will often know this and adjust instructions accordingly. Austerities and rigorous disciplines do not always help communing and inter-meditation; in fact, they can manifest as a form of abuse under the wrong combination of personalities, circumstances, and conditions. It's crucial to scrutinize yourself and recognize the distinction between a healthy and unhealthy relationship with a teacher or a congregation. It's like dating—you don't have to marry the first person that comes along. Self-deception is the bane of spiritual life.

Unfortunately, human nature being what it is, it is little or no surprise that not all teachers are altruistic, pure, and radiant manifestations of the holy ideals the major world religions and humanistic traditions proclaim. Some teachers eagerly hurry everyone they encounter into their particular fold. Fragile or unstable people are especially vulnerable when subjected to these autocratic, charismatic-yet-deluded, toxic, or even empire-building types of spiritual leaders. Over the years, I've had my own run-ins with cult leaders like Shoko Asahara of Japan, Reverend Moon of Korea, and Bhagvan Rajneesh of India; I've learned a lot from their outlandish, exploitative, and even criminal actions. Personally, I've found it useful to thoroughly screen my own students, and seek always to inculcate leadership rather than followership in them. We try to thoroughly prepare potential trainees who wish to participate in my Dzogchen Center's more intense silent meditation retreats and inter-meditation practices, observing them over a period of time in shorter retreats before encouraging them to become involved in long-term practice training sessions in rigorous conditions, which might prove to be to their detriment. I don't want to inadvertently turn a god into a demon through lack of conscientious guidance! Nor do I want to become a leader of an organization that has no honorable graduates but only shunned leave-takers—this would break my heart. To tell you the truth: I hate that shit!

There is not much professional oversight or organizational hierarchy in Buddhism. However, every authorized and qualified teacher answers to their own teacher and their own lineage tradition, stemming from Buddha himself, to a certain extent. Traditional monasteries in the East have their own systems of checks and balances, including communal monthly rituals and acknowledgments of wrongdoing. This has been the case for over twenty-five hundred years, since the time of the Enlightened Buddha. Eastern disciplines like Buddhism, meditation, and yoga are fairly new in our Western culture. We each have to rely on asking questions, research on the Internet, our own spiritual and emotional intelligence, and good old word of mouth to make intelligent decisions. And remember: far too often, the worst teachers are full of passionate intensity while the best are fraught with doubt and inner conflict. Again: rely on your open, inquiring mind, as well as your critical intellect.

His Holiness the Dalai Lama has told me that he considers himself "a simple Buddhist monk" (as opposed to a Pope-like figure), and he speaks out regularly "against ethical lapses, exploitation, abuse, and corruption among spiritual teachers, which is totally against what Buddha taught." He has advised me that "we should be Twenty-First Century Buddhists, socially engaged and open to science and psychology and other religions, developing critical thinking through modern education." He exhorts us to examine our teachers for quite a while before putting ourselves directly under their tutelage, and to be vigilant and discerning, self-critical as well as tolerant. We need to support each other in spiritual friendship, collegiality, and community. In this way, we can advance a balanced, harmonious, wise, altruistic, and actively engaged compassionate path of enlightenment that can bring significant benefits to the entire world.

> Don't point out the flea in someone else's hair while overlooking the yak on your own nose.

An old Tibetan saying puts it like this: "Don't point out the flea in someone else's hair while overlooking the yak on your own nose." St. Matthew said: "Why do you look at the speck of sawdust in your brother's eye and pay no attention to the plank in your own eye?" I myself try mainly to turn the spotlight of critical questioning and discernment *inward*. Everything we seek is within, as the scriptures say. It exists within each and every one of us, if we could only look deep and see it.

INTER-MEDITATION PRACTICE

Truth-Paring Debate or Mondo

A type of inter-meditation that helps determine if you and a teacher are a good match is what I call Truth-Paring Debate. It involves arguing, discussing, investigating, and exploring a spiritual proposition. Just as a teacher should test you, you might do well to test or at least check out the teacher by delving into questions like these:

- How did you become a teacher?
- Who were your teachers? What's their lineage?
- How long did you study?

- What do you teach, emphasize, consider most important?
- How can you help me progress spiritually, and find what I'm looking for?
- What is the path you put forth?
- Is there such a thing as God or ultimate reality?
- Is everything subjective, or substantially real, or what?
- Is there a fixed morality and code you follow and expect us to follow?
- Why do bad things happen to good people, and vice versa?
- What is the self, soul, spirit? What is the true nature of mind or personal identity?
- What, if anything, is my responsibility to others and to the world at large?
- Can we experiment and explore this together?

We can save a lot of time, trouble, and heartache if we just engage with honesty and conscious intent, a truth-seeking beginner's mind, openness, and genuine reflection. Some kind of wisdom dialogue like the one offered above can become a way of checking out a teacher, learning to internalize their teachings, and simultaneously allowing them to learn and adapt afresh from co-meditating with you. Please strive conscientiously to find answers to your own genuine questions—not just the ones I have posited here. It's the best way to discover the spiritual communion that can lead to direct transmission of timeless, essential teachings. It certainly takes two (not one) to tango, in this kind of co-meditation. There is no teacher unless there is a student, and vice versa; at least it's put that way in the lineage transmission traditions. Genuine self-enlighteners and instant awakeners are the exception to this rule, and such individuals are exceedingly rare.

In Tibetan this sacred question-and-answer session between a teacher and a student is called *shu-len* or *tri-len*. The word for teaching is *tri* in Tibetan. The Tibetan masters divide *tri* into three progressively deepening parts: *shay-tri* (regular teachings and oral commentaries), *ngon-tri* (experiential teaching advices), and *mar-tri* (esoteric pith-instructions—the one-on-one "whispered" secret, sacred heart-advice). *Mar-tri* literally means "naked" or "red teaching," suggesting life-giving blood, fresh flesh, and marrow. When my own blessed master Khenpo Rinpoche took me aside in the early 1990s, sat me down in front of him beneath some trees on a mountainside, chanted, and then transmitted to me his special one-to-one aural pith-instruction lineage, it was mar-tri. This was his heart-essence of awakenedness whispered to my ears only—not published and printed teachings and ideas. Later he wrote some of it in his own shaky handwriting for me to remember and have after he died. I still cherish those notes in my personal old prayer book, and keep copies in my Dzogchen Center archives and lamas' lineage and legacy preservation project.

Like a mountainside, a formal setting for inter-meditation—a monastery, a sanctuary or prayer room, a confessional, or a therapist's office—has its virtues. It gives us the structure, firm intention, safe space, and the freedom to focus. This is often the most efficient way to get from point A to B, but it doesn't have to be like that. Think of that all-night conversation in college that may have utterly changed how you saw the world, that sermon or Dharma talk that shook your foundations and transformed your life, or that intense argument that cracked you open or connected you fully with someone in the depths of your disagreement.

Moments like these illuminate new wisdom or understanding and make you a better, wiser, or more loving person as a result. There's no telling when the lightning of awakening will strike, but spiritual practice makes you more prone to it. It's a live thing—a flame. Beneath this blazing consciousness, my body is mere wax. But when this wax melts away, I pray that flame passes forward to light countless youthful lamps, just as my beloved master-teachers, mentors, sacred lovers, and spiritual friends gave me their flame of love and wisdom.

A Quintessential Awakening Presence: The Dalai Lama

Jon was the first mentor who made me a teacher, and what I learned from him enabled me to seek and find another important teacher—His Holiness the Dalai Lama. I first encountered him in June of 1972, when I was traveling through northern India. His Holiness wasn't as well known internationally then as he is now, especially since receiving the Nobel Peace Prize in 1989.

When I arrived at his residence in Dharamsala, His Holiness greeted me at the door, shook my hand, and continued to hold it while guiding me to sit near him on his living room couch. His actions felt so natural and genuine; he obviously intended to diminish the intimidation factor and sidestep the Tibetan custom of visitors prostrating themselves three times on the floor before him. On that first visit I spent forty-five minutes alone with the Dalai Lama and his right-hand man, Tenzin Getche. Once I got past being thrilled that a Jewish kid from Long Island could be in the same room as a living Buddha, his total presence and incandescent awareness overwhelmed my habitual conscious mind—all my hang-ups, preoccupations, self-as-heroic-protagonist stories, and ordinary perceptions. The Dalai Lama was awake, shining, alert, and simultaneously gentle, and even spontaneous and a bit boyish. He seemed to delight in the oversized, bearded American seeker he found before him. He was curious, humble, and respectful; he told me how much he appreciated me taking the time to meditate and investigate Buddhism, especially since he kept so busy with political duties, which severely limited his own time to practice, teach, and study. I began to see myself as he saw me, with a lot of potential and a great deal of purity and innocence. My best and highest self became prominent as my ego self receded, and we had a meeting of heart and mind, soul and spirit. He and I aligned intimately, intensely, and immutably; we felt completely connected. This feeling surpassed my wildest dreams and expectations of any world leader, esteemed elder or teacher, or even the fabled hierarch of Tibetan Buddhism.

I didn't expect much from popes and presidents after living through the shattering era of assassinations in America in the 1960s and the disillusionment of the Vietnam War, but my experience with His Holiness was something else entirely. I had rarely if ever encountered someone who was what he was supposed to be, who perfectly fit and seemed comfortable in the skin he was in, no matter how outsized or sacrosanct. The Dalai Lama was totally, utterly, unconditionally present, and seemed to have eyes and ears for no one but me—the person sitting before him. Lately others too have remarked on this incredible capacity of His Holiness to be utterly present for and with whoever is before him. Years later, when I asked him about this habit of complete compassion and attention, he responded, "What else is there to do?" It was so matter-of-fact and commonsensical that it took me aback. The wisdom of that simple statement has stayed with me ever since.

Yes, friends: what else is there to do except to love the one you're with? Co-meditation provides the fitting vehicle for us to be intimately engaged with whoever and whatever appears, through incandescent, moment-to-moment presence of mind. Being totally attuned and aligned is love.

I didn't have a name for it in those days, but sitting with the Dalai Lama on his couch was co-meditation—one that has never ended. I still feel it, right now. Our inter-meditation remains with me in a timeless way, elevating and informing my discipleship as well as my spiritual practice, and particularly my meditation. I always feel him with me and around me, guiding and protecting me, buoying me up. Seeing his picture or hearing his name affirms for me that nobody meditates alone, even if there is no *body* nearby. I can feel his hands on my head and gently patting my cheeks. My connection to His Holiness connects me to all Buddha-lamas and realized masters throughout space and time, and to all those on high, by whatever name or form we call or imagine them. Seen one, you've seen 'em all! Seriously, His Holiness is an archetype or icon of all that, the ultimate reality, the unconditioned and inconceivable in human form and condition. I have no other explanation. Nor has he ever failed me in that capacity over these last four decades.

How can I ever repay him? When I asked, he said, "Realize these truths, this liberating wisdom, and pass it on."

Co-Meditating with the Dalai Lama

- Think clearly of His Holiness the Dalai Lama (looking up to him).
- Visualize him right before you and with you, eye to eye, heart to heart, and/or look at his picture.
- Remember the gorgeous Guru-Lama (and his enlightened qualities) as the Compassionate Buddha and his pure, clear, warm, and loving presence.
- Pray to him / her / it (with or without words, from the heartfelt core of your being) for blessings, encouragement, inspiration, grace, protection, and guidance.
- Absorb the flow of spiritual transmission and timeless wisdom.
- Receive directly his blessings through a powerfully streaming light-beam of his sublime divine energy.
- Merge and dissolve with him in the Heart-Essence of sublime Presence.
- Rest joyously, radiantly, abundantly, and inseparably in that exalted expanse.
- Chant, repeatedly, *Om Dalai La-Ma Pray-Me Home, Om Mani Padme Hung.*
- Meditate in (breath) and out (breath) as the Dalai Lama, letting go and letting him breathe through you.

- See through yourself and free your bottled up, innate Buddhaness—let it manifest splendidly in the world.
- Re-enter the daily world with open arms, loving eyes, giving hands, and a kind heart— as an Awakening Being, Light-Bearer, and Bodhisattva—paying it forward, uplifting and edifying the world . . . like a young lama. Why not?

Inter-Meditating with Our Guides

Besides staying in touch personally with my gurus and sangha, I try to check in transpersonally with my spiritual guides and benefactors every single day through my contemplative practices, including inter-meditations, Vajra yoga, sacred lineage chants, devotional practice, and prayer. The Dalai Lama would be the first to tell you that you too can do this. You can learn to make this heartfelt, mystic interior connection, this inter-meditation with your Higher Power, your inner power, or whatever embodies and represents that which moves and transports you to your best self and higher ground. It's like a figure-ground shift: one moment I'm looking up at the stars in the sky, venerating and praying to the Buddha, Tara, Dalai Lama, or Gyalwa Karmapa; the next moment I'm looking down on this world and all its beings (including my little egocentric self) as if I'm using the eyes of the stars, or as if I'm an enormous transparent eyeball in the sky. How long have I been seeking the One, who has been looking out through my eyes all along! How amusing! *Emaho!* Wondrous, miraculous, eureka!

Accessing Big Mind, BuddhaMind, Divine I

- Begin by calling the sublime entity to mind—the Big Self, God, the Divine.
- Image-in it, visualize it, envision it—see it in your mind's "iye" (the ego "I" seeing through the eye).
- Visualize or look at a picture or object that symbolizes what I call Buddhaness, but you might very well name something else (Higher Power, Source, Totality, The One).
- Breathe; allow yourself to connect to its presence.
- Breathe out into it; breathe in, out of it.
- Repeat that (above).
- Tune in, sense, intuit, feel, be still, and know.
- Now proceed accordingly; let your innate wisdom-mind—Bodhichitta—be your guide, and travel safely.

We can never stray or fall from this path. The eye by which we see is the eye by which we are seen. This is the mystery of Divine Mind, BuddhaMind. Align yourself with it, and enjoy. Who do you think you're *not*?

The Miracle of a Teacher's Love

To successfully inter-meditate with a teacher we must have a healthy respect for that special, elevated plane of mutually *being with*. Whoever brings us to that acts like an awakener or enlightener to us, whatever kind of teacher or spiritual friend they may be. Remember that the miracle of seeing God in everyone and everything is the ultimate inter-meditation. This reveals and expresses divinity, lifts the veil of separateness, and helps us see beyond self and other, sacred and mundane, us and them. That's the true miracle of love, the all-embracing heart, the big inter-meditation beyond meditating. Tibetans call it *pure vision* or sacred outlook: perceiving the light of spirit in everyone and everything, every moment.

As I wrote earlier, one of my first teachers was Neem Karoli Baba, or, as we called him, Maharajji. I was just twenty-one and he seemed quite ancient when I met him at his ashram in Northern India in early winter of 1972. My older friends Baba Ram Dass and Krishna Das and Mirabai Bush, and all the Das brothers, were already there. So was Larry Brilliant and his wife Girija—decades before Larry became the head of the Google Foundation. I believe psychologist Daniel Goleman was there too. It was an extraordinary, karmically fortunate gathering of souls.

A few years ago, Larry was interviewed for a terrific movie called *Fierce Grace* about Baba Ram Dass. Larry's story can teach us about a teacher's love—for Maharajji's greatest miracle was the miracle of unconditional love and having a universal heart and seeing God in everyone and everything.

How do I explain who Maharajji was, and how he did what he did? I don't have any explanation. Maybe it was his love of God. I can't explain who he was. I can almost begin to understand how he loved everybody. I mean, that was sort of his job. He was a saint. Saints are supposed to love everybody. That's not what has always so staggered me. What staggered me is not that he loved everybody, but that when I was sitting in front of him, I loved everybody. That was the hardest thing for me to understand. How he could so totally transform the spirit of people who were with him and bring out not just the best in us, but something that wasn't even in us, we didn't know. I don't think any of us were ever as good or as pure or as loving in our whole life as we were when we were sitting in front of him.

The most common word that he ever said was "Ram," God's name, and the second most common was "Jau," "get out of here." And all the Westerners who would come to him, attracted like a magnet, he would always say, "Go away. Go away." No, I don't think he wanted anything ever from me or from any of us. We tried to give him things. You couldn't give him money. You couldn't do anything for him. There was nothing that he needed.[2]

That's the ultimate inter-meditation, being *with* _____ and *in* _____. You fill in the blanks: God, the Divine, and mutual reciprocity with/in that. That's why I call it inter-meditation or relational meditation. Mutual reciprocity—being with God is *being* Godly. That's what it says in the Upanishads.

Baba Ram Dass reminded me the last time I saw him in Maui: "When I forget who I really am, I worship you, Lord. When I remember who I really am, I *am* you, Lord." That's a great teaching from monkey god Hanuman on the principles of inter-meditation, of the mutual reciprocity of receiving and giving and sharing beyond separateness—of returning to the Whole and *convergitating* in intrinsic wholeness.

The Power of a Teacher's Transmission

In the early-mid 1970s, years before we'd get together for lunch in fancy hotels in New York City, I tutored a ten-year-old boy in English every morning at his refugee-filled little monastery composed of shacks on a tea-bush-planted hillside outside Darjeeling, India. He had a bicycle and a bunch of tutors and elders, and I taught him his ABCs. By the time I saw him in mid-morning, he'd already been up and at it for several hours, chanting his mantras, prayers, and liturgies, prostrating and doing energetic Tibetan yoga. Even as a child, His Holiness the Twelfth Gyalwang Drukpa was already recognized as a reincarnation of the Eleventh Gyalwang Drukpa, the reincarnate head of the Kagyu Dragon lineage that goes back to the early 1000s C.E. The insouciant boy I taught has now become an important and accomplished teacher, the master of the largest monastery in Kathmandu Valley, and an international humanitarian. He has monasteries and nunneries, projects, and Dharma centers around Asia and the world. A few years ago I asked him, "What is it about authentic lineage that is passed on or transmitted?" He replied:

> A blessing. The blessing is something very mysterious,
> actually. It is like a boost or encouragement. It is not
> only mysterious, it also has a lot of substance. There
> are also years and decades, centuries of experience
> here, amidst the blessings and teaching. There's an
> unbelievable sense of transformation of your mental
> state, liberating your mind and opening your heart.
> How can I express it, because it's like tasting honey?
> It's sweet; but sweet means what? It's inexpressible. I
> feel very happy, delighted, delicious, but I can't express

it—until you taste it, and then we can share something of the experience together. This is one aspect of the blessing, of course, which a book or mere words alone cannot give you.

But this is not the only important aspect. What I care about is that the blessing is truly transforming. Your life transforms into the divine state of mind. Even though you live the same way, everything is different—concepts, precepts, everything is different. Yesterday maybe you were unhappy; perhaps you were stealing, cheating, drinking, or simply dissatisfied or depressed. But last night perhaps by good karma you have seen the appropriate guru and have been inspired to change and today you have changed.

> May I meet this moment fully. May I meet it harmoniously as a friend.

This is not necessarily overnight; it may take years or decades but time doesn't matter. It changes everything, the whole world, your whole attitude. Your whole life can be transformed. From my point of view, if there is no guru, there is no way to get enlightenment. I'm one hundred percent sure. You have to have a personal transmission from a qualified genuine guru, one who has the lineage and is qualified to give this. If you don't have the lineage, your practice and path is uncooked, unfinished. If you don't have a human master who gave you the lineage, it cannot be received from a book.[3]

We can put this into terms of inter-meditations such as Tonglen: *Feel what we feel; feel what other feels,* because it's a two-way street—not only can we connect to our teachers, our teachers can and will indubitably connect with us. Formalizing the connection can have applications to any student-teacher co-meditational relationship. We plug in and make the connection, align ourselves and get on the same wavelength, merge and mingle with our Higher Power and inner power; then release *selfiness,* relax, open, and blossom, catch the updrafts and spontaneously soar together in Spirit's infinite space.

Receiving the Gift of Awakening

The Buddhist masters of Tibet regularly practice a rite in which they use their accumulated spiritual energy and self-mastery—accrued and consolidated from years of meditation and related psychic-energy practices—to help transfer their consciousness and awareness to their disciples. They also offer this practice to guide the recently deceased to higher forms of existence and what Buddhists think of as better rebirths.

These sacred ceremonies transmit energy from the source through the master to the disciple. Any priest, rabbi, imam, healer, shaman, or other sort of wonderworker (almost without exception) will necessarily and even joyfully connect with and share their source and Higher Power. In doing so, they learned how to set aside their small self so that, with the shadow of separateness and self-interest out of the way, higher purposes can be fulfilled. We Buddhists and lamas usually say chants and prayers while invoking and envisioning the entire invisible array of our lineages above and around and within us in order to help channel, direct, and focus this stream of blessings and energy to empower others. We definitely find a mutual reciprocity here, a potent co-meditation, between the person requesting transmission or help and the intermediary (priest, lama, practitioner). It's a way to tap the highest imaginable power source and share that ineffable energy. This is not merely a metaphor; it's a literal truth.

And it's not just the Buddhists. We learn of this transmission in other spiritual traditions as well, like the laying on of hands in Christianity. My friend Father Michael Halloran, a Zen Buddhist Catholic priest in New York, told me the Shingon school of Buddhism teaches a technique of mirroring where two people meditate together and each can meaningfully impact the other's meditation. Think about any encounter that leads to a real breakthrough or epiphany—with a psychotherapist, piano teacher, or baseball coach—that moment when you finally get it but you couldn't have gotten it alone. This inter-meditation helps precipitate a quantum leap in consciousness.

Chögyam Trungpa Rinpoche put it like this:

> In order to avoid charging up the ego, it is necessary to ask some external person to give you something, so that you feel that something is given to you. Then you don't regard it as your wealth, which he or she is giving back to you, but as something very precious of his or hers. So one must also be very grateful to the teacher. That is a great protection against the ego, since you do not look on the awakened state as something discovered within yourself, but as something which someone else has given you. In reality, the transmission is simply discovered within oneself. All the teacher can do is to create the situation.[4]

The Jewel Internet of Indra and Webitation

In Buddhism we refer to the Jewel Net of Indra, an ancient cosmic metaphor that illustrates how we're all interconnected. Writer and translator Francis Dojun Cook explains it beautifully:

> Far away in the heavenly abode of the great god Indra, there is a wonderful net which has been hung by some cunning artificer in such a manner that it stretches out infinitely in all directions. In accordance with the extravagant tastes of deities, the artificer has hung a single glittering jewel in each "eye" of the net, and since the net itself is infinite in dimension, the jewels are infinite in number. There hang the jewels, glittering "like" stars in the first magnitude, a wonderful sight to behold. If we now arbitrarily select one of these jewels for inspection and look closely at it, we will discover that in its polished surface there are reflected all the other jewels in the net, infinite in number. Not only that, but each of the jewels reflected in this one jewel is also reflecting all the other jewels, so that there is an infinite reflecting process occurring.[5]

Those shining, mirror-like precious jewels are each of us. Despite my Luddite moments, I've always thought the Internet works as a technological Jewel Net—in which each of us can mutually interpenetrate and reflect back on the other through the remarkable structure of bytes and signals and electricity. Since the mid-nineties I've become interested to see how the Internet can be applied to teaching and transmitting the Dharma. Is it another means of inter-meditation? Or inter-webitation?

Maybe it's not the same, but who knows? I've had some modest success with my websites, Ask-the-Lama columns, and blogs over the years. Now I wish to help make social media include spiritual media and to share my webitations.

One time, as we were toddling around the local pond amid the glorious autumn sun-bronzed divineness of New England, my astute friend Lila said to me, "The online courses and webinars and all are fine, but isn't it hard to stay riveted to your screen when you're alone, as opposed to the deliciously gluey force of practicing together? Can the real sacred work happen without face-to-face human interaction?"

I see her point entirely. *Where* are people actually doing their online trainings? I've seen advertisements for "online retreats," but what's the user's experience? Are they seated comfortably in front of their laptop away from everything else for a time, perhaps in a clear and dedicated contemplative space, or cradling their iPad in a contemplative moment, perhaps in bed or alone on the couch, or outside in nature? Or are they ensconced amid the towering piles and files of the average person's workspace, crammed with electronics, books, and paper? Perhaps they're viewing the event on a small handheld device, wherever they happen to be—perhaps in a subway or plane, or even walking or, worse, *driving*?

Lila said that when she and her friend get together for their far-off Buddhist teacher Namkhai Norbu's streaming and beaming meditation instructions and transmission, they definitely feel a lot tighter together and more closely aligned with the transmission taking place than either can experience alone. I'd say that this kind of spiritual partnership through webitation—verging on consorting—certainly bears out the old adage that I newly made up: "Co-meditation with benefits."

In recent years, someone asked the Dalai Lama if a traditional tantric initiation transmission could be as effective over the Internet as in person—an interesting question indeed. Many traditionalists and rationalists would say no. His Holiness responded, "Yes, if it takes place simultaneously." In other words, if people align in real time, and the transmission is not just recorded and received later. He and other Tibetan lamas of great repute now give initiations and esoteric teachings online—inter-webitators all. First they did it only for their students, but now they offer these teachings to the public. You can log in and see the Karmapa sitting under the Bodhi Tree at the Monlam Tibetan Buddhist prayer festival every winter in Bodh Gaya, and see the monks and nuns around him chanting. It's almost like being there; whether it's exactly as effective or not I'll leave to you. Just remember what Jesus said to Doubting Thomas in John 20:29: "Thomas, because thou hast seen Me, thou hast believed: blessed are they that have not seen, and yet have believed." Like me, some of us have seen, but still find it hard to believe. So much of this sounds too good to be true! With a little help from my friends, I have come to find that believing is seeing, and all the senses get involved.

These webitations presage a new era of possibilities for global co-meditation via webitation, which we're just beginning to explore. I've been delighted and surprised to find that, despite my hesitations, technology is starting to work for me as a lama. In fact, one of my most powerful inter-meditation encounters happened via the Internet.

Deathbed Co-Meditation:
Skyping as a Way of Intimate Connection

I'm often called to attend people's deaths. Skype has really helped me do my lama duties as required and requested, especially on short notice. For example, one day I received an email from Greece from a woman who introduced herself as the wife of a friend I hadn't seen since my days in India—Vivekananda, a.k.a. Evangelos. She said, "It's nice to connect with you. Evangelos has always talked so lovingly of you and the time you traveled together and shared a room in Benares in the seventies. We read your books and look you up on the Internet." We exchanged a few more sincere appreciations and memories, and then she said, "Anyway, I'm calling you because Evangelos is in the hospital with lung cancer and he's dying, and he's got an oxygen mask on and can hardly talk, and he asked if you could help him cross over. Because you're his old lama friend, and he trusts you." I said, "Of course. How can I help?"

She invited me to fly to Greece at her expense, but we decided to get together virtually via Skype. Evangelos was connected to so many apparatuses that he couldn't talk, so the telephone or speakerphone—which I usually use with people in hospitals, hospices, or their own homes—wouldn't work. So his wife set up a Skype call and put the laptop on the tray over his chest. I talked to him a little; he nodded his head and soon began to cry. We hadn't spoken in about thirty years, but that didn't seem to matter; we were still pals, comrades, and brothers. And so I began to chant. I sang some beautiful chants that we had done together in our ashram in India. And I chanted a little bit from the Tibetan Book of the Dead, which guides the "mental body" or "light body" through the in-between (*bardo*) state after death.

I was there with him and he was there with me, even though I was at home in Boston and he was on the island of Mykonos in Greece. He continued nodding and crying as I chanted, as if chanting along, and we experienced a gorgeous inter-meditation. I consider that face-to-face encounter a blessing and teaching for both of us—one in spirit and one at heart—even though our corporeal forms seemed 4,700 miles apart.

Inter-meditating with the dying is one of the most mysterious, important, and meaningful things I do as a lama teacher. It's not hard; it comes naturally. People in this place of great transition pull the absolute best out of you, if you can just be there for them and with them, agenda-less and attentive, openhearted and caring—it's love's imperative. At that crucial juncture, it's no longer expectation, obligation, appearances, preference, or desire; it's simply a privilege and a boon for people to request help at that point in their journeys. And it helps me a lot, too. Sitting with those in the process of dying is often the most meaningful thing I do all month. Still, I'm not entirely sure why that is.

The Biggest Teacher

Using technology like Skype makes me think of those flying, golden-robed lamas of Kathok Monastery gliding throughout the Himalayan sky amid the sun's rays. Remember Atisha's provocative slogan: "Be like a wizard of illusion, a skilled magician, while remaining as innocent and full of wonder as a child."

Almost every child seems to have an invisible imaginary friend. My dear goddaughter Linda had Anthony, a large pink and white rabbit. Imaginary companions answer a primordial, archetypal need. My Indian holy friends (sadhus) refer to "The Constant Companion" who is always with us. Some grownups see it too—this ascendant being or presence, like the anima and animus—as their guardian angel, ally, or spirit guide. Others experience it as their patron saint, benefactor-like ancestor, guru, or angel. Others realize it as their Higher Power, god, goddess, Buddha, Bodhisattva, or Jesus leading them forward, upward, and deeper—illuminating their way. This is not mere superstition, I can tell you.

This kind of communion or relational meditation allows us to loosen the knot of dualistic mind and enter into the tantric world of non-separation or oneness, completeness, totality—what Buddhists generally refer to as non-duality ("not two"). It allows us to inter-meditate with everything, utilizing and integrating every single thing—outer, inner, and incredibly subtle—as nourishment for the contemplative process. This warp and woof of everyday reality with all its polarities, dichotomies, choices, attractions, and antipathies becomes the very spiritual fabric of our brocade rainbow-light sacred body. Thus we co-meditators regularly pray, resolve, and affirm with friendliness, nonaggression, and loving-kindness in our hearts:

> May I meet this moment fully.
> May I meet it harmoniously as a friend.

In this way, we can befriend the whole world by befriending each other and ourselves as we learn better to cleave to the higher ground of I-Thou relationships in all of our relationships and states of mind, making everyone and everything our teachers, friends, and benefactors. The wise learn from the wise as well as the foolish how to be and how *not* to be; thus, everyone and everything is grist for the mill of incandescent self-awareness. When we awaken in the morning and receive life's gifts again, every day becomes a good day.

INTER-MEDITATION PRACTICE
Your Constant Companion

Here's an inter-meditation practice that you can do with whoever embodies or archetypically represents your Higher Power. (Or skip the go-between and do it directly with the Divine.)

- Call a teacher to mind—the lama on the cushion across from you, the cleric at the front of the church, or the memory of anyone who connects you with your transcendent and best self, the Big Self that's wholly good, incorruptible, and complete.
- As you meditate, visualize or look at a photograph of your teacher or holy representative (I like to use a picture or mental image of the Dalai Lama).
- Tune in to their presence. Be still and listen to the silence within. "Iye"-gaze with them, mutually inter-meditating and convergitating.
- Let their presence seep into you on all levels—outer, inner, subtle, and invisible. Embrace inextricable oneness and blessed union with this form of the Beloved.
- Let your Big Self and their Big Self become one—together as inter-self—fully aligned, interwoven, and interbeing.

- Enjoy the natural great perfection of things left just as they *are*, as the rising inner sun of wisdom naturally radiates its warm light rays of loving, compassionate action into the world, as needed and wanted.
- Stride forward, gently yet firmly, fearless and awake, into the shining waves of life, brandishing the brilliant sword of discriminating awareness.

Buddha said that transcendent peace exists in things left just as they are. I have found that all things are already at rest and at peace, inasmuch as one's own inner life remains fit, flexible, and attuned. Tuning in to this actuality, we can take action in manifesting genuine power, without bias, sloppiness, or compulsion.

It's one thing to work contemplatively with masters, people like the Dalai Lama whose jobs, missions, and personal narratives include lobbying for both universal spiritual enlightenment and human rights. Additionally, they take the time to inter-meditate with us to help us get in touch with our Big Selves—this is the very essence of co-meditation. And while we should rely on our teachers, we must never forget to return to our own wisdom and practice. Again: We are the ones we've been waiting for! Occupy the spirit. There definitely comes a time when we have to take it off the cushion or yoga mat, out of the therapist's office, home from the church, temple, or classroom, and into the real world where it truly counts. This is where the rubber meets the road on the spiritual path. How can we really gain traction on the path, our path? Why not start with the living Buddha in our own bedroom?

4

A Passion for Oneness

The Tantra of Co-Spirituality

According to Hindu scriptures, when Shiva (He) looks at Shakti (She) and Shakti returns that glance, whole worlds are enlivened, co-created, aligned, ignited, and illumined. Passion blazes up and consumes the universe, transforming and transmuting the dull lead of our own human-animal bodies into the gold of sacred spirit and gnosis. That sensation of irrepressible bliss of first falling in love, that complete experience of no-separation—*right there*—that's co-meditation, a sense of complete interpenetration without barriers or separateness. Who hasn't felt that?

Co-meditative inter-awareness allows us to relax, relent, and dissolve into that which far exceeds our small selves, as if bursting a bubble and recognizing that there's no difference between the air inside the bubble and the air outside—it's all air. Some might call popping that bubble surrendering our will to a Higher Power. I usually think of it in a more non-theistic

Buddhist way as mixing Spirit or Dharma inseparably with the reality of day-to-day life. Doing this in every moment—recognizing that nothing is impermeable and no separation actually exists between others and ourselves—that's the ideal of an intimate, coupled relationship. It implies integrity and intimacy, the sacred bond of Two I's, beyond the third i of egotism. Partners, consorts, and soul mates help elevate each other through co-meditation, inter-meditation. I've coined my own word for this experience—*convergitation*. It's not as simple as becoming one together, but includes making each other better and more vitally whole and enlivened (if not enlightened).

Nowadays in Western society, although marriage remains a beautiful and prevalent institution, the term "couple" does not necessarily mean husband and wife; the term no longer strictly refers to traditional forms of marriage, nor to any particular sexual orientation, but rather indicates a dedicated romantic, trusting, soulful, intimate, and committed partnership. In fact, coupled relationships today are not necessarily limited to our chosen spouse or to any one person at all. In Tibet, polyandry was not uncommon—generally with a Tibetan woman marrying multiple brothers—and that culture is also known for consort practice, the sacred yogic relationship often found outside of marriage.

I recently enjoyed meeting a wonderful woman, the consort of a very realized Tibetan lama and now his wife. She told my partner and me that the job of a consort is to elevate and support the lama, in whatever way possible, thus aligning with and further enhancing his altruistic work and Bodhisattva mission. My partner asked, "Isn't that supposed to be mutual and work both ways?" The realized consort exclaimed, "We [women] are already elevated." She wasn't boasting; she was sitting in her (Buddha) seat, coming from divine pride and deity-like dignity rather than simple egotism or superiority. I felt privileged to be included in this conversation between these two *dakinis*.

This pith-instruction echoes what Sangyum Kamala, the wife of the oldest living Dzogchen master, Nepal's Jatral Rinpoche, told a gathering in no uncertain terms at our recent nonsectarian prayer-fest called Rimay Monlam in Garrison, New York: "Women have more challenges and difficulties in this world, generally, but they are superior to men, when they've raised their spiritual heart and awakened body and mind, energy and spirit." *Superior and pre-enlightened already . . .* it's the dakinis' mystery, no explaining it. Homage to the Mother of Immanent Wisdom, Prajna Paramita, womb of all the Buddhas.

French and other European societies have long accepted lifelong romances like these, outside traditional marriage and nuclear households, particularly before couples could legally divorce, or when love partners could not marry for reasons of law, social status, or other constraints. Moreover, in our society, polyamorous people exist in respectable social roles and positions. Regardless, when considering any coupling along these lines, I'm sure we need to consider the fourth moral precept of Buddhism: "I shall refrain from sexual activity harmful to self or others, and cultivate healthy, honest, discerning, and responsible relationships."

But what does this mean, exactly? This precept has been open to interpretation for over two thousand years. We must become clear on its intent and import as well as the letter of any such vow, rule, or law; this is where wisdom and insight become extraordinarily helpful, and even necessary. Our real nitty-gritty lives take place mainly in the colorful areas of the wide spectrum between the poles of black and white. That's one reason I feel that the Buddha's main teaching is the Middle Way—balance, moderation, and appropriateness, free from dogmatism and other extreme forms of thinking, such as all or nothing, heaven and hell, materialism and nihilism, us and them.

Who am I to act like an authority on coupled relationship? In the previous chapter I presented my Buddhist teaching transmission lineage, but for obvious reasons of privacy I can't share every detail of my relationship history. However, I think you can identify with much of it. As a boy, I learned about sexuality and masturbation from "the guys" in the American tradition of sports clubs, locker rooms, swimming pools, and summer camp. We innocently and almost transparently swapped our experiences in humorous and sometimes boastful ways, as young boys are wont to do. I think I got as much misinformation as information! From there, I went off to Cape Cod during high school to work with another summer camp counselor, and that led to the first mysteries of actual sex with a woman. I'll skip over my learning-rich youthful escapades, but suffice it to say they occurred in the normal range of growing up. And I've continued that way, albeit with some less-than-traditional phases like living abroad in other cultures or studying Tantra (sacred sex and subtle energy) yoga under the guidance of masters, which informs the practices I describe later in this chapter. I feel proud and happy to say I still have caring

> In the moment of love sudden-arising, enlightened mind dawns.

and warm connections with almost all of the significant loves in my life. I'm divorced and unmarried now, enjoying a long-term committed relationship with my partner. However, I still chew on the koan of how to enjoy a workable relationship for me and my loved ones, all while striving to continuously grow, integrate, heart-open, and deepen as I do my best to put this book's principles and enlightened wisdom into daily practice.

"In the moment of love sudden-arising, enlightened mind dawns," sang the Third Karmapa Lama named "Spontaneous Thunderbolt" in Tibet, hundreds of years ago. How can we use inter-meditation to bring love's dawning and enlightened mind into the culture of "hooking up," new romance, "friends with benefits," or the bedroom? Or to the breakfast table after staying up all night with a sick child? Into an argument with our partner, or divorce? Into every aspect of our coupled lives?

Making It Sacred

Real partnership—real comm*union* and attunement—is the *co* in co-meditation, the *inter* in inter-meditation. One of the best ways to expand as well as deepen our practice into daily life is with our passionate partners; doing so, we follow the path of transformation through the mystical power of relationships—integrating masculine and feminine, self and other, yin and yang. Co-meditating and convergitating can awaken their hearts as well as ours, breathing life into my favorite Lojong slogan:

> Only a joyful, open mind and
> attitude, always sustaining you.

A Burmese master asked one of my friends, Vipassana teacher Steve Smith (who had been a monk under the master's guidance), if he was marrying his wife Michelle due to *kamma*—lustful desire—or karma and *yezed sounde*—water-drop connection and natural adhesion. *Water-drop connection*—what a great image for relationship! We want to work toward that, because pure relationship of this water-drop kind implies a feeling of adhesion and cohesion, an intimate recognition, as if of deep past connections, along with the sense of seeing and being seen. Is there a more satisfying feeling than being *gotten*? Is there a more mysterious sense of completion than watching infinite snowflakes, one by one, settle naturally on a peaceful lake, merging and dissolving in continuous flow, and continuing on their course back to the sea? This analogy of unity and oneness is so rich, dynamic, evolutionary, and even ecstatic. Who can comprehend it with the conceptual mind? So stop trying so hard! Conceptual mind has its limitations, and there are other ways to know and intuit things.

I once thought that satisfying a woman or being co-conspirator to mutual satisfaction was the best I could do when it came to coupling, but I learned that there's more to it than that. Losing all sense—of who's doing what, who's kissing whom, or even who's having the orgasm—delivers us beyond the pedestrian realm of physical sex to that of the gods and goddesses. Recall this applicable Lojong aphorism: "Happiness comes from putting others first, thinking of them before oneself. Unhappiness comes from preoccupation with one's own happiness and satisfaction."

Since most of us engage the spiritual journey as laypeople, and not as renounced monastics, intimacy is an extraordinarily important part of the path of awakening.

I find that whenever I give either traditional or more inter-denominational teachings the subject of love and relationships usually comes up. That makes sense—our lives are all about discovery, collaboration, and partnership. I like to remind my students that I am not handing down advice from some remote, exalted lama-cloud. Continuously working on these moments of awakening in my relationship with my intimate partner, I know firsthand that having someone to share with serves only as the beginning and not the ultimate goal of relationship. Co-meditating means remaining related to all and everything in the spirit of sacred view, seeing the light through all and every-thing—and that includes the shadows. Fear of the dark can keep us from the light.

That's one huge difference between ordinary relationship and sacred relationship: How much space does our self take up? How much room do we make for our partner? How much hon-esty, directness, and private personal reality do we dare to share? How much energy do we devote to the play and dance of rela-tional intimacy and independence, and ultimately the evolved relational consciousness of autonomy within interdependence? Where the dance of coupling really leaps ahead is in co-creating the sacred third in the country of We. It's all about the *we*-ness, not just the penis or vagina.

We don't have to fall into the trap of thinking that intimate relationships hinder our spiritual development in some way. We actually don't need to take a vow of celibacy in a monastery, ashram, or hermitage; we don't need to go into isolated retreat, cut off from society and the things of this world; we don't need to remove ourselves in any way. But we should definitely con-sider a partnership that means more than just "us"—more than a companion, partner, or roommate to help with the bills and childcare. Don't we want to reach beyond that? Think about weddings—whether they occur in a temple or a cathedral or a justice-of-the-peace's office, or just among two people in a private and sanctified moment, there's more to the ceremony than "Let's hook up" or "Let's share mortgages and car payments and fight over whose family's house to go to for Christmas." There's taking the *me* and making a *we*. With this union—intimate, transcendent, and sacred—we create the opportunity to bring something larger and more important into the world.

We all can and probably should seek to realize God and perceive the Divine, or Bodhichitta, that awakened spiritual heart, in our husband, wife, or lovers. Just as the small self is not separate from the Big Self, romantic love is not separate from Divine love—it's a part of Divine love, an aspect—like the hot tip of an unusual iceberg. Human nature is also Divine nature, and by becoming our genuine selves we can make a heaven here on Earth. I consider this the purpose of authentic relationships: to break through the walls separating us—individually and collectively—and enter into that sacred power and co-creation. It takes a village, co-meditators! Don't overlook the profundity of ordinary people and everyday experiences and relationships.

INTER-MEDITATION PRACTICE

Ten Keys of Inter-Meditation Applied to Relationships

Earlier in the book I listed ten keys of inter-meditation; let's go over them again with relationships in mind. Pick one each day and take a moment to express your intent to and with your partner. These co-meditations can transform your relationship into a sacred one:

1. We promise to give our true attention, honesty, and incandescent pure presence to each other, bringing forth our relationship and family with genuine authenticity.

2. We will be selfless together and trust our higher nature, stretching from competition and confusion to caring, commitment, and collaboration.

3. We'll be generous, giving of ourselves—not just things and time, but our hearts, emotions, respect, and best understanding—evolving from ego to eco-system.

4. From generosity comes patience, and we renew our grounding in forbearance, tolerance, acceptance, flexibility, stick-to-it-iveness, and resilience in our cherished relationship.

5. We value mutual respect, trust, and support, and see each other as a gateway to the Divine.

6. Our love is a genuine love based on honoring, delighting, and cherishing each other, with empathy, compassion, and caring.

7. We will never lose sight of the joy, pleasure, and fun of togetherness with our significant and very

special other—and we won't take all of this or
ourselves so seriously.

8. We'll seek out the passion, enchantment, and
    interest we have in the other—remembering that
    this is different from fascination.

9. We'll remain open to the mystery, to the innocence
    and possibilities inherent in not-always-knowing
    and not always having it all worked out beforehand.

10. We want to live a meaningful, shared life, moving in
    the same direction, combining our values, intention,
    and Big Selves, as part of Life Lived Large, a better
    world, and sustainable, equitable future.

You can apply these when you take your next step in inter-
meditation, practicing the yoga of relationship.

The Yoga of Relationship

> Only connect! That was the whole of her sermon.
> Only connect the prose and the passion, and both will
> be exalted, and human love will be seen at its height.
> Live in fragments no longer.   E.M. FORSTER

Tibetan yogis use the Sanskrit term *yoga* to mean "reunion with
the natural state," and not necessarily union with God or the
Divine, as wonderful as that certainly can be. In this way, non-
theistic masters experience that which is beyond any of us—yet

immanent in each and all of us—without imagining a separately existing supreme being or creator. Re-union, or convergitation, is more like a homecoming, a return to the source or wholeness, than a journey to some far-off holy land. For this reason, Vajrayana masters of Himalayan Buddhism teach about the Vajra Body—the immutable diamond-like essence of being, indomitable, unborn, and undying—the subtle energy body of rainbow-like transformation that transcends the impermanent, physical body.

We can transform our pairings, our couplings, our collaborative partnerships with something I call the Yoga of Relationship. It's a traditional way of awakening within Buddhism, and also in the Hindu and Taoist energy practice traditions. Even the evangelical Christians are getting interested in it these days! Couples of all sorts can use the Yoga of Relationship to integrate all that they bring forth into spiritual life. "For the ignorant person, this body is the source of endless suffering, but to the wise person, this body is the source of infinite delight,"[1] sang the Hindu sage Valmiki in the Yoga Vasistha more than two thousand years ago.

The Yoga of Relationship is a path to union and reunion, a path of re-experiencing, realizing, and actualizing wholeness and self-authenticating conviction through inner spiritual realization. Although I have known numerous spiritual masters from various schools and traditions, some of my best gurus were my lovers—the beautiful, sensitive, smart, giving, and strong yet vulnerable women in my life. Intimate relationships have provoked many moments of growth and awakening for me; I think most people can relate to this. In intimacy there's nowhere to hide; we can pretend and delude ourselves about our spiritual progress, but it's hard to fool our mate for long, isn't it? Relationship acts like a clear mirror in which our own blemishes become immediately apparent.

If we explore the Yoga of Relationship, we'll see that the way most understood and practiced in India is *not* the way followed by saints and celibates. By contrast, I'm referring to the path of husbands serving wives and wives serving husbands. Homes become temples and coupling a sacrament; marriage vows are considered as sacred as priestly vows. Women learn to worship their husband as Lord Shiva (Mr. God) and husbands similarly learn to worship their wife as the cosmic goddess Shakti (Mrs. God). It's a beautiful ideal of spirituality for couples—serving God through serving one's mate, and by extension one's family, one's community, and all beings. It's one of the main inter-meditative ways to awaken.

How do we know if we're taking our relationship to a place of sacred union, of co-meditation? Discuss these questions with your partner:

- How do we live our partnered/married life together?
- How do we as a couple reflect and embody our love for one another to our world?
- How loving and caring are we toward each other, our family, our colleagues every day?
- When people see us in ordinary circumstances, do they see a couple in love and loving their way toward heaven and a better world?
- Do they sense our spirituality in our togetherness, faithfulness, commitment, tolerance, acceptance, patience, and respect for one another?
- Is there an extra special aura of kindness and caring around our relationship?
- What shared dream or higher intention and aspiration do we—or might we—share?

Noble-Silent Nature Walks as Co-Meditation

As you work with the questions above and co-meditate on them, try bringing them into a walking practice. My partner and I make a point of taking silent nature walks together most Saturday or Sunday mornings. Any day of the week can serve as a shared Sabbath if we decide to co-create and dedicate it in such a way, just like a retreat: a day of rest, a day of mutual spiritual—not worldly—work.

- Make a decision together about where you'd like to walk—perhaps your favorite sylvan spot, although it could be almost anywhere, even in a mall.
- Turn off your electronic devices for the designated hour or two of inter-meditation, and instead plug in and get wired to your internal and mutual network, a higher frequency.
- Walk together in what Buddhist practitioners call noble silence (not just quiet), without speaking. Gently tread the path in this shared silence-walk, using eye contact for *communitation*.
- Walk the walk, as they say, and don't talk the talk. Listen, hear, and receive.
- Breathe deeply, settle down; give space for autonomic emotional resilience. Calm and relax, almost agenda-less. Let everything relax and clear.
- Here's the secret of noble silence: let your mind fall still and clear. Don't just silence your mouth, note-taking hand, or texting thumbs.

- Have a wonder-full, meandering walk! Appreciate the use of uselessness.

---

1 + 1 = **Oneness**

In spiritual intimacy, 1 + 1 = oneness. This goes beyond the simple nut and bolt fitting-together idea of pairing. When two beings become complete within themselves, they are drawn together into a dance of unity, wholeness, and spontaneous co-meditation. "Oneth me with thee, oh Lord," prayed a female Christian mystic long ago. I love that! It's the practice I call *one-ing*.

Here's an inter-meditation that can take us from me to we—from self to us—to the *sacred third* that far exceeds the sum of its two parts; it's the Big Self, like the country of We co-created by two individuals in unconditionally loving couple-hood. In this sacred dance (which can sometimes be quite motionless), we journey from head to heart, body to spirit, outer to inner and beyond. Almost effortlessly, we are drawn ineluctably into the infinite and the infinitesimal, simultaneously dissolving through the union of all polarities and dichotomies while connecting with all that is and can be.

- Find a private place. Be sure it's somewhere no one can see you, for practical as well as spiritual reasons.
- In this practice you can either visualize the ideal consort or work with an actual person—perhaps your main squeeze, mate, or designated yogi training partner.

- Sit facing one another. You can sit cross-legged and touch knee-to-knee. Or try something subtler—not touching. It's up to you. You can also sit in chairs or *yab-yum* style—that is, the first partner in lotus position while the second sits in his or her lap, legs wrapped around the waist of the first.
- Close your eyes and begin to synchronize your breathing. Inhale and calm the heart/mind. Exhale, relax, and smile.
- Again, breathe in. Breathe out. Let go. Let come and go. Let be. You'll begin to notice you're feeling centered and focused.
- Then, open your eyes. This is not a staring contest; it should feel light, comfortable, and natural. You can blink if you need to. This is a technique I call eye-gazing.
- Bring your focus deep into the other—really look into their eyes without judgment or evaluation, becoming aware of your projections and imagination, letting them go. Abide beyond separation and union, oneness and none-ness.
- Continue your synchronized breathing and become attuned to the other senses—smell, touch, and sounds.
- As you move toward inter-awareness, relax into it. Let your thoughts come and go, letting them be. Just sit, breathe, and be wholly aware together. Attentive. Luminous. Merging and mingling the subtle energies. You should begin to feel a shift from me to we—what I like to call *transrealescence*.
- Now close your eyes again. Notice how you can still feel the other person there—whether it's the

after-image in your mind, the sound of their breathing, or the warmth of their presence.

- Go deeper. Tune in to and be completely aligned with your partner—permeable, interwoven, and inseparable. Let go of selfiness and separation, simply being whatever arises in this twosome of paired oneness.
- This is relational- or inter-meditation.

Ultimately we want to reach a place of *embodied resonance*—a somatic reaction, rather than the more common responses of thoughts, feelings, fantasies, and dreams. When two people generate embodied resonance, it awakens a larger alchemy within them and all they come into contact with. It's like tuning forks blending into harmonious shared resonance, totally aligned and attuned.

Coupled Yoga is a superb co-meditation practice, and a few teachers do offer it today. Almost everything we do alone we can do as a couple, or pair, along with other exercises that accommodate the presence of two torsos, four arms, and four legs. This can take the form of peaceful and staid yoga *asanas*, as performed in hatha yoga studios. Or it can resemble more challenging postures, with two people aiding and abetting each other into super stretches, balancing acts, and position-holds akin to gymnastics, acrobatics, or even the Cirque du Soleil. It can also look like joint kundalini breathing techniques, intensive mantra workouts, or tantric yoga sessions with one partner sitting in the other's lap. All of these examples of co-meditative yoga can be learned, understood, and mastered. When practiced with integrity and compassion, this type of yoga produces marvelous benefits on various levels: outer (physical and behavioral), inner (attitudinal and energetic), secret (subtle and spiritual), and top secret ("suchness"—sublime non-action and organic primordial great perfection).

The Meeting of Thou and I: Committing to Stay Faithful to Our Partners and Selves

When we make a genuine commitment to our partner, we move beyond comfort and preference and enter the spheres of authentic love and devotion that result from elevating our intentional awareness to this level. We leave the separations of like and dislike behind; authentic love is so much larger, greater, and immeasurable. Love is big enough to deal with the stuff we don't like, as well as what we might like too much; love can draw sensible limits and boundaries, including both moderation and also moderation-in-moderation! If we truly want to experience new depths of relationship, we ourselves must change. Have you ever noticed that when you change, somehow—as if by magic—you attract different people and situations? Or familiar people react differently? That's karma, cause and effect. Like attracts like. This authentic power, born of self-mastery, is in your hands. And commitment is the first step.

Just the other day in Boston, I heard the Dalai Lama quote the Lojong exhortation to look at every adversity as an opportunity. Here's the problem: when we run away from difficulties in our relationship, we're actually running away from ourselves and our own path of potential breakthroughs. Constantly escaping discomfort like this keeps us moving in circles, not forward. Avoiding the wounded places in ourselves because we don't think we can handle them is a form of self-sabotage, self-rejection, and internal weakness. Personal intimacy is like a spark flashing out across the divide between self and other; the spark's development, growth, enhancement, and continuity depend on strong, courageous individuals making warm, personal contact, mutually sparking and enriching each other with complementary qualities and synchronizing energies throughout the entire dance of relationship, regardless of temporary ups and downs or sidesteps. This is the meeting of I and Thou elucidated by Jewish philosopher Martin Buber—not an impersonal spiritual union, but a personal communion rooted in deep appreciation of the other's sacred otherness. It's a transpersonal and companionate love not unlike directly encountering God in person.

Buddhist Lojong practice resembles giving ourselves a daily "iye" exam. This contemplative daily discipline teaches us to investigate each moment of an encounter, each instant of relationship arising. It encourages us to consciously connect to whatever life presents us in any given moment and to look into who we are, as well as acknowledge responsibility for our own actions (outer, inner, and subtle). Who *are* you, really, in this moment, as you relate to whatever dawns and appears to your "iye"? Who experiences your experience in this very moment? What stands in the way of love, of your loving? Maybe fear? Anxiety or busyness perhaps? Hurrying

> Everyone is responsible for creating their own karma, their own subjective experience. Their happiness and suffering don't depend on me.

through life definitely thickens the veil and obscures the fine details, genuine feelings, inner meanings, and subtle intuitions.

The purpose of different awareness practices is to attain inner clarity. Our egos obscure the inner light and dawning sun of reality. Love is a verb, not an object to obtain or acquire. Intend to love and accept love, and love shall find you. This doesn't mean, however, that all you need is love; obviously, you don't need to hang on to every relationship and work on it forever. It's more a matter of where we skillfully draw the line. When is conflict constructive and growthful, and when is it destructive and stultifying? Here's a slogan to recite, as needed; it will help you cultivate equanimity and spiritual detachment:

> Everyone is responsible for creating their own
> karma, their own subjective experience. Their
> happiness and suffering don't depend on me.

What a relief even to just think and write that! *Hey: You mean others' unhappiness and dissatisfaction aren't my responsibility? Phew!*

Drawing and maintaining healthy boundaries—both flexible and firm—is important. Responsibilities are not necessarily synonymous with obligations. It's better to disappoint by speaking truth than it is to poison a relationship with dishonesty and resentment; saying no is an art form well worth learning. People-pleasing can become a disease, and even ruin your relationships and your precious, gifted human life. Only you know when enough is enough; contemplate and explore this—understand this issue in a thorough and nuanced way. Show up for yourself. Know what you can and can't change. You might wish your partner all the best, you offer all you can to help them, but you can't fundamentally fix or change anyone. If we diminish, undermine, or limit each other, even unintentionally, rather than generating compassionate growth and producing Bodhichitta together, why stay together at all? Lojong practice can help you clarify these issues and develop healthy emotional management, self-regulation, and self-awareness. One can transcend habitual codependent tendencies and the disease to please, and still give care and love and be loved without inhibition, illusion, or expectation.

Partnered relationships end in different ways. Often, they break apart by one partner seemingly running away from his or her companion, while in fact he or she is running away from their own demons. Too often this comes out messy, painful, and sad; moreover, this kind of breakup can result in lasting anger and grief, not to mention other problems (like custody battles, expensive legal bills, and the like).

But sometimes despite the best of efforts and positive intent, a couple's fundamental needs for their own authentic life and well-being—or how they have changed, or how they are currently able to show up in the relationship—makes it so that the two are no longer compatible to a workable degree. When a couple has thoroughly examined and concluded that their union is unsaveable and they are no longer generating Bodhichitta together—or, on an even more fundamental level, when they no longer get along in a friendly, collaborative, and acceptable way—I like to recommend a little ritual to celebrate the good aspects of the relationship and the time the two spent growing alongside one another, sometimes with family and children. I recommend mindful, balanced, mature, and possibly mediated rather than adversarial parting, which can preserve the dignity and integrity of each half of the couple and the family fabric. This ritual can take any shape you like, but here's one version to consider—it's my co-meditative model for conscious separation and compassionate divorce:

Conscious and Compassionate Uncoupling

Say to the other, one at a time, while the other listens most respectfully and attentively, without responding or reacting:

Our time together is done for now. Thank you for being my sacred partner and companion on the path, and for all your love, patience, understanding, sharing, caring, and support. We've had some great times, and now it's time to say goodbye and to go, without regrets or resentments. I now release you, forgive you, and set you free, accepting you just as you are. All our accounts are balanced and cleared, without further expectations. As the Buddha once said after his enlightenment had been achieved: "Done is what had to be done." We no longer want or need each other in close proximity, or to aid and abet our purposes in life. I wish you well, and trust that you wish me well, too. So goodbye, have a safe trip. Happy trails! *Sayonara. Vaya con dios.*

Then reverse roles and have the other say these sentences back to you, while you listen silently and provide them with an excellent sounding board and opportunity to get on with life themselves—no regrets, no resentment, and without looking back. On to life!

Why Sex?

It's always sad when relationships come to an end. Life contains perpetual change, loss, growth, and transformation. But let's go back to the relationships that end up flourishing—at least for a while—in which sexual intimacy necessarily comes into play. Just like our work life, family life, and spiritual life, sex life is important to us, individually and even collectively. Sex is part of the rich tapestry of society and social life as well as personal life. Some people experience this energy and aspect of life more keenly than others, in different phases and stages of their lifetimes, according to their upbringing, biochemistry, habits, and psyches. It's both simple and not always so simple, isn't it? And, of course, there are times in our lives when we don't have sex—it's kind of like fasting, abstinence, or practicing noble silence or sublime solitude. According to general spiritual thought, we accrue more good karma and beneficial spiritual growth by fasting intentionally rather than simply by experiencing hunger and not finding food. The distinction is all in the motivation and intentional commitment, self-discipline, and practice—practices that we cultivate. Intention and vows combined with Bodhichitta and altruistic resolve all create a different kind of karma than just falling into something positive, although that too can have its own merits and ensuing benefits.

Even if we don't act on them, it's important that we learn to communicate and even express our sexual feelings in a wholesome and nonjudgmental fashion in order to avoid hypocritical gaps and contradictions between our words and beliefs, on the one hand, and our actions on the other. As with every activity, some significant personal scrutiny and self-inquiry regarding the nature of our sexual desires, feelings, behavior, and relationships can prove extremely rewarding.

Sexual energy pulses in almost everything we do, and it can certainly be constructive. When I felt slightly confused and hung up about sexual desire as a young man, living for years in my twenties and thirties in Himalayan monasteries and Indian ashrams where celibacy was respected and even recommended, the abbot of our monastery in Darjeeling said, "But Surya, sex is just a part of life." It was a tremendous relief to hear this from a venerated Tibetan meditation master and yogi who was a celibate monk, an impeccable pure renunciant, and a Buddhist saint in the making. I'd bought into the ancient venerable Hindu *sannyasin* tradition of *brahmacharya* (noble celibacy)—much recommended by Indian gurus and saints of the time—and I struggled mightily to stay chaste through my young adult years in India, even while living in monasteries and ashrams, retreats, caves, grass-roofed huts, a garage, and a goat-shed. Yet, as time went on and I studied more about other aspects of myself and the path of awakening, I discovered there was more than met the eye—as usual—and I realized that I didn't need to be so rigid. It turns out that there were icons such as Tibet's beloved Sixth Dalai Lama and Bhutan's native saint and sage Drukpa Kunley who were renowned as tantric sexual yogis. Apparently, every night, this particular young Dalai Lama would slip out of his Potala Palace under the cover of darkness and visit the houses of ill-repute in Lhasa, the capital city. The houses where he chose to sleep would proudly paint their doors a special shade of yellow—the brilliant golden yellow worn only by the Dalai Lama in that stratified medieval society. In Bhutan, even today families paint oversized depictions of Drukpa Kunley's erect penis on the front doors and outer walls of their houses. I'm not making this up! Maybe that's one reason travel brochures proclaim Bhutan the happiest country on Earth.

These anecdotes might come across as shocking to some of us. Many of us—particularly Judeo-Christian Americans—still struggle with an inclination to treat sex as something disconnected from who we are—or worse, we consider sex as sinful, shameful, or necessary but somewhat unclean. I think most of our parents raised us to believe that what goes on behind closed bedroom doors is separate from everyday reality and should remain unspoken, extraordinarily private, and in shadow. If we want to fully experience the entire rich tapestry of our lives, become true inter-meditators, and connect to the inherent sacredness of every aspect of our world and ourselves, then we must open to the possibility of sexuality as a meaningful, potentially gorgeous, and often revealing step on the path of spiritual evolution. Conscious sexuality—body and mind, heart-energy and soul—can even serve as a booster rocket to authentic transformation.

Love and sex together have no peer in this world as we know it—it goes far beyond temporary pleasure or gratification. We can develop the sex-with-love practice through the early stages of mutual satisfaction and growing closer, strengthening our connection and bonding, accomplishing intimacy together at the most private and deliciously secret levels. From there, we can move to opening and trusting, letting down our guards and defenses, dissolving, transforming, and re-emerging as infinite regeneration and cosmic energy flow, as if immortal, deathless, and indomitable. The Chinese characterize this energy as the Immortals—often confused with Ancestors, but more akin to the birthless and deathless, unborn and undying Dharmakaya nature in each and all of us. This ongoing and recycling divine sexual energy, once unleashed and channeled appropriately, can last far longer than the brief satiation of desire commonly achieved through physical climax, entering the vaunted realm of what ancient tantric practice manuals term "the sixteen kinds of bliss."

There are various types and levels of sexuality, intimacy, and loving. These include but are not limited to biological and biochemical, generative, emotional, cultural, interpersonal, social, yogic, spiritual, and transcendent. On one hand, the most basic evolutionary purpose of sex is to procreate, which involves the fundamental desires of getting what we want and helping others get what they want, need, and desire, including offspring, closeness, and the short-term relief of physical desire through orgasm. At the other end of the far-reaching spectrum of sexual energy, the purpose is to liberate love and unselfconscious energy in realizing oneness, wholeness, and something ineffable—akin to dissolving and connecting totally at one and the same time—and transcendence, enlightenment, a cosmic epiphany. This is enlightened lovemaking, which may or may not even involve *two* people, bodies, or orgasms. One can learn to make love to the entire body of life, caressing all of her curvaceous, bodacious, and blissful forms. By encountering natural *Samadhi,* we can open to this path of sexuality as awakened enlightenment.

Natural Samadhi

Think about it: how often in your life are you as attentive, as present, as *with* it as when you're surging toward an orgasm, close to the point of no return? When you arrive at that place, you don't need to *practice* mindfulness, you just do it. It's not usually a time when, in order to remain present, you have to call on all of the self-conscious techniques you learned in meditation class. In other words, you're practicing *natural Samadhi*.

Samadhi is a state of intense meditation, concentration, and total absorption—the opposite of being overwhelmed, distracted, absent-minded, or scattered. Through a small turn of attention, Samadhi becomes total awakening—that flutter of going beyond you and me to *us*, which wings our "selves" over the brink. That's the moment when the clear light dawns for us, even though it's always there—like the set sun, unseen. The brilliant intensity of Samadhi is there in uninhibited passion, in holy union, and in the total self-emptying, self-surrender, and even "ruination" that medieval mystics have talked about. Thus, it's a tremendous innate natural resource we can call upon and exploit for all kinds of purposes and results.

Do you ever find it hard to concentrate when you meditate? As an antidote, try becoming more interested in your practice. Add an intriguing question like "Who am I?" or "Why do we suffer?" Similarly, you can try new approaches to your sexual experience by turning your awareness upon itself immediately before or precisely at the moment of climax; it's like joyfully speeding along in a car and choosing to slam on the brakes. This practice makes everything in the subconscious come rushing forward and achieve release. It's even said that this practice is one of the best ways to empty the whole realm of samsara—our cycle of births and rebirths. Think about that. Speed it up as much as you can and then put the brakes on totally, then look directly into the experience and see who's experiencing it. This backwards step, or tantric turnaround, can actually precipitate cataclysmic awakening. This tantric turnaround can also usher forth a personal *we*-volution with great implications for each and all of our relations. Challenging and provocative as the practice may seem, I believe we are up for it today, and we can't just relegate this incredible spiritual method of tantric practice to the dustbin of history, particularly in this secular, scientistic era when our passionate, poetic heart and soul seem in danger of being eclipsed by hyper-rational thought, material values, and vocational-oriented education too often short on humanism and magic. This is not simply a post-modern problem, but symptomatic of the creative friction between heart and mind, body and soul, Heaven and Earth, yin and yang, amid the ceaseless waves of time, space, and life itself.

Tantra: Diamonds and SkyDancers

The teachings of tantric Buddhism compose some of the most powerful, transformative, boundary-stretching, and outrageous contributions to world spirituality. Specifically, these enlightened instructions actually take the human body seriously, and they skillfully provide inner sciences to heal, wholify, harmonize, and awaken the various levels or dimensions of our mortal coil—exploring and exploiting this physical fabric and its subtle energies as resources for enlightenment. The Sanskrit word *tantra* has roots in the word "union" and warp and weave, implying interwoven; perhaps it can best be translated as yoking together or inseparability. Sounds a little bit like the ancient word *yoga,* and also how I've described inter-meditation. For tantric practice I have coined the term *merge-itation.*

The Tibetan tantric tradition abounds with teachings on coupled relationships and co-meditations—with deities, and later with visualized consorts and embodied (human) ones as well. Yeshe Tsogyal the SkyDancer, for example, was the young queen of Tibet, main Dharma heir and enlightened consort of Master Padma Sambhava; she developed a potent lineage of secret dakini practices in the eighth century for people of tremendous passion, like herself, who were also profoundly devoted to spiritual awakening. Even at eighty years of age, she took a handsome, youthful yogi as consort, Atsara Sale from Bengal. The two lovers accomplished the unique fierce-goddess inner heat (*tummo*), mystic incandescence, and rejuvenation for longevity and deathless bliss Tantra practice together in sacred caves and hot springs, as did another accomplished Guru-consort with Padma Sambhava in the Maratika Cave in eastern Nepal many decades earlier. This potent transmutational subtle-energy transmission is still alive and well in those springs and sacred sources, and I can attest personally to that. My elder master-teachers and lama friends still journey to Maratika to practice those recondite secret techniques. Through practicing his powerful longevity empowerments there, one realized master keeps his elderly parents alive and well beyond all medical expectations. The path of the SkyDancer—sacred-energy Tantra—is one of true spiritual partnership between men and women as equals and mutual enhancers and edifiers, integrating ecstasy and blissful unity consciousness into their daily lives, suffusing all aspects with luminosity, awareness, the fierce inner heat of Samadhi (contemplative absorption), and the exalted sixteen kinds of bliss.

Tantra is a path of union and integration—pairing, sharing, and synergizing—not withdrawal or escapism. This is why it's so pertinent to our modern era, and especially to this theme of developing co- and inter-meditation practices utilizing the encounters of daily life as practical, organic supports and even catalysts to higher consciousness and deeper wisdom. Tantra is about relationships, especially vitality, longevity, healing, and subtle internal energies—masculine and feminine, yin and yang, Shiva and Shakti. In our own light-body and energy field we become the rainbow bridge between Heaven and Earth. Genuine practice of this discipline can prove an exceptionally powerful tool to harness, boost, and utilize the natural concentration or Samadhi of intense passionate desire to connect more deeply to another, to ourselves, and to what lies beyond—whether we conceive of it as Higher Power, Buddha Nature, oneness, the Clear Light of reality, or spiritual transcendence. But we can't just talk about it; we have to practice it—which is why I have included a number of simple yet effective basic meditations in this chapter. Of course, please remember that no book can replace the personal guidance and instructions of an experienced, qualified teacher—especially in such a sensitive and esoteric area as the tantric teachings.

Tantra implies non-duality or inseparability—the warp and woof in a single weave. Many people think the tantric texts merely instruct us on how to magnify love and fullness of heart through sexuality, that the teachings focus mostly on finding a cosmic portal into love's incomparable wonder, joys, and ecstatic union. But that's just part of the story. Tantric sex is just one popular example of how to unite with non-dual awareness-meditation and cosmic energy communication. It refers to fundamental unity or interwovenness of the fabric of reality, of all of life. Tantra yoga traditionally is known as a practical discipline for unifying the mind, or one-ing (*yoga* means yoking, *joining*) with God. Tantra vastly helps resolve the disharmony and split between matter and spirit, God and man, time and eternity, life and death/eternity, and assists in the re-integration and harmony of all such conceptual dichotomies and polarities. Historically it has been considered the most powerful esoteric way in which to resolve all conflicts—outer, inner, and subtlest—and make peace within oneself.

"Tantra's body-positive approach is the direct outcome of its integrative metaphysics according to which this world is not mere illusion but a manifestation of the supreme Reality," writes Georg Feuerstein, one of America's foremost Tantra scholars and author of *Tantra: The Path of Ecstasy*. Tantric sex with orgasm, however delayed, is only one of the five families or substances comprising the authentic timeless ritual, and it's most commonly enacted by men and women trained in those tantric arts. As delightful as they feel, and earth-shaking as they may be, multiple orgasms, full-body orgasms, and extended climaxes are not the main point of tantric spirituality. My own Tibetan Vajrayana masters actually consider tantric practice a strenuous austerity (*tapasya*) and intense advanced self-discipline due to its rigors, sacrifices, necessary renunciations, risks, and necessarily thorough course of training and development. Confusing tantric bliss (*maha-sukha*) with the pleasure of physical orgasm is a huge distraction, a perversion of the truths of Tantra yoga; this mistake can lead one into sidetracks, pitfalls, and even worse. I can tell you from personal experience that tantric yoga practice is not always easy or comfortable—and let's let it go at that!

The Potent Purposes of Tantric Co-Meditation

1. Raise ordinary (dualistic) consciousness to unity consciousness and oneness-vision by allowing us to see through the illusion of separation

2. Boost and transform inner energies—both gross (physical) and subtle (spiritual)

3. Sacralize sex into a practice of awareness, heart-opening and energy-sublimating

4. Revitalize the physical body and vital energies, prolong life, heal, and liberate blockages and frozenness

5. Rebalance, harmonize, integrate, and actualize the masculine and feminine energies in oneself so as to experience inner wholeness and completeness

6. Help one learn to love everyone and everything, as it is, inseparably merged with all of it; to love and be loved, to love life and unstintingly live to love

7. Harmonize and re-integrate heaven (divine masculine principle) and earth (divine feminine) within oneself

8. To re-unite us with the natural state of inherent freedom and primordial being, our true intrinsic nature

9. To facilitate the experience and assimilation of everything as part of the path of enlightenment, beyond dichotomies and dualities such as sacred and mundane, worldly and spiritual, pure and impure

10. To help us lighten up and brighten up in the ever-present brilliance of innate luminosity, leading to collective illumination

Four Great Moments

The four great moments of awakening taught by the tantric Tibetan masters are death, falling asleep, sneezing, and orgasm. What these four share in common is the great relief attendant upon total loss of control and ego-death, however temporary. These splendid occasions of release compel letting go into absolute acceptance, not knowing, and not trying, even for the most driven and hardened among us. Many of us seek this very place when we meditate.

If our minds and bodies fall away, as they do when we die or experience orgasm, we might well take a moment to wonder precisely who we are *in that moment*. Who experiences that experience? Orgasm is not just a pleasurable inter-meditation technique; it can truly help precipitate that falling away of mind and body. Just as with a midnight trip to the emergency room, or going into labor, or headlights coming at us in the dark—we are suddenly, precipitously, even terrifyingly startled out of being who we think we are and our usual round of semi-sleepwalking. This experience can point toward the incorruptible, changeless underlying nature of our true Selves. If you become truly aware at the crescendo of any of these moments, you will undoubtedly experience a breakthrough beyond bounds of any kind. Zen Buddhists call this *satori*—peak experience.

> Die before you die, and you shall never die.

God-loving mystics assert that emptying yourself leaves a lot more room for God's love to enter. Sufis say, "Die before you die, and you shall never die." This refers to ego-death and self-transcendence, realizing the greater Self or whole that lives in and through each and all of us, by whatever name we call it. Dying in someone's arms in bed is one way there, I believe, either literally or metaphorically—falling asleep or climaxing. Orgasm is a useful metaphor for death and surrender—the big letting go, the ultimate release (the "little death" in French). Hopefully you too have experienced that. Chanting *Ahh* loudly while breathing out is an easy co-meditating-with mantra that I highly recommend to instantly replicate, from time to time, the Great Death Moment experience, and to reproduce similar results. Try it:

Ahh . . .

Many of us are familiar with the essence of what Zen master Dogen taught:

> To study the Buddha Way is to study the self
> To study the self is to forget the self
> To forget the self is to be enlightened
> by the ten thousand things
> To be enlightened by the ten thousand things is to
> free one's body and mind and those of others

Here's another translation:

> To forget the self is to be intimate
> with the ten thousand things
> To be intimate with the ten thousand things is to
> free one's body and mind and those of others

To be intimate with the ten thousand things. Certainly passion, love, and orgasm are included among the ten thousand things and serve as powerful methods into and through them, to alignment, oneness, and flow. All are parts of a whole that we need to be one with, and not avoid or ignore, if we want to have a well-rounded and complete spiritual life. Intimacy and oneness *are* the path and the goal, not mere sidetracks or impure diversions. Of course, this isn't the right path for all people—monks, nuns, swamis, and *sannyasis* have chosen celibate, solitary life paths. They enjoy other Dharma gates, different access points and epiphanies, no doubt, as well as wondrous ways of becoming intimately one with themselves and all that lives. I certainly hope so. However, for most laypeople, co-meditating via the path of intimate relationships is crucial, as relationship is such a prominent element of our lives. Our instinctual desires, energies, thoughts, and feelings are like fuel which can burn us or power our progress, contributing to our total awakening along with that of this floating-dewdrop world.

INTER-MEDITATION PRACTICE
Bringing Tantra into the Bedroom
With Tantra the first step is having the experience of touch, of profound contact—with things, with ourselves, our

partner, the universe—without mental commotion. When you touch deeply, you no longer need to let go—that occurs naturally as you relax, soften, trust, let go, let be, dissolve, illuminate, and connect.

When we arrive at that place of unity, oneness, and wholeness, we find more practices and opportunities conducive to sustaining natural Samadhi in the present moment, spreading and circulating the subtle energies, thus further focusing and intensifying lucid undiluted attention. You might want to try co-meditating without orgasm while in sexual union, at least now and then, to build up increased sexual charge; or try going two or three times longer than usual with both foreplay and especially penetration in a lovemaking session. There's a range of possibility to this practice: from simply making love a few minutes longer while "edging" (up to the brink of orgasm, then backing off) without giving in to pleasure's culmination, to remaining coupled for thirty minutes without moving, four times a day, while visualizing yourself and your partner as two deities making love as if the entire universe of light and dark, Heaven and Earth, god and humanity were one and inseparable. Four times a day may not be a logistical reality for most of us, but even the idea of doing so can open us up. Why limit ourselves with mind-made mini-suits, like mere flesh-sacks, when we can don superhero costumes and assume sensational avatar-like roles together?

Tantric lovemaking is the ultimate physical act. It brings body and soul, heart and mind, together in harmony and oneness in a collaborative, co-created dance. All of our spiritual energies unite for one sole soulful purpose and passion: higher, deeper, more conscious evolution and awakened progress; Tantra is far more evolved than mere biological, procreative, and pleasure imperatives.

Here are a few more practices to try:

- Use the Hindu *maithuna* position—like the scissors posture of modern love-fare, but side by side and facing each other without scissoring, contemplatively, with penis inside vagina for thirty minutes without much movement.
- Visualize each other as deities, facing each other and eventually inside each other.
- Breathe together and circulate the subtle prana energies, recognized and felt as well as super-subtle and subliminally sensed and intuited.
- Anoint and massage each other with warm, fragrant oils and unguents, using extra-mindful intent—from the toes, one by one, up to the navel, chest and heart, shoulders, neck, and up to the head.
- Trace sacred signs and symbols on each other's skin, especially on the seven chakras and any other erogenous zones.
- Offer up the light of candles and fragrance of incense.
- Explore this inner, shared co-meditational universe, and plumb the infinite without going outside at all.

Tantric Role-Playing

There's a tantric meditation in which we visualize ourselves as exalted archetypes or deities in order to cultivate those qualities personified by the icons. As a man, you can visualize yourself as a goddess, like Tara, Yeshe Tsogyal, Vajrayogini, Maya, or Kali; conversely, as a woman you visualize yourself as a male deity. It "trans-personalizes" us so we don't get stuck in our habitual gender-based personalities while trying to meditate and so we don't self-consciously judge ourselves while worrying about if we're getting it right. We come to feel that it's simply the archetype meditating, and not just our small, separate, insecure selves trapped in our limited mortal coil. We become confident that all is well, regardless of whatever momentarily seems to be happening, abiding in non-conceptual awareness, the oneness-mind of the deity. Vajrayana meditation manuals call this "Vajra pride" or "deity dignity."

Through this co-meditation with an archetype or chosen deity (*yidam*, in Tibetan) representative of your own Higher Deepest Inner Power, having transformed your identity—however temporarily—into one of the spiritual superheroes of the ascendant pantheon, you realize the experience of being That and seeing with BuddhaVision, unity consciousness. You see through the deity's eyes, or the view from above, and experience an entirely different perspective, along with the feelings and perceptions, wisdom and insights, and even psychic powers and abilities that can come with it. This is a major part of the tantric transformation practice, or Vajrayana Deity Yoga, including sexual Tantra. It opens the chakras and channels, unties knots in the psyche, liberates the frozenness and hang-ups within, makes the ordinary ecstatic, and thereby unleashes the magic of everyday life.

If we think of the Buddha's historical teachings as a vehicle of deliverance, Tantra is a rocket ship; it's an anti-gravity, laser-enabled, fourth-dimensional means of space travel through the boundless infinity beyond time, space, and mental knowledge. That's why the Tantras all promise enlightenment in a single lifetime for the assiduous practitioner who maintains his or her vows and commitments to profound ongoing practice and liberating activity. Moreover, Tantra's non-dual or direct-access instant-enlightenment pith instructions reveal how to make the direct journey from here to totally and completely *here*. How long does that kind of quantum leap need to take? Thus it is often called the Vajra (Diamond) Shortcut to enlightenment.

With diligent regular practice, we can take it pretty far—not just imagining or visualizing, but actually manifesting and enacting the deific powers, virtues, and marvelous enlightened qualities. We can do this by circulating energy through the chakras: masculine energy flows clockwise, in general, and feminine energy circulates counterclockwise. We can also intentionally reverse these flows and have the different yet complementary experiential perspective within ourselves, almost like a flower's stamen and pistil self-complete for reproductive purposes. It's a powerful way to bring out more of the other-gender aspect of your own energy.

This exercise doesn't have to be completely formalized, esoteric, or rarified. One straightforward inter-meditation practice based on Tantra is changing our relational roles. For example, in any relationship, one person may typically take on a caretaker role, while the other person plays more needy; or one partner may be the provider and the other seemingly more dependent; or one makes decisions and gets things going, while the other assesses and nurtures the relationship; or maybe one's the martyr and enabler and the other is the indulger. Couples tend to find their own equilibrium and have their own karma and preferred co-personality. As a co-meditation practice, switch positions and experience your partner from the other side; you will start to find your partner in you. Then you can truly love and explore together from the fullness of being, and not from neediness, fear, or partiality, immaturely hoping for the other to bring you completion. In this way, you can evolve tremendously together. You don't have to remain stuck in the habitual fight-or-flight animal level, or the tit-for-tat lower human level. You can transcend these mundane ways of coupling and keep moving and evolving beyond the dichotomies and trade-offs of the usual giver and taker, or sharer and carer, and unfold the possibilities of mixing and matching, enhancing and synergizing, and arriving together at a place you could never reach alone. There are even more refined ways of exploring togetherness and Vajra-impeccability; you can indeed become like the grand Bodhisattvas of old, who gave nobly without expectation of return, recognition, or even explicit result, and lived spiritual life large as an inevitable result.

When I cultivated so-called feminine energies as a monk in cloistered meditation retreat, by performing female-Buddha practices, I experienced a similar sense of belonging and inalienable wholeness that I'd found through love, sex, or even merely when hugging a real woman deeply without agenda, expectation, or complication. Practically speaking, in those tantric co-meditation practices I felt like I was actually embracing the woman within me, the feminine energy, inside-out and topsy-turvy, yet completely in balance and alignment: laying my head on her breast, in her lap, and making love with her. I felt inexplicably fulfilled, as if from the opposite direction I'd been seeking and expecting, reaching and striving—or from the complementary polarity. This inter-meditative *mergitation* totally stopped my mind and unclenched my heart, freeing me from gender identification or bias, releasing joyous bliss throughout my entire being.

INTER-MEDITATION PRACTICE

The Nine Stages of True Intimacy

I've developed a practice based on Tantra called the Nine Stages of True Intimacy that models how, through sexual relations—with an actual partner or visualized consort—we can make every contact meaningful and achieve oneness—true co-meditation and mergitation. As you move through this book you can bring these steps to situations beyond your sexual relationships, ultimately achieving genuine intimacy—step by conscious step—with other people, friends, pets, nature, the world, the universe, God, or whatever you consider your Higher Deeper Inner Power. Here are the stages:

1. Find a place to be alone with your partner and then begin breathing together, calming and clearing, opening up your chakras naturally while relaxing together.

2. Pay true attention without touching as you focus on each of your chakras—those points through which your vital life force moves.

3. Gently approach one another.

4. Make contact.

5. Enter and penetrate, or feel somehow more physically connected, genuinely and deeply.

6. Engage, going deeper, experiencing, feeling the feelings without separating them into yours or theirs.

7. Go even deeper, sustaining, resonating together and attuning, trusting, softening, allowing, becoming vulnerable and permeable.

8. And now, even deeper: communing, exchanging, melting, and flowing.

9. Reach that place of mingling and joining, a state you can't arrive at without the preceding stages.

10. Merge and dissolve: simultaneously feeling more present and disappearing, ceasing to exist.

11. Experience unity, oneness, wholeness, the luminous cloud of unknowing. This is natural Samadhi. Savor the moment, this very moment. *Emaho!*

Now remove sex from the picture. Think about how you can apply these steps to a conversation with your boss or an argument with the guy who took your place in line. How can we transform our passion into compassion? How can we open, soften, approach non-aggressively, connect, and inter-connect? Try it. Start first with someone you know and like, someone safe, familiar—a friend, close relative, or neighbor. Dare to try this Tantric co-meditation with God or your Higher (deepest) Power, your sacred archetype, or guru (and not necessarily in person).

Everything Must Be Meditated = Non-Duality

"Bring your spiritual practice into your everyday life." "Be mind-ful of everything you do." "Cultivate loving-kindness." "Serve others." "Take a deep breath, let go, and let be." How often do we give and receive advice like this? It's all important, of course, but what do we do with the wildness—our passion, our sexual-ity, our dark sides, and conflicting emotions?

Beyond the mindful anger management we've already dis-cussed, working with all of our hot, messy, illogical, primal feelings often requires something sharper, like a sword or dia-mond. Specifically, I'm referring to the Diamond Path—the tantric teachings that utilize all parts of our lives as tools of awakening. We can use Tantra not only to fully embody ecstatic states of sexuality, but also to expand our potential as human beings. Moreover, as we mature in this way, we bring an authen-tic naturalness and inherent freedom to others as a genuine possibility, thereby making a wiser, safer, and more liberated world more possible. Without a doubt, we need a better future for all of us, especially for the generations that will follow us. If we want to survive on this endangered planet, we must make a quantum leap in our priorities, from ego striving and selfishness to altruism and the grand *we*-volution. We can start with a social policy more concerned with the whole than the sum of any of its privileged parts. I'm talking here about inter-meditation on a grand scale—the fruition of dedicated, compassionate practice—and I'm offering these tantric instructions as one practical and accessible means of arriving there.

But we must exercise caution. For all of Tantra's superlative advertising and super-charged energy practices, riding the lightning of sexual energy can have its downsides. Tantra yoga scriptures and teachers traditionally exhort would-be practitioners to beware the pitfalls and potholes on this swift and joyful, provocative path. Tantra is risky and potentially treacherous because of its alchemical nature; we're not talking about gradual purification and safe, incremental change. In the fiery, mercurial forge of Tantra, our dense, dull, lead base-metal of animal instincts transmutes into the radiant gold of sublime consciousness—Buddha nature. Practicing Tantra resembles balancing on a high-wire without a safety net. Chögyam Trungpa Rinpoche described it like riding down a banister sharp as a razor blade. Tantric practice can even lead those seeking enlightenment into the opposite way—into greater bondage and delusion. Of course, on a smaller scale, we can see these risks in sideways attempts to integrate spirituality into daily life, resulting in more ego-centered behaviors, thoughts, justifications, and rationalizations. For example, a mind more concerned with self-gratification than liberation can easily turn the slogan "Everything must be meditated" into "It's all meditation—let's go get drunk at happy hour." As well, when the Dharma encourages us to become nonreactive and equanimous through radical acceptance of whatever occurs, the Buddhas and Bodhisattvas certainly did not mean for us to take this teaching as a license for complacent indifference, passivity, quietism, complicity, indulgence, ignoring necessary changes to the status quo, or exploitation.

But how do we know the difference? Which gauge detects such egocentric bending, spiritual materialism, and self-deception? In short, it is always suggested that we can rely on authentic teachers and discriminating wisdom teachings to help us maintain the integrity of our Bodhichitta and our truth-seeking, while we can also continually check in with ourselves and our own inner motivations and progress, honestly and fearlessly. Are we actually in touch with others, specifically their feelings—or are we cocooned in our own isolationism? When empathetic compassion is in play, we feel what others feel and naturally move in to help, share, cooperate, and co-create. Finally, if we're truly experiencing equanimity and spiritual detachment, then complacency and narcissistic laziness don't arise—they're incompatible with the path of enlightenment. Not that we don't know how to have a good time—I do encourage you to celebrate (not celibate)!

Tantra taught me that I can utilize and integrate everything and anything into the path of one-ing with the divine light of Bodhichitta at the heart of all. I have come to see shadows as nothing but aspects of light, and I have learned that I can stop running and reaching, hiding and avoiding, and just savor this moment as it is, this breath the only breath, and let the rest go by. When my head clears from this mental clarity practice, then

I can better discriminate how, when, and if to act, and all the rest that must ineluctably follow. Tantric practice confirmed for me that I no longer need to see anything in myself or in life as an impermeable obstacle or absolute hindrance, sin or defilement; I needn't worry or overburden myself with mistaken, habitual efforts to remove, purify, repress, or avoid what just comes naturally. In practical terms, tantric experience and insight powerfully empowered and challenged me to go beyond well-socialized notions and norms of rational religiosity and into inconceivable freewheeling responsibility and discerning insightfulness. Through Tantra, I come to know the groundless and boundless vastness of my own inner infinite BuddhaMind, Divine Heart/Mind, cosmic consciousness—right here in my self, my desires and thoughts, relationships and activities, the very locus of the hundred thousand peaceful and wrathful light and dark deities of the Tibetan Pantheon representing the varied forces—good, bad, and neutral. This astonishing path has helped me grow up and assume my own *mensch*-hood.

Perhaps the unboundaried, provocative, inconceivable, and even transgressive core of Tantra is why tantric masters often adopt a Buddhist version of an antinomian stance in the world, or why they sometimes seem so iconoclastic, trickster-like, and outrageous. We often associate tantric traditions with Crazy Wisdom, and delightful examples abound in both East and West. Chuang Tzu, the seminal Taoist philosopher of ancient China, famously said, "Everybody knows the utility of usefulness, but nobody knows the utility of uselessness."[2] These words are far wiser than they might immediately seem, and far less than crazy, which is precisely the outlandish terrain where Crazy Wisdom prefers to operate.

Passion Becomes Compassion

Intimate relationship is a path and dance of awakening. "This is how God prays: by dancing,"[3] wrote Benedictine monk David Steindl-Rast. Human love can open us to Divine love. As we work with relationships through co-meditation and inter-meditation practice we can learn to include our sexual passion, but there's more to passion than just sex. Our passion for creativity and imagination, our calling or vocation, and even our quotidian work in the gritty world—all become a gift we can contribute to the world. We can serve as passionate teachers, parents, activists, collaborative leaders, cooks, healers, or artists. That's when our passion becomes compassion—when we recognize every moment in life as a possible awakening, fertile ground for inter-meditation, for unified co-creativity within the entire interdependent mandala of people and things. And this holds true not just when I'm writing poems and haiku, or spiritual songs and prayers. When I work at carpentry or masonry, or when I build a stone wall, every single nail hammered or stone set feels like constructing a meditation temple sanctuary in the paradisiacal Pure Lands or Buddha-fields—particularly the Buddha-field renowned as the Holy Here-and-Now. This is the joy of co-meditation.

This is how God prays: by dancing.

Love is a spiritual practice—not just truth and intelligence, but *love*. When joined with wisdom, insightful gnosis and compassion form the two wings of the bird soaring in the space of enlightenment or awakening. Spirituality is all about the breadth and depth, the potential and actuality of complete love, infinite love—an authentic, warm, and heartfelt love larger than any one of us, yet within our heart and soul, body and reach. It's the most personal and intimate thing. Obviously, everyone doesn't learn the curriculum in the same way, according to the same timetable or guidelines. In no way should the path be simply one-size-fits-all, cheap, off-the-rack clothing that has to suit everybody without trimming, tailoring, or choice. It has to fit you. And when you lose or gain weight or age or change your style, you have to alter the wardrobe a little too, rather than wearing that tube-top or faded jeans like old habits and outdated prior ways of being.

Through our spiritual life we can marvelously use these human capacities of complete love, intimacy, trust, vulnerability, and sharing—as well as the incandescent inner longing for connection, belonging, and pleasure (and later, for transcendence and integration)—to take us beyond the ego and its habitual small-minded selfishness and deeply entrenched ruttedness. Cultivating these arts and co-meditative practices of freedom helps us to unfold and become our best selves, and to love, accept, appreciate, and forgive others, even when we don't like or agree with what they do. How they respond in turn is more their business than yours. Everything changes; nothing remains for long. Everything passes, while events and other developments don't necessarily adhere to plans—ours or anyone else's. Life's not fair, but it's lawful, karmically speaking. Abide by that universal Law, and fly free. People won't always be loving, reliable, consistent, or loyal, but learn these lessons and they won't have real power over you. Again, it's not what happens but what we make of it that makes all the difference. Therefore, please take up the rope leading from the ring in your nose, fellow brother- and sister-oxen, and find and follow your path, unalone and unafraid! Transformation is hard but not unattainable.

All of our relationships can stretch and move in that consciously evolving direction, from self to noble self, from ego to evolutionary consciousness, from ignorance to wisdom and darkness to light, from death to immortality. We can cultivate a love far larger than the both of us—an infinite love, a love for the ages greater even than death, as one Good Book says. *Amen.* And we can bring that loving intimacy, openness, sharing, and ever-sustaining joyful mind from the bedroom into the world—allowing passion to become compassion, as we inter-meditate with our families and co-meditate with the (divine) world in all its myriad delightful and terrifying guises.

¡Viva la We-volución! Co-meditators of the world, unite—don't subdivide! Throw off your chains, your concepts, your neuroses, and your differences. When I am awake, all is awakened—even my mother and yours, and the animals, the mountains, and the trees.

Row, row, row your boat,
gently down the stream.
Merrily, merrily, merrily, merrily,
life is but a dream.

The existence of a single number by itself is unthinkable. Morally or spiritually, this means that the existence of each individual, whether or not he is conscious of the fact, owes something to an infinitely expanding and all-enwrapping net of loving relationship, which takes up not only every one of us but everything that exists. The world is a great family and we, each one of us, are its members.[1]

D.T. SUZUKI

5

The Mama and Papa Sutras

Interbeing with Our Families

I have found through my work with Dharma students who are children of parents or parents of children that the parent-child relationship offers some of the most vital teachings of everyday life. Accordingly, it provides some of the best inter-meditation practices. Therefore, don't get discouraged that your dad and mom duties seem to fill up most of your hours. You might not have all the time you'd like to visit that retreat center, attend workshops, bask in formal prayer, practice yoga, or meditate for hours on end, but that doesn't mean that your path is being obstructed. Quite the opposite, in fact. Parents, children, and genuine intimate relationships of all kinds draw out the best in us; they lovingly force us beyond ego and its limitations and defense mechanisms. Imagine if you were restricted to following little else than self-will and your wants, needs, and desires. I can tell you, there are plenty of selfish single men and women living in monasteries, ashrams, seminaries, and meditation centers. I've been there; perhaps I've even been one. Although we might not all be parents, we're all mentors, uncles and aunts, or somebody's child, sibling, colleague, neighbor, or constituent. Regardless, we enjoyed the good karma of family—including the role of parenthood—in past lives.

We Are the Offspring of Both Murderers and Doting Mothers

All of us—every single person alive—has been parented. The marauding thirteenth-century horseman-warrior of the Asian steppes, Genghis Khan, was one of history's great military strategists. He was also a mass murderer. He must have had a mother, at least, and a biological father as well. With his mounted Golden Horde, he raped and pillaged from China to India and Persia, and all the way to the cities of Eastern Europe. Khan sired hundreds of children; as a result, a predominant number of Mongolians and related nationalities carry his genes. Historians say he was probably responsible for the deaths of over ten million people. We may feel far from him, morally superior, and more kind and peaceful, but he is never far from us—we're all family. According to the *American Journal of Human Genetics* and *National Geographic,* Khan's chromosomes are present in "0.5 percent of the male population in the world, or roughly 16 million descendants living today."[2] This means that a number of us gentle vegetarians, Buddhists, peacemakers,

When your mother gave birth, where did you begin and she end?

and yogis have a direct lineage link to the notorious Khan. Let's reflect on that, my pacifist friends.

So when you start drawing imaginary lines and thinking "He's not one of us" or "She's not like us" in the black-and-white, us-and-them mode, ask yourself, "Who is really my family? My friend? My enemy?" Is there actually that much distinction? Are you not closer to some non-blood kindred spirits and beloveds in this life than to some of your own apparent flesh and blood?

Mahayana Buddhism teaches that all beings have been our doting mothers, fathers, grandparents, caretaking-guardians, children, friends, enemies, lovers, and neighbors throughout time in the endless cycle of birth and death and rebirth. This cycle resembles a huge waterwheel going round and round, refilling and emptying its compartments again and again. Or it's like how clay pots are formed, shattered, and dissolved—the same clay used, reformed, and reused generation after generation. "From dust to dust," as the Bible says. That's why Tibetan prayers all without exception include words such as "for the benefit of all motherly sentient beings." This refers to how we fit into God's cosmic inter-meditation and includes all in the embrace of our hearts' prayers and aspirations. My dear old mom is now laid to rest in our family plot in a Long Island cemetery, yet she remains with me always, in spirit as well as in genes and chromosomes. And particularly in her sense of humor.

When your mother gave birth, where did you begin and she end? Have you begun, really? Will I ever end entirely?

Being a Full-on Family

How can we tap into profound re-integration with others in order to overcome our habitual sense of isolation and lonely separateness, and to make ever more meaningful connections with our children, parents, and the world around us? When our kids are no longer sweetly sleeping toddlers, but angry, frustrating, ungrateful, and hormone-addled adolescents? When our parents are not simply wise elders and loving grandparents, but invalids who can't tend to their own hygiene and may even forget our names? Is that not the time for which we have been training and practicing, the real moment of crisis and opportunity for which our spiritual fire drills have prepared us?

Family and intimate relationships bring out what Tibetans call *shenpen*, the unselfish thinking-of-others attitude—an altruistic, benevolent concern for the well-being of everyone else. It is actually a synonym in Tibetan for Bodhichitta which, as I've discussed, is the most morally desirable behavior and character trait. This shenpen is a ready-made action-path to inter-meditation. When we parent, care-give, mentor, or serve with our full hearts, we're often as present with another as we are with ourselves, pulled out of our heads and self-centeredness into the world of *we*. This irresistible self-giving process and mutual reciprocity, whether explicit or implicit, can sometimes elevate us to superhuman places. Think of the story of the ninety-five-pound mother who lifts a car off her child. Shenpen implies wishing well for and doing well by others, unselfishly and without expectation of return. We inter-meditate to feel what others feel and intuit what they want, like, and need as if from within them. This is the magic of unconditional love, empathic warmth, patience, and generosity—Bodhichitta.

Use Tonglen to Do What Matters

I could write a whole book applying Lojong slogans just to families and relationship dynamics. Here's a favorite slogan that a friend of mine uses when she is having a hard time with her parents or her child:

> This time do what matters; put others
> first, practice Dharma on all levels, develop
> genuine compassion and selfless altruism.

Or as the musician John Cage once said, "No why. Just here."[3] It is always now. It's now or never, as always. If you won't do something now, you probably won't later. We know this as the karmic law of conditioning. In this moment, instead of meeting a child's defensiveness with anger or an elderly parent's criticism with hurtful retaliation, make the interaction an inter-meditation by breathing in the negativity or unwanted through nonreactive mindful acceptance, and generously exhaling the good, positive, and desirable. Have a moment of attention, make time for a sacred pause, and let the fresh air of detached awareness blow through and carry away the cobwebs that obscure clear vision. Then choose how, when, to what degree, and if to respond.

Tonglen practice kicks in when we realize self and others as inseparable in the ultimate sphere of oneness. It cuts the root of our dualism, our egotism, our self-centered willfulness, and our ignorance. As this gap heals, it reconciles the illusory separation we feel between others and ourselves. Instead, we bridge the gap; we return to our inalienable interbeing and interconnectedness, and even

This time do what matters; put others first, practice Dharma on all levels, develop genuine compassion and selfless altruism.

oneness. As the saintly master Paramahansa Yogananda chanted, "I am the Bubble, Lord, make me the Sea."

Momitation

One night a couple of years back, I sat chatting in my cousin's home after dinner with a newish member of our family—my nephew's wife, Helen. She spoke of how much she longed for peace and stillness, and a modicum of quietude and centered-ness in her intensely busy mom-a-thon of a life. She lived with my nephew and their little kid, worked a full-time job in marketing, and helped care for her aged mother in an assisted living home nearby. I let her know that, as a matter of fact, I actually work in the "inner peace and stillness-finding" spiritual business.

The more we gabbed and joked around, the more we connected. How could she find extra alone time and space in her stressful, busy, chock-full-of-commitments day in order to meditate or pray, exercise, commune with nature, read, or do yoga? She asked me about my meditation practice, and if I had a meditation room or a regular group or institute. I suggested that, rather than trying to imitate my routine—forty-five minutes or so every morning—she might just try the following practice:

INTER-MEDITATION PRACTICE
Momitation

- Inter-meditate by sitting in your kids' room at night after they go to sleep.
- Breathe slowly and mindfully, relaxing, slowing down by just breathing.

- Let go of tension and to-do lists, should-haves and stress.
- Begin by centering your attention upon mere breathing and your attendant physical sensations, breathe gently and relax; allow your heart to open and unfold naturally, like a lotus flower blooming in the warm sunlight of awareness.
- Practice really feeling *with* the sleeping kids, breathing in the feelings and releasing them. Think of it as inter-meditating with the angels, or co-meditation *en famille.*
- Watch their chests rise and fall with each precious breath.
- Breathe with them, as them, and do your best to carry that moment into their waking lives.

Helen readily tried this practice and emailed me a few days later to thank me and tell me how well it worked. She said it changed her relationship to her children not just at night but during their waking hours, even during the less quiet and joyful times. She planned on doing that "Momitation" every evening for the rest of her life. "Even after they leave home and go to college, their room will still be there!"

And I thought, gratefully: how simple it is and can be, *when we are.* The real Holy Land, the Pure Land, paradise, is everywhere, even right where we stand. Everything can be meditated, grist for the mill of spiritual awareness—nothing and no one is excluded. This Kingdom of Heaven is within.

Realization through Our Proximity

There's some interesting science behind this Momitation and all of inter-meditation. Rollin McCraty and other researchers have demonstrated how people's heart rates and rhythms influence each other when they're in proximity. The heart sends out the strongest electro-magnetic field of any of our bodily organs, stronger even than our brains, and it can influence those near us. McCraty says that the heart actually gives more neurological information to the brain than the brain does to the heart. Who knew?

According to the Institute of HeartMath where McCraty is the director of research: "Using a technique called signal averaging, researchers were able to detect synchronization between a mother's brainwaves (EEG) and her baby's heartbeats (ECG). The pair were not in physical contact, but when the mother focused her attention on the baby, her brainwaves synchronized to the baby's heartbeats."[4]

We know this intuitively. Think about a sobbing child. How do we hold him or her? On our hip? Facing outward? Rarely. We lift up the child and bring him or her toward us, chest to chest, heart to heart. It's the same when we comfort anyone; it's like instinctive heart-to-heart spiritual resuscitation.

The Power of Connection

My very first Dzogchen master was the great Kangyur Rinpoche, originally of Riwoche Monastery, who was revered for his voluminous learning and memory. He could recite and teach the entire Buddhist canon—the *Kangyur*—by heart. That's extraordinarily important in a nomadic oral culture like Tibet, where Kangyur Rinpoche lived until his escape from Chinese occupation in 1959.

His memorization of the canon also proved essential in Darjeeling where he lived later with no mass communication, printing presses, or libraries, and certainly no computers or Google. Even if books and texts had been more widely accessible, he couldn't lug them around eastern Tibet on a horse in the first half of the last century. I got to really know all of Kangyur Rinpoche's family during the 1970s and 1980s, and his oldest son, Tulku Pema Wangyal, was one of my main teachers during our three-year meditation retreats in the forest of southern France.

In 1975 Kangyur Rinpoche died of old age and was laid out in his bedroom befitting Tibetan Buddhist custom. His youngest son, little Tulku Jigme Khyentse, was devastated. A boy of eleven years old, he cried and begged and wailed through the night; it was absolutely heartrending. All he wanted was for his father to come back. Unlike what you might expect, the family didn't take him away, or tell him to be quiet and man up—they let him cry. After all, he may have been a *tulku,* a reincarnated Tibetan master-lama, but he was also just a little boy whose daddy had just died. He didn't care about esoteric post-death meditations, the bardo, or stoicism and non-attachment; the boy was totally grief-stricken.

And guess what?

After a day and a night, Kangyur Rinpoche woke up!

People called it a miracle and attributed it to Rinpoche's powers of compassion even after death. He lived for six more months and he joyfully said that he'd come back just for little Tulku Jigme.

It's a beautiful story—a father loved his son so much he returned from the dead. But how is this inter-meditation? It all comes back to karmic connection and intent.

Manifesting Genuine Intent Gets Results

You have to have skin in the game. You can't just want to inter-meditate with your parent or child or merely think about it—you have to actually do it and mean it. And, as I repeat throughout this book: you have to manifest genuine *intent*. When you do, there are spiritually verifiable and even scientifically quantifiable results.

In his fine book *How Children Succeed*, Paul Tough writes,

> Science suggests . . . that the character strengths that
> matter so much to young people's success are not innate;
> they don't appear in us magically, as a result of good luck
> or good genes. And they are not simply a choice. They
> are rooted in brain chemistry, and they are molded, in
> measurable and predictable ways, by the environment in
> which kids grow up. That means the rest of us—society
> as a whole—can do an enormous amount to influence
> their development.[5]

In other words, cuddling our babies, showing up at soccer games and piano recitals, reading before bedtime, and active loving—the most basic opportunities for parental inter-meditations—can have radical positive effects.

Nicholas Kristof explored this when he wrote in the *New York Times* about the Nurse-Family Partnership: "It sends nurses on regular visits to at-risk first-time moms, from pregnancy until the child turns two. The nurses warn about alcohol or drug abuse and encourage habits of attentive parenting, like reading to the child. The results are stunning: at age fifteen, these children are less than half as likely to have been arrested as kids from similar circumstances who were not enrolled."[6] This happened because these mothers practiced being present for their children with explicit conscious intent; they began by taking the time to meet with the visiting nurses and then applied what they'd been taught. There have been dozens of other studies like these.

From diapers to bar mitzvahs, inter-meditation can help us become better parents. It's one thing to feel bliss and spiritual connection with a cooing baby, but what about with a sullen adolescent? When we inter-meditate we commit to being fully present *with* our child or those in our charge. As opposed to dwelling on the spit-up in our hair or a return visit to the principal's office, we stop and breathe—inhaling and opening, exhaling and releasing. In doing so, we give our children a spacious pathway of pure presence and unobstructed clarity through which to connect with us as we connect with them to whatever extent may be possible in any given moment or situation. Whether they do it or not is mostly up to them. Regardless, we provide the opportunity and back them no matter what, while getting out of their way because we love and cherish them. This brings me to one of the most basic yet effective inter-meditation practices: hugging.

INTER-MEDITATION PRACTICE

Hugging as a Nowness Meditation

Sometimes we may have genuine conscious intent, but not a lot of time. Our lives are a hustle and bustle. Take mornings for example—parents prepare breakfast, find lost homework and shin guards, make sure the dog has been walked, sign permissions slips, pack lunch, plan play dates, argue about inappropriate clothes, answer the phone, schedule doctors and tutors, charge computers and phones . . . it's a lot! But there's always time for one inter-meditation and it only has to take a few seconds: *hugging*.

The late Japanese Zen master Sasaki Roshi, who lived to be over one hundred years old, called hugging the American Nowness meditation—and it is!

Three Seconds to Bliss

According to an article in *Science* magazine, a hug usually lasts three seconds—the same average amount of time as a baby's babble or a wave goodbye.

> Ever wondered how long a hug lasts? The quick answer is about three seconds, according to a new study of the post-competition embraces of Olympic athletes. But the long answer is more profound. A hug lasts about as much time as many other human actions and neurological processes, which supports a hypothesis that we go through life perceiving the present in a series of three-second windows.

The article goes on to explain:

> The results reinforce an idea current among some psychologists that intervals of about three seconds are basic temporal units of life that define our perception of the present moment. Put another way, what one psychologist called the "feeling of nowness" tends to last three seconds.[7]

Yes, they said *nowness!* (And you thought I was making this word up.) That's what gets me—although I think time is less relevant than quality of presence. As the Dzogchen masters say, one moment of total awareness is one moment of freedom and enlightenment. Whether or not it takes exactly three seconds may be immaterial, but so many opportunities for greater consciousness and connection certainly abound when you break them down into three-second increments.

There's a whole area of research devoted to hugging. Other scientists suggest that a hug should last twenty seconds. According to Stan Tatkin at UCLA, twenty-second hugs release oxytocin—the "love hormone" that bonds mothers and babies, lovers, friends, and maybe even people and their pets. It also lowers blood pressure and relieves stress for both the hugger and the hugged. Count me in.

But again, it comes back to intent. As reported in the *Daily Mail:*

> Neurophysiologist Jürgen Sandkühler said: "The positive effect only occurs, however, if the people trust each other, if the associated feelings are present mutually and if the corresponding signals are sent out.
>
> "If people do not know each other, or if the hug is not desired by both parties, its effects are lost."[8]

That's the inter-meditation principle—synergy, beneficial mutuality, and enhancement. So your mom and grandma were actually on to something. They knew that hugging could resolve conflicts, ease the pain of skinned knees, end a tantrum, take the fear out of nightmares, quiet the agitated mind and heart, and connect two people on a profound level. It's one of the best inter-meditations we can do. I still remember the feeling of my dad's big arms around my boyish shoulders after bad things happened, and him saying, in his authoritative father-voice, "It's gonna be alright, Jeffy. Don't worry; everything's gonna be alright." I take refuge in that embrace, and I sincerely feel for those who lacked that in their own upbringing.

Grouped Together in Sacred Activity

It goes beyond mother and child. *Inter* can mean more than one on one—it can span siblings and parents and generations. Look at how group activities like dancing or singing or cooking or barn-raising together can become an inter-meditation and take us to a place of true connection when done with sincere, sacred communal intent. Think about a father dancing with his daughter at her wedding. Or think about a family singing grace before dinner: "Praise God from whom all blessings flow." Or joining voices in Kaddish: "Blessed, praised, glorified, exalted, extolled, mighty, upraised, and lauded be the Name of the Holy One . . ." I refuse to believe these are examples of *just* dancing or singing—something more important is happening here. Consider your experiences, those moments of familial unity, like any favorite holidays or family gatherings, and the unexpected yet delightful nature of how they actually unfold, beyond the outer organization and routines. Or think about cooking together—preparing your father's last dinner before his cancer surgery, cutting the crusts off the sandwich for your child's lunchbox, or baking your daughter's favorite cookies before she leaves for college. Isn't selfless love the secret ingredient in these magical victuals?

As usual, don't just take my word for it. Andrew Dreitcer, the executive director for the Center for Engaged Compassion at Claremont University, recently said in an interview in *Spirituality & Health* magazine that these kinds of embodied inter-meditations and rituals evoke "a neurophysiology that really responds to intimacy," and "if you have the capacity to pay attention without condemning—even unconsciously—it opens up all kinds of possibilities."[9]

Inter-Meditation Games

We can go beyond dance steps, prayers, and rituals and inter-meditate as we find the joy and humor in family life. I love inter-meditation games, which are really far more than just games.

As a young child playing hide-and-seek outdoors with my cousins and siblings in Brooklyn, the Bronx, and suburban Long Island, I learned an early meditation lesson: the more I stopped and became quiet and tuned in to the bare immediacy of the moment, the more focused and still and clear I became. And when I became clearer, *everything* became clearer. This was my youthful introduction to the harmony and oneness available via a heightened, wakeful awareness. When we adults utterly calm our own body, mind, and breath, we can engage this way with children as well. This secret, in combination with regular batting practice, made me a fearsome hitter on the baseball diamond because I could completely close out all distractions at home plate and just concentrate on the ball, as if the ball and I were not two and it was attracted to my bat.

Try my adaptation of a Dzogchen inter-meditation practice called sky-gazing with your small child or elderly parent:

Sky-Gazing Together

- Find a comfortable seat outside, preferably with a view looking out on nature or buildings, or at least find just a little sky, perhaps through a window or skylight.
- Ask your co-meditator to close their eyes, gently, trustingly, and then do the same.
- Inhale deeply, and exhale fully, letting go totally.
- Now do it again, twice more (three is a magic number).
- Let go and just be, as you are. Rest naturally and at ease in your body and mind, heart and soul, and enjoy the natural state—or whatever state you seem to be in.
- Let your body and mind settle in their own places, in their own ways, just as they are.
- Now slowly open your eyes and quietly ask your partner to do the same.
- Gently raise your gaze. Look through your eyes— really look!
- If you're inter-meditating with a child, ask them what they see. It could begin as a game of "I Spy." For example, "I spy a sparrow." But what do they spy when the sparrow has flown into the clouds?
- Encourage them to see more, further, deeper. You'll be profoundly amazed at how this can open up sensitivity and awareness.
- You could just sit, listen, hear, and wonder. Where do sounds come from, really? And where do they go when they're gone?
- Shift your gazes beyond objects, upward to the infinite. And then let the infinite dissolve.

- If your partner gets distracted, encourage them to breathe a few times, focus, and relax back into the spacious openness of newness-awareness as things naturally unfold, settle, and clarify.
- Enjoy the serenity, relaxation, harmony, and pure joy of meditation.
- Remember: natural meditation ain't that hard. If you try, you just can't miss!

Finding Caregiving Balance through Equanimity

I'm well aware that family life isn't all about songs and dances and dinner parties, free from challenges, misunderstandings, and conflicts. Another benefit of inter-meditation seems at first to be the opposite of connection—spiritual detachment, or what Buddhists call *equanimity*. But this is not synonymous with complacence or cool indifference. Equanimity helps us smother less, mother (and father) better, and keep our lives and relationships balanced and in tune with reality. The Tonglen meditation of sending and receiving—seeing things through another's eyes and equalizing self and others—is a way to avoid the co-dependent caretaker pattern of "hijacking all the giving" in a relationship, which is a sure recipe for parental or filial burnout. One becomes a better *caregiver* and love-sharer rather than an over-invested and even manipulative *caretaker*.

Only you can do what you do. We Bodhisattvas strive to do our best and be our best selves. But overdoing it and becoming demanding, perfectionist, or too idealistic shifts the balance and causes us to keel over, sooner or later. We can easily lose the *inter* in inter-meditation. We need to remember the delightful sharing of breathing in and breathing out—in balance and together—in healing and harmonizing mutuality, and co-maintain this healing cycle.

Just as we wouldn't want to neglect those we love, we don't want to overdo it either. There's a term for this: *pathological altruism*. According to Barbara Oakley and her co-authors, "Pathological altruism might be thought of as any behavior or personal tendency in which either the stated aim or the implied motivation is to promote the welfare of another. But instead of overall beneficial outcomes, the 'altruism' instead has irrational (from the point of view of an outside observer) and substantial negative consequences to the other or even to the self." Oakley and her colleagues go on to warn about the dark and possible downside side of altruism.[10] Extremes of pathological altruism might even range from suicide to genocide; in our daily lives it can manifest as co-dependency, giving until we over-sacrifice for our loved ones to the point of abandoning and stunting ourselves. Think of the mother who exhausts herself to the point of illness in taking care of her family until she can't care for them at all.

It all comes down to balance, equanimity, resilience, and ultimately to loving all beings equally, including ourselves. Here's a basic mantra to deliver us there:

INTER-MEDITATION PRACTICE
Equanimity Mantra

> Everyone is responsible for creating their own karma
> and experience. Their happiness and suffering
> doesn't depend on me.

My happiness and suffering don't depend on them.
I accept them as they are, and bless and
release them from all expectations.

Resolving Conflict

Inter-meditation heals divisiveness and conflicts between self
and other, and changes the entire relational atmosphere. It
effectively erodes our habitual tendency of separateness. Practice when things go well. Then, when difficult situations come
up—a custody battle, substance abuse, a daughter acting out
sexually, or a grandmother lost to dementia—you'll be able
to handle those vicissitudes, fearlessly breathe that misery in,
let it dissolve internally, and breathe out joy and generosity.
An extraordinary healing transformation can and most often
will occur.

This is an advanced, potentially scary practice. If you're in
actual physical danger you need to—first and foremost—get
safely out of it. Meditation is a tool, a means; it isn't necessarily instant magic. Mindful awareness can't fix a broken bone or
cure a viral infection. I'm skeptical of those who believe they
can treat serious illnesses with prayer and prayer alone. Please be
kind to yourself by being sane, practical, and realistic.

INTER-MEDITATION PRACTICE

Riding Conflict with the Breath

- Bring yourself to a place of restful awareness.
- Let every thought float by like a dream, mirage,
  or an old and cancelled sitcom.

- Inhale all of the negativity and stress of the difficulty at hand—whatever the current source of conflict, anger, fear, and tribulation.
- Breathe deep, inhale, and hoover it up like you're vacuuming dark clouds. Take it in and then let it dissolve in the inner luminosity of your infinite, radiant, empty nature of mind.
- Exhale fully. Breathe out love, forgiveness, understanding, loving-kindness, empathic compassion, and life-giving healing energy.
- Direct this positive breath specifically to perceived obstacle-creators and troublemakers. *Poor humans* . . . generating their own bad karma and sorrow, seeking happiness and fulfillment in all the wrong places!
- Simply breathe in and out. Let the natural flow wash away and re-harmonize all obscurations on the windshield of your inner "iye."

When we get used to doing this, it opens up the entire situation. We no longer fear meeting our most difficult problems, and we no longer dread that we're going to explode or fall apart if someone gets mad or critical of us. We can face it and deal with it; we don't have to get away and hide from it. We don't have to try to escape from our families or our responsibilities and challenges—we can find Nirvana, Heaven, our Higher Power, or our deepest inner strength with them even when the going gets tough. We can see the light even within the shadow side of life.

While Family May Be Family for Life, Everything Changes

Here's how I would put it: No feeling is final; everything changes. Fear is a liar and a cheat. Anger is like bubbles in a soda bottle—the more you shake it, the more the pressure builds. We are not always punished for our anger, yet we are always punished *by* our anger. Shame is a self-centered rip-off. Guilt's a bastard, without legitimate claim. Thoughts and beliefs are mostly illusory and meaningless, except for what you choose to invest in them—why get entangled in momentary impulses, moods, and ideas? The mind is fickle and feelings are fleeting, like the changing light and shadows playing upon a mountain range. Better to rest, calm and clear, in moment-to-moment conscious awareness, and act as needed from that spacious clarity and objective detachment.

I have found that when interacting with family, my head is not the best neighborhood for me to live in. Personally, I like to ponder and analyze things, but I much prefer to try and live mainly from the heart. In this mysterious world, rational knowing must often take second place to trusting, accepting, surrendering, and flowing. I invest energy in thoughts and emotions that beget more positive energy in the direction of my values and principles; I trust in this nonviolent and tolerant way of being. Together and unafraid, everything is possible. Every day is a good day. Every heart is a good one at the core. Everyone's mother loved them, speaking generally, and saw at least some goodness in them, even Hitler's. I see the light, the Buddha, the god or goddess, the good and goodness, in everyone and everything, regardless of how they momentarily appear. I consider this my practice, my way, my truth, and my guiding light. In this way, in this light, I am carefree, content, and easy. *Emaho!* Wondrous.

Just as love is not enough, anger and sorrow aren't necessarily the end of the world. It goes back to the ebb and flow, the inhale and exhale of Tonglen. More complex intimacies and shared vulnerabilities—not to mention other practical considerations, values, and biochemical and emotional affinities—must be explored and mutually inter-coordinated for authentic long-term relationships to flourish and thrive. We also come to realize that no relationship really lasts forever, or even very long in the bigger scheme of things. We strive to savor and appreciate what we have while we have it, without taking it for granted or overlooking the miraculous gift of genuine intimate sharing. We have been given so much! Mastering co-meditation practice with those we love—even when we dislike or momentarily feel as if we hate them—lays excellent groundwork for inter-meditating with those we might never imagine loving. Patience is active peacemaking. Nonjudgmental attentive openness and forbearance can be a necessary austerity when it comes to enjoying and appreciating life, with all its blotches and blemishes.

> May I meet this magical moment
> fully and embrace life as it is,
> beyond notions of good or bad, liking and disliking.
> May I dance with life and meet her all along the entirety
> of her gorgeous, sinuous body.

Patience is active peacemaking.

We are all in the same boat, brother, so you can't
rock one end without rockin' the other.

AFRICAN-AMERICAN SPIRITUAL

6

Closing the Gap

Conversitation with Our Enemies

The Dalai Lama's late tutor, Serkhong Rinpoche, loved circuses. He often said that if a bear could be taught to ride a bicycle, then with skillful means and patience, a human being could be taught anything—including how to inter-meditate with his or her enemies. All of our connections and interactions are sacred and meaningful—nothing happens by accident; sometimes our adversaries and enemies prove to be our most profound teachers. They need not even be human. They could take the form of an infectious disease, a weather crisis, a disaster, tragedy, misfortune, grievous loss, or even just a daily disappointment. Any undesirable circumstance or outcome can have the face of an enemy simply because we consider it negative.

To make the journey from the big head to the big heart—from perceiving unwanted circumstances as enemies to regarding them as teachers and change-agents—we must take conscious steps to loosen our egotism. If we do this, eventually

Since unwholesome thoughts and harmful actions are everywhere, integrate them into the path of transformation leading to enlightenment.

we will behave like the Methodist minister from Texas did when she encountered the robber in the parking lot. She empathized with the would-be mugger and trenchantly perceived what was beneath his violent mask. She connected with his pure and uncorrupted innermost spiritual essence, as a troubled and lost child of God—to use her words—and chose love, in that very moment, eschewing fear in favor of connection and the divine embrace of interbeing. This is how inter-meditation opens us up into Divine love in human form. The minister embodied this Lojong aphorism:

> Since unwholesome thoughts and harmful actions are everywhere, integrate them into the path of transformation leading to enlightenment.

But there's a little more to her story. Ten years after that robbery, a guy in a suit approached her after Sunday service in church. He was polite and respectful to the point of reverence, and then he asked, "Do you remember me?"

The minister answered honestly: "No."

And the man said, "I remember you. You totally changed my life."

With a flash of realization, she recognized the man in that dark parking lot so long ago. And then he told her the story from his side; although he had taken her money away, what stayed with him much longer was her message.

The minister's words, her actions, her stopping to breathe in the evil and release the good in that very moment transformed the man and opened up a better path for him. I can never think about what she said without tearing up:

> I wish I had more to give you. I love you.

We Are All Born Able to Change

The minister's compassionate actions and spiritual goodness show her side of the inter-meditation, but what about the robber? We know he changed and what changed him, but how did this profound personal transformation actually occur?

Northeastern University psychology professor David DeSteno suggests, "If we see a commonality between ourselves and someone else, we are more likely to act with compassion toward them." In this way of understanding, the robber participated in the minister's actions—he wasn't just the subject of her goodness. DeSteno goes on to say:

> Some people believe that criminals are "born bad" and that they cannot change. If they commit a crime because they were not able to see the humanity in someone else, then who is to say they will ever see it again? Science.
>
> Developments in neuroscience have shown us that the brain is plastic and malleable, a phenomenon called neuroplasticity. What neuroplasticity teaches us is that change, growth, and understanding is always possible. A criminal is often a person who has experienced hardships and violence that led to a life of crime.

Similarly, just as experience may have turned them into criminals, in the same way experience can help them turn around.[1]

There are countless examples of this innate ability to change through fresh experiences. Gabriella Savelli, director of Prison Smart, a non-profit organization that brings yoga and meditation into prisons, explains that even some of the toughest inmates can undergo transformation. She says,

> One instance that comes to mind is in New York City. The course was an absolute zoo at the beginning. On the first day the twenty-five participants were very rowdy and noisy. Many couldn't close their eyes during the processes or stop bothering people around them. By the end of the week, the same group sat perfectly still in their chairs while they did the breathing and meditation exercises for a very long, quiet, peaceful time. When they finally opened their eyes, one man stated, "Now, when I look around the room in these other guys' eyes, all I see is me!"[2]

This particular inmate—someone with a long history of aggression, reactivity, and anger—became a far more compassionate, patient, and understanding person through mindfulness meditation and hatha yoga.

I'm a big fan of Father Greg Boyle, the Jesuit priest who founded Homeboy Industries in Los Angeles in order to help former gang members start new lives. He explains, "This is not work of helping, but of finding kinship, because the point of Christian service is about our common calling to delight in one another."[3]

There's also the work of the restorative justice movement which legal scholar John Braithwaite describes as "about hurt begetting healing as an alternative to hurt begetting hurt. Some restorative justice advocates argue that shame has no place in restorative justice because shaming is a kind of hurting and shame is a destructive kind of hurt that can make crime and injustice worse."[4] These Bodhisattvas and so many more are inter-meditating with people perceived as enemies and truly *changing their hearts and minds*, and for the better. This healing power is a precious gift, and one that we all can learn to participate in. Change is universal, but changing oneself for the better requires sincere effort, perseverance, and patience.

I wish I had more to give you. I love you.

The Truth About Taking in the Pain

I am often asked: If someone is harming me, should I try to practice nonviolence (*ahimsa*—nonaggression) and Tonglen sending and receiving to take in the other person's pain? Won't breathing in their hate fill me with hate?

No, it won't—that's the short answer. That's over-reifying what's basically *sunyata*—empty, hollow, insubstantial, like a dream, a mirage, a fantasy. First of all, we might actually have to make a choice whether or not to defend ourselves or even protect others from danger. We might have to take action, and forcefully in some cases. The peaceable elderly Dalai Lama, champion of radical nonviolence, has bodyguards, due to realpolitik and threats to his life. They are not hesitant to spring into action, if necessary. What they tell me is *he* is their actual protector, who guards their spirit and Bodhichitta, keeping them from aggression and other forms of negativity.

Our altruistic Bodhisattva Vow and practice compel us to cultivate and sustain equanimity, and moreover to treat others as like ourselves or our beloved children. In co-meditation practice, we become aware of the other's pain or struggles, experience it, and let it pass through, dissolving into the spacious sunyata (void, mystery) from which it originally arose. Similarly, we practice Tonglen with the dead, the sick, the dying, the insane, and also the emotionally toxic and aggravating. We don't inhale their germs and viruses, per se, in a material sense, nor receive their unwanted gifts of anger, prejudice, and violence. However, we do "inhale" and invite all their suffering and pain into our spacious clarity and unguarded vastness of internal being, taking their burdens upon us. Then we give back to them all our peace and happiness, joy and hope. And all the while we ride the breath, breathing in and breathing out, and experience the feelings as a healing without driving them away. We simultaneously rest in the emptiness and openness of unborn BuddhaMind at our heart's soulful, luminous core. In the actual Tonglen practice, we're almost like air conditioners: we're going to take in all the heat and transform it into a cool breeze that heals the separation and resultant friction and conflict, to unify and harmonize the universe. With strength of inner mind and pure, clear intention, this can definitely happen.

To reply with kindness and compassion to negativity and harm is the swiftest way to progress in overcoming ego and fulfilling the Bodhisattva path.

Troubled relationships and adversaries provide wonderful opportunities to inter-meditate. However, a troubled relationship is not meant to be a life sentence; we should exit from truly destructive situations. Yes, we could very well learn to feel empathic compassion for everyone—unfair employers, friends who have betrayed us, political enemies, competitors, and critics—but we also need to let go of futile battles and the need to prove who is right or wrong. Sometimes our biggest lesson is learning to walk away from anger or conflict. A spiritual master does his or her thorough best, and then lets go. Whatever happens *happens*. No regrets.

Would you rather be right or happy? I have chosen. So can you.

Sweating the Small Stuff

If we can change a criminal's mind or rehabilitate an addict through recovery and helpful community, what about those people who don't present grave threats but just, well, irritate and kind of tick us off? Let's start small and bring it back to inter-meditation—not with hardened criminals but with our unreasonable employer or someone whose extreme political opinions make us crazy, or maybe even the IRS or INS, or some other large, faceless government agency theoretically dedicated to the common good but infrequently perceived that way. I have a friend named Cecil who, in the midst of an ugly tax audit, turned a combative relationship into a productive encounter, and ultimately into friendship, when he and his auditor took a break from paperwork, went for a walk outside in the yard, and connected over a mutual love of gardening. They put into practice the heart-opening words of my late compassion-master, Dilgo Khyentse Rinpoche of Derge, Eastern Tibet:

> To reply with kindness and compassion
> to negativity and harm is the swiftest
> way to progress in overcoming ego
> and fulfilling the Bodhisattva path.

Didn't Jesus say something similar? As the Venerable Thich Nhat Hanh teaches, Buddha and Christ are brothers. If we contemplate them, these truths are universal and almost self-evident.

We can practice less complex levels of inter-meditation in preparation for the big moments, like fire drills—since anger and resulting violence often burn us and can become so destructive. "One spark of anger can burn down a whole forest of good deeds," said the Peace Master Shantideva in his classic text *The Way of the Bodhisattva*. When we inter-meditate in a skillful fashion with a bitchy boss or someone who cuts us off in traffic today, we're training for the really bad stuff—people who truly hurt us or hurt the ones we love, or perpetrators and abusers. It's like a dress rehearsal, helping us to entrain these highly positive values, preparing to respond as we would wish when push actually comes to shove. In this tough real-world classroom, the test comes first, then the lessons are explained, and not vice versa. However, mindful anger management, emotional resilience, self-awareness, and equanimity can truly help to iron out life's difficulties. You're hearing this now from the lips of an elder whose teenage motto was *kill the quarterback!* Change is possible.

Who knows if someone cutting us off in traffic isn't hurrying a back-seat stroke victim or birthing mother to the local hospital? Why fall prey to road rage and suffer from its harmony-destroying internal poisons when we know so little about what's going on with other people in situations that bother us? We hardly need to waste time and energy on lower-chakra reptilian-brain reactivity. There are so many other ways to be! I promise you, if we saw the whole situation all at once, as if from above—with God's eye or BuddhaVision—we would almost certainly have different feelings, reactions, and opinions. Remembering this small but telling insight helps me stay calm and clear most of the time, and definitely furthers inner peace and harmony. Some of my friends think that I am preternaturally calm, that I never get angry; little do they know what lurks inside the heart of man!

INTER-MEDITATION PRACTICE

Taking the Small Stuff in Stride

My own practice for not sweating the small stuff entails utilizing a few homemade quotes and potent slogans that speak to me. I keep yellow sticky notes and index cards on my desk, bathroom mirror, dashboard, wallet, and computer. I practice what I call *remindfulness* by remembering to look at these handwritten adages; they help me recall what is important in the bigger picture and the long run—my values, principles, vows, practices, and goals. I let the wisdom of these maxims sink in, inevitably defusing the situation before it gets anywhere near out of hand.

This too shall pass.

Among these potent pointers, here's my favorite:

This too shall pass.

> How much will this matter to me a year or two from now?

This slogan reminds me to practice patience, acceptance, and forbearance in the face of irritation and disappointment. I also remember to stay in touch with the long view, because things are cyclic and nothing happens without causes, even if not immediately apparent to me. Here's another one I like:

> How much will this matter to me a year or two from now?

I also like to echo the Diamond Sutra, the world's oldest printed book, which quotes Buddha saying:

> See things as like a dream, a fantasy, a mirage.

I usually add the word sitcom or movie, just for fun. This traditional Dharma teaching helps me remember to regard everything as like rainbows or the divine dance of illusion. It helps me take things a lot less seriously and leave room for my inner child and little Buddha within to stand up, play, dance, and sing.

Probably the most effective, practical yoga- and meditation-related maxim is this:

> Breathe, relax, center, and smile.
> Nothing is as important as it
> seems at this moment.

That really cools my jets, and allows for more intelligent decision-making and clear-headed thinking to proceed.

I've gotten my friend Amelia into the habit of singing (often in her head) the great nursery-rhyme mantra guaranteed to defuse any difficult situation:

> Row, row, row your boat, gently down the stream.
> Merrily, merrily, merrily, merrily, life is but a dream.

If I have a good amount of time and feel inspired to co-meditate with the Masters for further spiritual relief and sustenance—perhaps when I'm sitting in a waiting room at the airport or somewhere—I either close my eyes and chant Tibetan mantras and prayers to myself, so only my collar can hear it (as Dudjom Rinpoche once advised), or I recite Buddha's Metta Sutra (Maitri or Loving-Kindness Sermon) which includes the line:

> See things as like a dream, a fantasy, a mirage.

> May all beings be happy and at ease!

Or I might take St. Francis of Assisi's Peace Prayer out of my wallet and read:

> Make me an instrument of your peace . . .

I invite you to try my small-stuff slogans out, one at a time, and see how they work for you. Or find other one-liners in the appendix of this book and make up your own.

When Facing Enemies, Pause to Share

Before you enter a confrontational meeting, or a complex interpersonal situation like a doctor's diagnosis visit or court appearance, research shows that you can dial down the stress and tension by acknowledging and sharing your worries, doubt, and anxiety with someone else. It's especially helpful to connect and commune (inter-meditate) with someone who may be similarly afflicted or burdened. I've found that even talking to my dog has beneficial results.

Sarah Townsend, assistant professor of management and organization at the USC Marshall School of Business, found that sharing stress and worries with another person can provide relief and buffer us against stress by normalizing our emotional state. Many others suffer from similar feelings and also manifest physical stress-symptoms when encountering similar situations. So, when we face a challenge or even a threat, interacting with someone who feels similar to us decreases our stress.[5] I believe that "sharing" is the operative word in the researcher's conclusion; the participants in the study were no longer battling alone. Isolation is a terrible thing, and some famous people throughout history have faltered on its shoals. We need each other—in so many ways, and for so many reasons. "No one is an island . . . "

The Honesty Beneath Anger

Anger has its own logic, penetrating intelligence, and insightful wisdom; it often points directly at something that is actually wrong. We can intentionally hone attraction and aversion—or desire and anger—to help us choose more intelligently which way to go, and decide which options assist or hinder our aims, goals, and purposes. All emotions contain their own particular wisdom or special feature; we need not reject or indulge them. Before we self-righteously leap into action, perhaps precipitously, we might learn to consider things first in the calm light of lucid awareness and via our objective inter-meditative principles. For instance, if we feel mad at somebody, before jumping to conclusions and retaliating, we might first try to put ourselves in their shoes for a moment and look at the situation through their eyes. We can open up to this experience and imagine what the other person must be feeling. More information can also be helpful.

May all beings be happy and at ease!

Empathy is said to be the root of compassion. Empathy means feeling *with* another—feeling what they feel. Doing so attunes us and allows us to find a way to connect and convey our side of the story as well. Can you imagine revealing your own tender underbelly and making yourself vulnerable by telling your enemy, critic, competitor, or someone you're in conflict with that you're afraid? That's what inter-meditation practice involves—opening oneself, unzipping the wetsuit, experiencing the natural elements, and unmasking all sides of the story while escaping the death-grip of our constrictive ego and self-centered habits and defenses.

Remember that Tonglen practice goes both ways—giving *and* receiving—so just as you should take a walk in someone else's shoes, you should let them try on yours. When given the opportunity, we can put the *inter* into inter-meditation by developing mutual empathy, genuine connection, identification, and oneness. We can choose this over alienation and the self-protective barricades we too often build and reinforce with our subjective, self-interested storytelling. We can do this practice—nonverbally, or even beyond rationality and conceptual mind—in order to dissolve the separation between others and ourselves.

Make me an instrument of your peace...

Here's a first step in getting out of that selfish point of view—it's a practice I love. I call it "Wishing Others Well" or WOW. It's the essence of loving-kindness meditation, also known as *metta* or *maitri* practice taught by the Buddha 2,600 years ago. *Maitri* means friendliness, love, and openness. Maitri entails a lot of joy, and it's a way to truly attune and empathize with others.

Maitri expands from concentration and inner-meditation to inter-meditation, and it forms a key component of the Buddha's life-changing wisdom-development teachings. Anyone can do it. You can add it to the end of your daily meditation, or use it whenever you like—while washing dishes, waiting in line at the bank, sitting in traffic at a red light, or when you see that you're about to get into an argument. I have taken the basic sacred phrases from the Maitri Sutra (Metta or Loving-Kindness Scripture) and added to them over the years as insights and aspirations have arisen in my own prayer and meditation practice. I encourage you to do the same; make WOW practice your own.

INTER-MEDITATION PRACTICE
Wishing Others Well (WOW)

Start by saying and praying:

May I be happy, content, and fulfilled.

May all beings be happy!

May I experience the joy of mental happiness
and the ease of well-being.

May I be peaceful, centered, and serene.

May I be free from suffering and dissatisfaction.

May I be free from harm, danger, and fear.

May all beings be free from harm, danger, and fear.

May I/we walk the path of wisdom and compassion.

May I be understanding and learn to listen.

May I respect all other people, as well as myself.

May I be patient and loving.

May I be loved and let the love in.

May I practice loving-kindness.

May I practice equanimity and mindful nonreactivity.

May I grow each day in being less judgmental,
more tolerant and open-minded.

May I be happy, peaceful, and liberated.

May my family flourish.

May our lives be filled with joy.

May I be free from suffering and enjoy peace and ease.

May my heart remain open.

May I enjoy and appreciate the holy now.

May I awaken to the light of my own true nature.

May I be healed and whole again.

May the planet itself be healed and restored.

May I be a source of healing and harmony
for all sentient beings connected to me.

May I be grateful and reverent.

May I walk in love, joy, and peace.

May I experience the beauty and wholeness of
my own intrinsically sacred true nature.
May I feel connected to all other beings.
May I live in a state of gratitude and grace.
May I love deeply, with full acceptance, and
may I open my heart to receive love.
May I know peace and be peace.
May I forgive and be forgiven.
May I be free from harm, danger, and anxiety.
May I be free from suffering.
May I be free from the illusions that keep me bound.
May I be fearless in pursuing and speaking truth.
May I live in boundless joy.
May I see the light in all things.
May I and all other sentient beings, near
and far, known and unknown, walk in
beauty, truth, courage, and wisdom.
I bow to my true Buddha Nature [or Jesus Nature,
or Sacred Nature], innate in one and all.
I dedicate the merit of this maitri practice
to the ones I hold dearly in my heart—may
they be edified and awakened!

Now, imagine or visualize the people you care about
most—your partner, your family, your dearest friends—
and bathe them and yourself in the warmth of your
love. Pray for their health, happiness, protection, and
enlightenment. Use the same well-wishing benedictions,
replacing the word *I* with the word *you* and focus on loved
ones one at a time.

Continue chanting and begin to think about other people who touch your life and help serve your needs—the mailman, your neighbor, your favorite musician or athlete, your kids' favorite teacher, the mayor of your town. Open your heart and offer each of them your love and service, blessings, support, and benevolent well wishes. Be generous and expansive; why be stingy? Breathe it out, and breathe it in, almost simultaneously. WOW!

When your openhearted love has grown along with the subtle energy of the chant, extend your compassionate love even further—to acquaintances and strangers. Let your love reach as far as you can—eventually even including people who get on your nerves, who frighten or manipulate you. Finally, let your love expand to the people who have harmed you, including those you consider your enemy, abuser, critic, or bogeyman.

Imagine that warmth emanates from your heart. Feel it inter-connecting you with everyone and everyone with you. This is one wow of an inter-meditation, interbeing with each and everyone, one by one and then collectively!

Then recite:

> May all beings have happiness and the cause
> of happiness, which is virtue.
> May all beings remain free from suffering and the causes
> of suffering, which are non-virtue and delusion.
> May all beings remain un-separated from the sacred joy
> and happiness that is totally free from sorrow.
> May beings come to rest in the boundless, all-inclusive
> equanimity beyond attachment and aversion.
> May all beings be happy, content, and fulfilled.

May all be peaceful in harmony and at ease.
May all be protected from harm, fear, and danger.
May all have whatever they want, need, and aspire to.
May all be healed and whole again.
May this planet be healed and whole again,
restored and replenished.
May all beings awaken from their sleep of illusion
and be liberated, enlightened, and free.
May all realize their true spiritual nature and thus awaken
the sacred connection within.
May all equally enjoy, actualize, and embody
the innate great perfection.
May we all together complete the spiritual journey, all
the way to enlightenment, Nirvana, freedom, and bliss.
As I have lovingly prayed and resolved, may it be so!

Play Your Hand Well

No matter how much loss, pain, or joy we've experienced, it's not what happens to us that determines our character, destiny, or karma; it's *what we do* with what happens to us. It's not the cards we're dealt but how we play the hand. Some people come out of horrible experiences embittered, no longer believing in anything, cynical, and alienated from the Divine and from other humans, too. On one level, who can blame them? Yet consider other people, like Nobel Peace Laureate Nelson Mandela. He emerged from his lengthy imprisonment and turned the atrocities he endured into maitri—loving-kindness and benevolence—as he became an advocate for both truth and reconciliation. Most people probably fall somewhere in between. It all comes down to how we relate to our experiences—what we make of our suffering and difficulties.

> What lies behind us and what lies before us are small matters compared to what lies within us.

Why we each make the choices we do is a mystery; I wouldn't want to trivialize it by providing platitudes. However, I do feel strongly that our choices—which arise from our levels of self-understanding, faith, and hope—can cause vastly different outcomes. In a way, we can look at the suffering in our lives as an opportunity to open up or to shut down; for better or worse, we'll be transformed either way. I, for one, would much rather see creative results than self-destructive degeneration. If "life is but a dream," as the song says, I'd prefer to try and make it a nice dream for the children of this world rather than a nightmare. Who wouldn't?

This is where inner wisdom and character maturity comes in. One of my favorite native Bodhisattvas, the seminal early American thinker Ralph Waldo Emerson, put it simply: "What lies behind us and what lies before us are small matters compared to what lies within us." Again, we see the *inter* in inter-meditation. Emerson didn't say lies *within me*. His all-embracing word *us,* two hundred years ago, includes you and me, today. He lived and loved large, for the ages.

Sympathetic Joy

I want to put in a word here for living large and joyfully, and especially for *positive* Buddhism. I've had my fill of *dukkha* (life as suffering) and death, sacrifice, restraint, renunciation, emptiness, and no-self—enough already! I give. Stop. I'm Jewish on my parents' side, sure, but I didn't leave Brooklyn and the Western world in 1971 just to hear more depressed holy rollers kvetching and whining about the infernal vicissitudes of life! Get over it. Personally, I'm not going to stand on a table and rail against fate, like the famous mystic Rabbi Levi Yitzchak of Berditchev, who remonstrated with God daily for how badly He treated His people, the rabbi's flock. No wonder God died around the turn of the last century; it may have been from heartbreak, or simple neglect.

Instead, I want to propound the joy of awakening together through inter-meditation. The *joy* of meditation, not the chore of strenuous self-discipline and the ascetic practice of trying not to think, which some *schlemiels* mistake for meditation. What could be better than the buoyant joy of spirit, ecstatic and never static?

The antidote to envy, covetousness, and egotistical competiveness is the Buddhist concept of joy traditionally called *Mudita*—sympathetic rejoicing. *Mudita* means to experience joy when others feel happy or when they succeed—not mere pride about how others might reflect positively on you, but actual sympathetic joy. This means selfless enjoyment for their virtues and accomplishments. One could even extend this attitude to one's competitors, critics, and even enemies. Good sportsmanship is an excellent example, in a practical and worldly way. Shaking hands afterwards and genuinely congratulating others for the excellent fight or performance they gave in outclassing you—no matter how much you may have wanted and even fought to win. This virtue builds character in

Drive all blames into one(self) [and give to others your profit and victory].

an extraordinary way and reinforces our happiness hormones and goodness genes.

In Yiddish, Mudita might be called *nachas*, which means "receiving joy from." Similarly, the term *kvelling* means "reveling in another's success." Rejoicing in the good fortunes of others is the royal road beyond envy and covetousness, bitter competition, and resentment. It is the polar opposite of *schadenfreude*, enjoyment of the troubles of others. Mudita is a boundless trove of good karma, too; that so-called good luck I often hear of, which is actually comprised mainly of preparation, skill, timing, and connected inter-meditation. Mudita increases our good karma portfolio, particularly when we appreciate the success of our enemies and detractors. It's the hidden gem of the four aspects of Buddha's boundless love: loving-kindness, compassion, sympathetic joy, and impartial equanimity. Buddha himself said that when you rejoice in the virtues and meritorious good deeds and successful accomplishments of others, you get a full share as well. How great is that? A free windfall profit bonus for unselfish Mudita co-meditation. Don't leave home without it.

Sympathetic joy means unselfish appreciation, which celebrates and savors the blessings and virtues that others may achieve or already have, even those that you may lack. Again I'm reminded of Atisha's admittedly difficult Lojong slogan:

> Drive all blames into one(self)
> [and give to others your profit and victory].

This is not easy for losers to live up to.

Shantideva taught that the greatest suffering is thinking only of oneself, while the greatest happiness is thinking of others.

Now there's a radical concept. Where we find ourselves on the selfishness spectrum makes an enormous difference to our quality of life and happiness quotient. Humongous. Some even say that obsession with happiness is one of the greatest causes of discontent and unhappiness.

Joking and laughing together—Laughter Meditation groups and gatherings currently take place all around the world—or offering a gift, even something small or as simple as a smile, can plant the seed of enlightenment and become a fruitful inter-meditation. Lightness is one of my favorite noble qualities, to be appreciated, recognized, and cultivated—but not too seriously.

Smile Mirroring

A smile is said to be the shortest distance between two people. Since ancient times, smiling has signified friendship and disarmament, just as a handshake signifies no weapon in hand. Modern scientific research shows that even a simple smile helps release the pleasure-inducing hormones and other chemicals associated with happiness, health, and sensual gratification. Who knew it could be so simple, easy, and delightful? The most ancient scriptures of India teach that we all exist as part of a universal web of light—all interconnected, co-emergent, and interdependent. In the Buddhist Flower-Garland or Avatamsaka Sutra, each and every one of us comprise the cosmic Diamond Net of Indra like shining mirror-like jewels reflecting the light of the whole, all in each and each in all—not unlike a shining hologram. We are each like flowers in God's garden, or strung upon Buddha's rosary, blooming and blossoming in our own way, time, and place.

Science and common sense tell us that aversion, aggression, or harsh judgment all tend to generate mutual antagonism. If I respond to someone with affection, respect, and appreciation, good will arises and cooperation and collaboration become much more possible. Neuroscientists have found that mirroring a facial expression—like a smile—stimulates hormones like oxytocin and dopamine which biochemically lead to the almost immediate physical and mental experience of happiness or contentment.[6] So when I smile at those drivers on the country road, I'm changing their brains and consequently their hearts, and they're changing mine in return. Good deal!

You can take the phenomenon of conscious mirroring and explicit soul-searching one step further by intentionally practicing mirrored dialogue. Mediators can also apply this inter-meditation technique to conflict resolution, focusing upon imagining what the other feels and thinks about the contested subject, as well as feeling into the other's fears, needs, and goals. I love this type of meditation because it doesn't come across as esoteric—you can do it at work, on the soccer field, on the phone, or while stuck in traffic. It can help a troubled marriage or even a border dispute. The intrepid Quakers have a long and successful history of this kind of inter-meditative empathic witnessing as a form of conflict resolution in contentious situations, including political and military crises.

First, we need to sit down with someone in the courtroom, boardroom, bedroom, bullpen, or airplane seat, and consciously breathe the same air deeply—actually as well as metaphorically. In this way, we can turn conflict into collaboration and cooperation; at the outset, we establish at least some common ground and collaborative process before delving deeper into developing genuine vulnerability, openness, interest, connection, truth-telling, fruitful dialogue, and ultimately inter-meditation. This gradual process of softening and permeating can lead to working together rather than adopting adversarial stances on the hot topic or problem in the usual us-and-them, either-or mentality, even where other more traditional means and methods have fallen short.

Letting Go into Isness

First, assume the position. You choose where and how.
Face each other, in a friendly yet respectful and
slightly detached yet mutually collaborative stance,
seated or standing. Don't think of this as a face-
off, but as a co-meditation and collaboration.
Begin to relax, let down your guard, and unmask—
slowly, gently, and patiently.
Breathe and let it all go.
Let it all come and go, and just be.
Let it all happen—for it is!

Start with eye-gazing, gently, not a staring contest,
for a minute or three.
Relax your face and jaw muscles.
Smile a little, without expecting or
seeking anything in return.
Contact, connect, and release.
Notice any tendency to turn away
or run and hide inwards.
Now relax and close your eyes.
Notice the afterimage and retained presence
of your dyad partner in your inner eye.

Breathe in and breathe out, perhaps starting
off together but without working too hard
to coordinate or communicate.
Just breathe, smile a little, center, focus gently, and relax.
Breathe out and let go. Relax.
Let the ordinary natural magic happen.
Let the spirit move through each of you.
Feel what you feel, with naked awareness.

Now open your eyes and maintain
a natural frontal posture
as if doing co-yoga, the Raja (Royal) Yoga of just sitting,
and allow things to go as they go
and be as they are
as you feel into it—
and just be with it, not agin it.
Inter-meditation means with it,
getting with it
and getting it,
grokking the vivid truthiness of this very moment—
so come as you are,
without props, masks, or role-playing,
simply naked and unadorned,
at home and at ease
in the explicit here and now.
How beautiful thou art, Bodhisattva and truth-breather!

Just breathing, feeling and healing;
center yourself on the breath
and physical sensations, and let

all other fancy notions and practices
totally go. Know nothing.
And go nowhere, be nothing
and no one,
for a change.
It will change you, for certain.

No worries about the other's thoughts or opinions,
reactions or process.
Recognize all the waves of experience
as your own mind projections
and its conscious and unconscious workings,
as if there's no one there—the lights are on,
but no one's home—
not to mention no other (person).
Just don't know. Enjoy ignorance
for a change, rather than trying
to become a know-it-all
or improve your mind
and get enlightened.
No Enlightenment here!
(That's your new Zen name: No Enlightenment.)
Savor this serene shared moment, and this breath
together in a fresh new way.

INTER-MEDITATION PRACTICE
Stand in the Other's Shoes

To complete this conflict resolution exercise, try to put yourself
in the other's shoes, the other's seat.

Imagine seeing things through their eyes;
How does it look?
What do they see, think, and feel?
Besides seeing you, what else
do they perceive, feel, identify with,
think about, worry over, plan or hope to do,
achieve, get, or become?
Try to reach out through your eyes and with your heart,
and sense intuitively
what goes on with them.
How will they look when they grow old?
What did they look like when they were little tykes?
Feel what they feel as if your own,
in the very present and numinous
life-giving breathing zone
of open, incandescent, moment-to-moment
undiluted awareness,
choiceless, lucidly alert, and interested
yet withholding all judgment and
imaginary interpretation.
Feel and heal, without suppressing
or judgmental evaluation,
without manipulation or interference of any kind—
rest in the fertile oasis of pure instinctual
somatic feeling-sensations
without straying into the arid desert of
thoughts and conceptual elaborations.
Why try to tie knots
in the sky?

(Do not interact explicitly or verbally with your partner;
allow them to continue doing similarly with you,
according to these inquire-ful inter-meditative instructions.)
Allow the transpersonal inter-meditative magic to happen.
This is the royal road, the Royal Yoga,
the unity and free-flowing harmonious aliveness
and alignment
of inter-meditation.

Overcoming the Emotions of Self-Fixation

Me, myself, and I . . . "What about me?" Isn't this the mantra of our modern age, and the heart of our predicament? We think so much these days, yet we know and understand so little, either about ourselves or how things actually work. I'm talking about the karmic law of cause and effect, which makes of our life either a heaven or a hell, or more commonly a purgatory.

The real hero is not one who conquers material enemies of flesh and blood. The real hero is one who overcomes the inner enemies, the kleshas, conflicting emotions and delusion.

This obsession with the illusory self is not necessarily new. In Buddhism we call negative, unwholesome, and self-centered states of mind the five poisons, or *kleshas*—greed, hatred, delusion, pride, and jealousy. Some call them the five conflicting emotions or deluded obscurations. These habitual elements of our deeper consciousness arise due to ignorance about our true nature and how the world actually works at the causative level. In Dzogchen texts, wise masters point out how the five afflictive obscurations are actually inversions of the five insightful wisdoms—discernment, equanimity, mirror-like awareness, panoramic oneness, and all-accomplishing activity. These wisdoms comprise the unique and coherent BuddhaMind, or cosmic consciousness.

By working with these five poisons—inner enemies and emotional obscurations—we come through the back door to enter the mansion of innate wisdom. We can see more clearly where we need to go, how to get there, and with whose assistance. As Shantideva states in the *Guide to the Bodhisattva's Way of Life*: "The real hero is not one who conquers material enemies of flesh and blood. The real hero is one who overcomes the inner enemies, the kleshas, conflicting emotions and delusion."

Inter-meditation can help us do just that, as we face and get to know ourselves better, both within and without, alone and in relationships of all kinds. If we approach any situation with an inter-meditative mindset, the most difficult person can become our greatest teacher, our greatest opportunity. The enemy or fearsome adversity can connect us to the extensive suffering of the world, open our hearts, and sensitize us to others and experiencing what they feel. Inter-meditating in this way results in genuine compassion. It can turn us away from the evil of harming others as it furthers our patience and forbearance—offering us an opportunity to go more deeply into the sacred mystery of loving even those we don't necessarily like or agree with. As we find our balance between sensitivity and equanimity, we become fearless servant leaders, real Bodhisattvas, and edifying awakeners.

Mindful Anger Management

As a teacher, I've discovered that people have the most trouble with the klesha of anger, which includes hatred, aggression, and basic aversion. Anger can so easily flare up and become a major affliction. It has the power to take over a personality and an entire life if a person is unprepared to deal with it or manage it in a healthy way. Anger and rage are just emotions, albeit powerful ones, and we *can* handle these energies, for example with Mindful Anger Management. Day to day, anger can seriously impede inter-meditation, close off or burn up open communication, and assail healthy relationships of all kinds. But we need to remember that anger has its own function, intelligence, and logic; therefore, we should not try to suppress or eradicate it entirely, even if we could. Referring to acts of anger, the fifth-century Indian Buddhist scholar Buddhaghosa states in the Visuddhimagga: "By doing this you are like a man who wants to hit another and picks up a burning ember or excrement in his hand and so first burns himself or makes himself stink."[7]

Anger is not synonymous with aggression and violence, although anger can lead to them. It is merely an internal, organic energy and emotion we can learn to simply experience; we can handle it, without needing to avoid or suppress it. We learn how to just feel anger in our body as physical sensation, before we become caught up in its grip and inevitable reactivity. We can cradle such feelings lovingly, with patient acceptance and tolerance and without judgment or over-reaction. When we experience anger as a mere sensation in our body, it allows us to release the mounting internal pressure and helps us attain the healthy emotional-energetic experience of re-integration. We can process lust, anger, or even rage in this mindful way before deciding what, if anything, to do with it, and how, when, and if to express it externally.

Anger can make us sick, cloud our judgment, and take us to a place far from the harmony and interbeing of inter-meditation. It can drive us to sudden, surprising actions even at the risk of our lives—actions we later regret. On the other hand, as an antidote, patient forbearance and radical acceptance help soothe and heal our hearts and untangle the knotted mind, opening the door to inter-meditation and superior communitation.

Buddhism teaches that pure good and bad don't exist, only the wanted and the unwanted. Shakespeare also expresses this sentiment in *Hamlet:* "For there is nothing either good or bad, but thinking makes it so." This means everything is subjective. Buddhism encourages us to practice patient forbearance even in the face of harm and recrimination. To begin to practice patient forbearance in the face of upset, disappointment, or irritation, ask yourself: How much will this really matter to me a year or two from now? This practice of what I call *perspectivising* helps me moderate some of my most intense reactions and over-involvements. The challenge of healthy mindful emotional management is to slow down our conditioned, knee-jerk reactions to unwanted and provocative stimuli, while simultaneously sharpening and speeding up our conscious

> By doing this you are like a man who wants to hit another and picks up a burning ember or excrement in his hand and so first burns himself or makes himself stink.

mindful awareness. How can we mind the gap between stimulus and response? How can we contemplate alternative, proactive responses as intentional actions rather than just falling again and again into habitual conditioned reactions?

After much trial and error, I have come up with my own self-awareness practice for regulating strong emotions; it helps me become a better and more patient person as well as a far more present and accountable inter-meditator. I've definitely found that creating mental space for conscious, intentional, principled responsiveness—the opposite of blind reactivity, which so often leads us to regrettable actions—has consistently saved the day and saved my ass too, from all sorts of unintended and even disastrous consequences.

INTER-MEDITATION PRACTICE

The Six Rs of Intentional Responsiveness

We can open the door to inter-meditation by practicing what I call the Six Rs of Intentional Responsiveness: *recognize, recollect, reframe, relinquish, recondition,* and *respond.* In combination, these six gestures of freedom are like a cool, fresh breath of mindful awareness, helping us to relax and let go, releasing a large amount of built-up negativity that comes from the tumultuous bumper-car ride of modern living. They can free us from falling into all kinds of regrettable reactivity and the undesirable outcomes caused by knee-jerk retaliation to anger and harm—what we might call "tit for tat."

1. **Recognize:** Notice with equanimity the stimuli that push your buttons and trigger an unfulfilling, retaliatory

response. Things like abuse and harsh words, false accusations and betrayals, or unfair treatment might very well provoke retaliation in kind. Stop for a moment, however brief, and breathe and collect yourself—for the moment, at least.

2. **Recollect:** With remindfulness, remember the downsides and disadvantages of returning hatred with hatred, anger with anger, harm with harm. The Buddha taught that hatred is not appeased by hatred. Hatred is appeased only by love. Recollect the significant advantages of practicing patience, forbearance, tolerance, and acceptance of karma and its repercussions. In this second step, find and use the sacred pause. Take time to pause and mindfully reflect, between any stimulus and your response. Rest in the space of the sacred pause, as if counting to ten before striking back. Take another breath. Breathe out, release, relax, rest, and smile.

3. **Reframe:** Reframe the situation and see things from the other's point of view; begin to cultivate feelings of genuine compassion for those who harm you. Acknowledge that—through their harmful actions, words, attitudes, and the like—they are just sowing the seeds of their own unhappiness and bad karma, *not yours*. This is a genuine cause for compassionate concern. To take it one step further, recognize the adversary or critic as a teacher, friend, or ally who helps you develop patience and overcome unconscious, habitual, and unproductive reaction patterns. Think, notice, and

inquire into this statement: *There must be some reason this karma is ripening upon me, some karmic debt or implication for me to explore and become better aware of so as not to perpetrate further unwanted consequences.*

4. **Relinquish:** Give up habitual conditioned reactivity and let go of impulsive urges in favor of dispassionately chosen responses. Accept the fact that such instinctual and discomfiting feelings and urges naturally arise; neither suppress nor indulge them. Let them be without acting on them; reflect upon them and watch them pass by and dissolve. It's not external things that entangle us; over-attachment and fixation are what trip us up.

5. **Recondition:** This is a way of redirecting reactivity through remindfulness. Mentally replay the entire situation while relinquishing its power; reflect on how little it will matter in a few days, months, and years. Actively let go of unwholesome reaction patterns. Remember to remember what's most important and hold firmly yet flexibly to your principles and practice commitments.

6. **Respond:** Opt for intelligent, consciously chosen thoughts, words, and behaviors; be proactive rather than reactive. In some cases, this may translate into doing nothing, or in other cases it might mean responding with equanimity. Ultimately, this practice helps you make more skillful and creative decisions based on conscious awareness and experience. At other times,

action is clearly called for; physical self-defense may even be called for.

Fresh, Friendly Awareness

Shantideva said that anger is the greatest evil, because it's the most virulently destructive passion. Conversely, he taught that patient forbearance acts as the best remedy, however difficult to apply in practice. As we grow as inter-meditators we learn to heal the divisiveness, the conflict between self and other. Accordingly, we can change the entire dynamic from struggle—with its ups and downs—to self-sustaining, naturally motivated maintenance and natural flow. If we practice the Six Rs of Mindful Anger Management and Intentional Responsiveness in the situations that make us most angry, we can stop, breathe, and let the anger—and the fear that usually feeds it—dissolve to reveal a place of calm and joy; here is the dynamic *inter* in inter-meditation. This potent practice can be extraordinarily healing and transformative. It will help you hang in there and go beyond anger, rather than suppress or deny it. Then you can see, hear, feel, and understand much better than when under the influence of anger and hatred, or any intense emotional energy.

It's good to imagine being in the company of the troublesome other—for example, someone who is quite angry with you—before actually encountering them. This goes back to Wishing Others Well so you can ultimately communicate more easily in reality, not just in your mind. As a dress rehearsal, to ready yourself for the big performance, picture the difficult person. Visualize them with you, and inhale all of their negativities. Hoover it up like dust and reveal the underlying maitri, the friendly loving-kindness and benevolent openness. Breathe out love, forgiveness, understanding, and empathy. It doesn't mean that what they've done might not be wrong, but they are not wrongness themselves—nor are we necessarily the designated arbiter of right and wrong, especially for other people. As we get used to this kind of inter-meditative being with the challenging person—and the difficult feelings and reactions they bring up—this kind of open, fresh, friendly, and even innocent attitude of agenda-less present awareness opens up the whole situation. We're no longer afraid to meet them. We're no longer afraid that their anger might destroy us. We can face and work with anything, anyone, anywhere; all becomes possible for us.

This fresh, friendly awareness helps us bridge the gap between self and others. Our demons are really nothing more than parts of our psyches. Remember that inter-meditation means seeing through and beyond the illusion of separation. It's a sure route to making peace between our small selves and our Big Selves, our friends and our enemies, revealing our interconnectivity and divinity.

INTER-MEDITATION PRACTICE

Wisdom-Development Dialogue with Ourselves

After we've worked our way through the Six Rs, our small self is ready to co-meditate with our Big Self.

> Perform your daily morning "iye" exam.
> Look in the mirror or simply turn your
> attention inwards, upon yourself, rather than
> looking outward at people and things;
> Breathe, relax, focus, center, and smile a little.

Now, turn toward yourself, and perceive the perceiver,
see through the seer, and be free.
Rest freely and nakedly in the here
and now, in nowness-awareness,
upstream from mere thoughts and concepts.
Naked as the day your mind was born,
enjoy the natural sublime perfection
and completeness
of things just as they are
in the natural state of (Buddha)mind,
free and clear.

Our Enemies Teach Us About Reality

A broken bone heals stronger than it was before; scar tissue is tougher than ordinary skin tissue. Similarly, the inner strength that we gain from learning to process our personal hurts and emotional wounds helps us mature into better, wiser, and more resilient individuals. As for this, I have no doubt.

I call the kind of transformation that our enemies can unintentionally cause the "Pearl Principle." Inside of an oyster, it takes an irritant—like a grain of sand or a bit of shell—to stimulate the oyster to produce the mucous juices that engulf and surround the irritant as it eventually hardens into a bright and luminous pearl. It is the same for us. Difficulties and suffering produce the aspiration for spiritual enlightenment, motivating people to inter-meditate and seek help and merge with others along the way as they follow the path of self-awareness, self-transcendence, collective awakening, and ultimate enlightenment. According to Buddhist cosmology, the gods and demigods are incapable of spiritual practice; they can't be bothered to think of anything beyond their exquisite experiences of bliss and sensual pleasure. They see no reason nor feel any need or motivation to undertake spiritual practice until their long, delightful lives start to come to an end, as their flower garlands and pleasure gardens start to whither and rot, and their faces sag with age. By then, unfortunately, it is too late to make new habits, friends, and allies. Perhaps the lords and ladies, oligarchs, dictators, and other power-mongers of this dream-like world are the human representatives of the gods and goddesses in ancient Buddhist cosmology. Or is it just we wealthy Westerners, rather than people in the developing countries, who are surfeited with pleasure and distracted from the journey toward awakening? In truth, most animals—including humans—live in desire most of the time and remain unmotivated to transcend their own familiar ways and habitual states of mind until faced with suffering, old age, and death.

The Dalai Lama meditates, prays, and chants each and every morning from about 3:30 or 4:00 until 7:30, wherever he may be on this planet. I used to practice together with my own teacher in the monastery during that time. As I've mentioned, these days I like to *virtually* join the Dalai Lama in my own morning meditations, in spirit, and co-meditate with him and/or my other main root gurus. Sometimes when I practice Lojong and compassion practice, I recall in my mind these oral instructions of the Dalai Lama:

> In meditation, imagine that in front of you are three persons—an enemy, a friend, and a neutral person. At that time, in our minds we have (1) a sense of closeness for one of them, thinking, "This is my friend"; (2) a

sense of dislike even when imagining the enemy; and (3) a sense of ignoring the neutral person. Now, we have to think about the reasons why we generate these feelings—the reasons being that temporarily one of them helped us whereas the other temporarily harmed us, and the third did neither. However, when we think in terms of the long course of beginningless rebirth, none of us could decide that someone who has helped or harmed us in this life has been doing so for all lifetimes.

When you contemplate this way, eventually you arrive at a point where a strong generation of desire or hatred appears to you to be just senseless. Gradually, such a bias weakens, and you decide that one-sided classification of persons as friends and enemies has been a mistake.[8]

In addition to how much I enjoy, savor, and appreciate spending time with the Dalai Lama—in spirit when not in the flesh—this co-meditation helps me even out my biases and prejudices, and enables me to cultivate a more unconditional sense of love, compassion, and universal responsibility.

Again, the deepest truth is that there are no objectively positive or negative things, no good or bad experiences or circumstances—there are only desirable or undesirable ones. It is almost entirely subjective. Conceptual mind cannot understand and penetrate all and everything. Remember that our karma—life experience, conditioning, character, and destiny—are not determined by what happens to us, but by what we do *with* what happens. Our response makes all the difference. This is where inter-meditation and intuition come in, especially when we move a step further, to inter-meditating with adversity.

Adverse conditions are spiritual friends.
Devils and demons are emanations of the victorious ones.
Illness is the broom for evil and obscurations.
Suffering is the dance of what is.[1]

JAMGON KONGTRUL RINPOCHE I

7

Coming Together
without Falling Apart

Unity through Adversity

Once, long ago, a spiritual seeker traveled to the Himalayas. He was on a quest for the last and best word on the subject of enlightenment. The seeker trekked and schlepped his bags all the way to the foot of an extremely high peak in Nepal. As he struggled up the mountainside, the stuff he carried grew quite heavy, so he threw his tent into a gulley and left his backpack under a tree.

Gradually, hour after sweaty hour, he stripped himself of almost everything as he climbed. He inhaled and exhaled hundreds of thousands of breaths. He was ready to arrive at the summit, ready to listen to the wisdom he felt confident he would hear at the top. The seeker pulled himself up over the final ridge of the mountain and looked into the mouth of a cave.

Much to the seeker's amazement, the Buddha was sitting right there!

Overjoyed, the seeker asked the Buddha his big question: "What is the most important truth and teaching?"

The Buddha replied, "*Dukkha*. Life is suffering; life is fraught with difficulties." The seeker felt so disappointed. He had come such a long way. He looked around wildly and shouted, "Is there anyone else up here I can talk to?"

I love that joke. I can relate to it, too. What do we do when we experience something that isn't quite what we had hoped for? Or, worse, when we experience something that is life-and-death challenging?

One of my *least* favorite inter-meditations is dealing directly with troubles and difficulties—meditating with adversity. Unlike a lot of other spiritual teachers, I'm not eager to tell everyone how great it is to face the hardest things, as far as spiritual growth is concerned—to experience disappointment and loss, illness, tragedy, and crises. The Venerable Thich Nhat Hanh says that everything can serve as a Mindfulness Bell—like a meditation gong or call to prayer—awakening us to the here and now, the miracle of this moment, including suffering. He lived through the French occupation and then the Vietnamese War, in his youth, in his own country. By contrast, I'm more of a card-carrying member of "The Ostrich Lineage" that teaches a bury-your-head-in-the-sand practice. "No gain if pain is involved" could be our childish motto. No one would rather avoid difficulties and pain more than I, and sometimes I catch myself avoiding pain rather than confronting it.

However, in the years of my gloaming I have come to learn better, the hard way, and understand matters a little more deeply. Luckily for me, Buddhism abounds with wonderful teachings

> Join whatever you meet with awareness practice, so even the unexpected becomes the path.

about life and its travails. These teachings provide both solace and guidance, and they can help us deal intelligently with loss, change, and fear. Additionally, they can guide us to find fitting answers to the big questions, like the meaning and purpose of our lives, and they instruct us about death, mortality, and suffering. For there is no Nirvana, no Heaven, no enlightenment outside of daily life, as countless masters attest. Here's a Lojong aphorism that can help us practice this wisdom:

> Join whatever you meet with awareness practice,
> so even the unexpected becomes the path.

We cannot spend all our time and energy striving to avoid the unpleasant and just experience the pleasant things in life, tempting as it may be to do so. Life has other demands and requirements. As they say, when man plans, Buddha laughs. Yet you can integrate whatever you meet unexpectedly into your life, bring it into your meditation through co-meditative awareness. It's like a bigger frame or perspective that can accommodate and embrace everything. As I love to say, it's all grist for the mill, like manure fertilizing and nourishing the fields of *Bodhi* blossoms. As Thich Nhat Hanh says:

> Everything we are looking for is right here, in the present moment. We don't have to go anywhere to obtain the truth. Every day we are engaged in a miracle we don't even recognize. Enlightenment is not separate from washing the dishes or growing lettuce. Walk slowly, don't rush. Each mindful step brings you to the best moment of your life, the present moment.[2]

Our path consists of all of the circumstances of our lives—falling in love, a sarcoma diagnosis, cuddling with puppies, and the atrocities of genocide and domestic abuse, too. Don't think that they're in the way of your path—there's no other path! The only way through is through. Please take a breath now, and absorb this. You're not in the way, obstructing yourself—though it can sometimes feel like that. You *are* the Way, and it runs right through you.

The Benefits of Suffering

Besides its numerous practical benefits, inter-meditating with adversity offers the remarkable spiritual benefit of reversing our tendency to cling to the wanted and avoid the unwanted—habits very much at the root of nearly all of our dissatisfaction and suffering.

"Pain is inevitable, suffering is optional." Buddhism teaches us to make use of adversity, to allow it to spur us on to become less fascinated by transient, unreliable, worldly things and turn toward perennial spiritual values. If we perfect our training in bringing both suffering and happiness into the spiritual path, then no matter what we face, our mind will remain calm and at ease, and we will experience inner peace and bliss, harmony, Nirvana, and carry this with us, wherever life and love may lead.

But to receive this benefit, we actually have to go and grow through adversity. I don't mean just blasting through like a torpedo. We have to integrate it, hear its message, learn the lessons, grok it, and assimilate it. We can't just go around suffering and avoid it; we can't just sweep things under the rug or make a spiritual bypass whenever our values challenge our ego. So, whatever we meet, we bring into the path. We face it and deal with it, head on. And that's where Lojong and Tonglen practice come in handy. Consider this relevant slogan:

> If you can practice even when distracted, you are
> well trained. Use difficulties to help you progress.

What's a bigger distraction than going through troubling times—illness, for instance, or losing a loved one, or a crisis like a fire or hurricane, or living with a significant form of pain, impairment, or misery? The remainder of this chapter offers several ways to use difficulties for your own ultimate benefit.

Who Makes Me Suffer?

The First Noble Truth of Buddhism is "Life is suffering" or as I like to put it: unenlightened life is difficult. And the Second Noble Truth teaches us that life is difficult because of attachment, because we crave satisfaction in ways that are inherently dissatisfying—in other words, we're responsible for creating our own suffering. Fortunately, Buddhism doesn't stop there—the Third Noble Truth teaches us that everyone can liberate themselves from difficulties by following the Fourth Noble Truth: leading a compassionate, awakened life of virtue, wisdom, connection, and meditation.

Taking responsibility for yourself as the source of your suffering and consequently your healing is not just the path to awakening from samsara, it's helpful in everyday life as well. It changes the whole atmosphere, especially if you have an intense crisis or suffering, like tragedy, illness, or pain. Here's how contemporary Tibetan Buddhist master Gyalwang Drukpa puts it:

> As you must have heard it millions of times from me, "We are the creator of our own sorrow and our own happiness." So it's better to start to be mindful and bring a "karmic mirror" with us all the time, so that before we blame our failures on others, let's take out this mirror and have a good reflection, "What did I do before, that I am now suffering?" This analytical understanding will at least help us not to continue to make the same mistake or the same decision and encourage us to always be mindful of our intentions, our thoughts and our actions.[3]

The Grace of Being Able to Let Be

There's a traditional Tibetan maxim: "That which is born, ages and dies. Those who have gathered will one day be parted. All constructions eventually come to ruin. This is the Law." Through inter-meditation practice, we come to better appreciate and enjoy the coming and going, the necessary changes and losses endemic to life as we know it. We learn to see the necessary losses in life—aging, separation, sorrow, and death—as inevitable, and understand that change begets change, that everything fluctuates, and that transformations are the constant for living organisms. "The more things change, the more they remain the same," as the French adage says. When we learn to take the heroic path of adversity instead of detouring around it, we lessen our suffering, enhance fearlessness and other character virtues, and intelligently modulate our expectations, hesitations, and resistances. It's a kind of graceful letting go, part of the practice of cultivating non-attachment and equanimity; but let's also try to remember that inter-meditation isn't just letting go—that's merely half of it. There's also the crucial piece involving the letting come as well, letting come *and* go, which implies *letting be.* This is the key. Letting down defenses and allowing in, through letting be. This is how we inter-meditate with things as they are, reality just as it is, and as it presents itself, moment after moment.

The richest and most powerful, famous, or beautiful people aren't exempt from suffering, either—it's part of the human condition. But then, so is happiness. In *Optimism*, the famous deaf and blind activist Helen Keller writes:

> Although the world is full of suffering, it is full also of the overcoming of it. My optimism, then, does not rest on the absence of evil, but on a glad belief in the preponderance of good and a willing effort always to cooperate with the good, that it may prevail. I try to increase the power God has given me to see the best in everything and every one, and make that Best a part of my life.[4]

That heroic, awe-inspiring woman knew of what she spoke. Suffering is the proximate cause for inner growth, enlightenment, and awakening. Without inner irritation, no pearl-like wisdom of experience gets produced. Here is the explicit virtue of adversity, not to be overlooked or bypassed.

How Grieving Is a Gift

I learned a lot about this from my friend, Boston College professor of Buddhism and contemplative theology John Makransky, who also happens to be a lama. He told me that when his father died it felt like his whole world collapsed. He wept uncontrollably all night, but his Buddhist-based spiritual practice became stronger than ever before, because everything other than taking refuge in spiritual practice and meditation felt meaningless and just fell apart. As John put it, "The power of that refuge emerged like a phoenix to transform that despairing grief into empathy for all who had lost loved ones before me, to whom I had paid little attention." Isn't that beautiful? "Every pang of my own grief through the Buddhist practice of Tonglen—exchanging self and others—got translated into a vivid feeling of what so many have been undergoing for so long, while I had been oblivious to them all, in my own dream. My father's death was my greatest door into refuge . . . " Non-Buddhists might call this making a spiritual commitment to the Big Self or God—the ultimate reliance and sanctuary, the safest port in all of life's storms.

Even if we can acknowledge adversity as a vital aspect of awakening, engaging suffering in ways that benefit us is an art unto itself. Here is a practice to get you started:

INTER-MEDITATION PRACTICE
Being with Pain

One of the best practices I've found for inter-meditating with adversity is "Bringing Compassion and Loving-Kindness into Areas of Pain" from my old friend Gavin Harrison's book *In the Lap of the Buddha.* For me, the fact that Gavin has lived with AIDS for over twenty years adds to the profundity of the meditation.

- Allow your eyes to close gently.
- Center attention on the breathing.
- Move awareness now to a part of the body where there is pain and discomfort.
- Rest there.
- Be aware of any sensations that there might be.
- Allow whatever you find to be okay.
- No fight.
- No struggle.
- Be with the truth, with acceptance.
- Continue attending to the breath for a while. If possible, breathe into and through the pain, as if this were actually the place where the breath enters and leaves the body.
- Direct the following phrases quietly to the area of pain (or use your own meaningful phrases):

    "I welcome you into my heart."

    "I accept you."

    "I care about this pain."

    "I hold you deep in my heart."

    "I accept what is happening right now."

    "May I be free from fear."

    "May I be happy, just where I am."

    "May I be peaceful with what is happening."

- You may wish to lay your hands gently on the area of discomfort.

- Allow feelings of loving-kindness and compassion to flow through the body. If there are no feelings of compassion, that is okay also.
- Continue repeating the phrases.
- End by returning to the breathing for a short while.[5]

Recognizing Our Universality Is Healing

The ancient Buddhist sutras contain an invaluable story about gaining through loss and learning through grief and compassion. The story involves Kisa Gotami, a young mother who lost her infant son and went mad with grief. The loss of a child is perhaps the most difficult adversity in the world, so it was natural that the woman went to the Buddha and asked him to restore her son—she couldn't go on living without him. The Buddha didn't say yes or no about bringing her child back to life or removing her suffering. Instead he asked the woman to go door to door and collect mustard seeds (prominent in India) from every house where no one was grieving over the loss of a loved one and bring all the seeds to him. After visiting hundreds of houses, the woman didn't receive a single mustard seed. But she received something else—the gift of compassion and empathy from all of those who shared her grievous yet universal experience. In all of those houses, behind all of those closed doors, the woman had been unaware that the whole world suffered as much as she had—the vice-grip of illness, aging, and death affected everyone. Because of this, heartfelt compassion and clear insight arose within her. She returned to Buddha with no mustard seeds, but with a heart full of wisdom, empathy, and compassion, and a little more equanimity and acceptance.

Acknowledging the suffering of others enables us to attend more closely to their feelings and needs; accordingly, we can give birth to heartfelt compassion for them, as well as for ourselves. Feeling with others is the warm, beating heart of intuitive responsiveness and altruistic compassion in action. I discussed self-compassion when it comes to inter-meditating with ourselves in chapter 2, but it's relevant when we deal with adversity too. Kristin Neff, Associate Professor of Human Development and Culture at the University of Texas in Austin, defines self-compassion as treating yourself as you would a dear friend. She examines self-compassion through the lens of three aspects—Self-Kindness, Common Humanity, and Mindfulness:

1. Self-Kindness vs. Self-Judgment
   - Treats self with care and understanding rather than harsh judgment
   - Actively soothes and comforts oneself

2. Common Humanity vs. Isolation
   - Sees own experience as part of larger human experience not isolating or abnormal
   - Recognizes that life is imperfect (us too!)

3. Mindfulness vs. Over-Identification
   - Allows us to "be" with painful feelings as they are
   - Avoids extremes of suppressing or running away with painful feelings[6]

I like how one thing leads to another in this schema: if we can act with kindness toward ourselves, we can recognize our common humanity in a healthy, permeable, undefended, yet strong and resilient manner. From this point, we can accept and face our own adversity and suffering, and the adversity and suffering of others, too. The organically arising non-separation pact between others and ourselves—and between *ourselves* and our *selves*—naturally includes identification and compassion for everyone.

Ten Steps for Gaining through Loss

Through my own practice and years of teaching meditation, I have developed a sequence of steps that can guide us through dealing with change, loss, and especially death. Here's the ten-step practice for inter-meditating with adversity I call "Gaining through Loss." Try it.

1. **Face the loss.** First, be aware of the problem. What is the adversity? What's causing the pain? This step may not sound like much, but we first have to overcome avoidance and denial. Face the difficulty fully. Be aware of the sorrow and disappointment in the experience rather than suppressing, repressing, or avoiding it. Pain, fear, anger, jealousy, anxiety, regret, anguish, despondency—whatever your experience, name it and feel it. Feel where it seems to sit in your body as a physical sensation. Awareness is curative. Let the light in, and you will find your way. This is the "inter" part. Why shut yourself off?

2. **Recognize the stages.** We can apply Elisabeth Kübler-Ross's five famous stages of loss[7] to any sort of adversity:

- *Denial:* We can't believe it's happened—somebody's died, we've suddenly lost our job, a relationship fell apart, our house burned down, or we're bankrupt.
- *Anger:* We rail against fate: "Why me?" "How could this happen?" "Why did it happen?" "Who can I blame?"
- *Bargaining:* We negotiate or argue with reality: "If only I could turn back the clock or have a do-over."
- *Depression:* We give in to sorrow, despondency, deep grieving.
- *Acceptance:* This means facing the facts, and feeling the entire experience, through and through, without hurry, painkillers, soporifics, or other end-runs. Not just trying to repress or forget the adversity, but also paying attention, staying attuned—pure physical and emotional feeling can be healing—and learning from it, gaining the wisdom of experience so one can move on, live again. This can take time—even years.

Who ever entirely recovers from the loss of a child? From holocaust, genocide, trauma, or abuse? Yet we must go on, one way or another. We must make this choice. This process culminates in acceptance; then we can move on—gracefully, gently, and slowly but surely. We can't spend our lives jilted at the altar, enraged from abuse we have suffered, or weeping in the cemetery over a cold tombstone. We face the adversity, go through the process of shock and loss, sadness and grieving, and then the aforementioned positive stages—or some version of them, in whatever order, at whatever pace. And we may still feel sadness, loss, and grief, even while we pick ourselves up again. Eventually we move on—as life goes on. It's in our higher Self-interest to do so.

Various cultures have processes for guiding us through mourning, and most often we undertake these steps together. For example, our ages-old heartening Jewish tradition of sitting *shiva*, where the deceased's immediate relatives stay at home and actively grieve together while friends come to visit, bring food, and join the family respectfully in their grief over several days. There are losses other than death—the end of a friendship or getting fired from a job, for example—to which we can collectively apply this step-by-step healthy grieving process. Of course, each person's path belongs to him or her alone. Acknowledge the spiritual legitimacy and emotional validity of your own natural process. But also recognize that you aren't alone in your suffering—it's a universal experience that can be marked by a sequence of traditional stages, passages, rituals—and even celebrations.

3. **Remind yourself that it's all impermanent.**
   Acknowledge the impermanence, the fleeting, dream-like nature of everything. In this you can recite the Diamond Sutra mantra: *Like a dream, like an illusion, like a mirage.* Everything resembles a mere echo, mirage, hallucination, or sitcom. As the

great American truth-teller and president Abraham Lincoln put it:

> It is said an Eastern monarch once charged his wise men to invent him a sentence, to be ever in view, and which should be true and appropriate in all times and situations. They presented him the words: "And this, too, shall pass away." How much it expresses! How chastening in the hour of pride! How consoling in the depths of affliction![8]

Based on your own reflections and experiences, is there anything that has not passed? These mantras and spiritual aphorisms apply to everything and everyone—your grief, your joy, those you love, and those you might not love so much, too. This too shall pass—imprint it upon your eyes, hold it in your heart. Remember to remember that everything is fleeting, so cherish it, enjoy the gift with delight, and let go, too.

4. **Learn the lessons.** Pay attention to the karmic interlinking, and notice how everything is connected. Focus on the loss at hand, its origins, its causes and circumstances, and how our habitual patterns or behavior or policies may have played into it. This can help us develop more inner harmony and outward reconciliation as we move toward adopting different actions that bring new results. Reflect on the pattern that may have enabled or contributed to

the adversity. Recognize the karmic concatenation or sequence concerning this particular loss. What led to it? And look for where you're most attached, seeing what it points to within yourself. Does the loss really change our essential situation? Or does it mainly affect only our popularity rating, our stock portfolio, or some other external measure?

Examine your own beliefs and assumptions about the painful situation, the meaning it holds for you, and its past and future implications. Even a death is not just an end, but a part of a larger process, and the beginning of a new relationship with those we have lost. Remember that love is greater than death. I still feel my parents' love, and I still love them in return, long after their departure from this fleeting, floating world. What a heartwarming, soul-nourishing, and fulfilling daily co-meditation—even just thinking of them, for a moment, and feeling that warm love-tide flooding in!

The guiding principle is to start wherever you are with awareness, patience, calmness, caring, and precision; then seek further intuitive understanding. Recognizing how things came about will help you steer a clearer course in the future, and also help you begin to see that suffering and undesirable things are not always and only unfavorable. Often it's short-term thinking and narrow perspectives that define things as good or bad, helpful or harmful, a success or a failure. Of course the death of a loved one—or any other grave crisis—cannot be remedied by these various reflections. However, prayer, contemplation, shared silence, and other spiritual practices—even amid great grief and anguish—can bring much solace, comfort, and ease.

5. **Practice patience and forbearance.** In chapter 3, when I wrote about inter-meditating with our teachers, I touched on the Buddhist virtues, or Paramitas—*generosity, moral self-discipline, patience, enthusiastic effort, mindful awareness*, and *transcendental wisdom*. Of these, I find *patience* the most essential when dealing with pain, suffering, and adversity because it leads to acceptance, forgiveness, resilience, and the moving-on necessary concomitant with letting things come and go. Patience Paramita can be one of the most difficult practices, but is perhaps also the most rewarding. Shantideva said that anger and hatred entail the worst negativity, but that patient forbearance administers the most effective spiritual virtue and antidote. It requires grit and audacity to expand, tolerate, and embrace dreadful people and events, rather than contracting, retracting, and separating. Developing patience and fortitude may take time and persistence, but I think that's the best way we become able to withstand pain and even unbearable sorrow.

It's foolish to seek short-term solutions, especially in bottles and pills, helpful as they may sometimes seem. However, we don't always gain from trying to fix a crisis or deep wound immediately; this can act as yet another form of avoidance. True healing work takes time and energy, effort and stick-to-itiveness, which includes patient forbearance, and doesn't usually happen overnight. How long does one need for successful physical healing or fruitful psychotherapy? Who knows? I don't like the popular cliché "What doesn't kill us makes us stronger," but when it comes to inter-meditating with adversity, there might be some truth there.

6. **Accept.** Bear the burden; take it upon yourself to become stronger. Like this Lojong aphorism teaches:

> Don't pass the buck; don't transfer the ox's load to a mere cow. Take responsibility for yourself.

Passing the burden is irresponsible. It also means losing an opportunity for honesty and maturity, both of which we need for spiritual awakening. Better to face up to situations, as needed, and focus on developing inner strength, fortitude, and the patient long-term view while working on practical solutions now and long-term systemic improvements, too. This approach helps us to foster an attitude of equanimity, objectivity, and dispassion, which allows us to better work with adversity in the long run—and the long run begins now. This does not mean acting like a martyr or ignoring the dark side, but rather accepting that difficulties come and go. Remember: pearls attain

their luster through
constant irritation inside
the oyster, and it all
happens in the darkness.
Recognize that the enemy
or obstacle can serve as one's
greatest teacher and precipitant to
inner change and transformation.

> Don't pass the buck;
> don't transfer the ox's
> load to a mere cow.
> Take responsibility
> for yourself.

7. **Investigate.** Examine and analyze exactly the nature of your kind of pain and suffering. What kinds of fears, anxieties, disappointments, physical sensations, and mental states does this particular loss or tragedy bring up for you? Look to see where you get caught and what you need to work on. Don't inhibit your growth; experience the dilemma. Examine, analyze, dissect, and reflect on it. Bring it close and learn from it. Why not? Do you have something better to do?

8. **Visualize what has been lost.** Use your imagination to bring to mind what has been lost, to see it better, to know it, to reflect on it, to intuit it, and to feel it as if it were still present. Appreciate what actually was better before, and try to genuinely call up and feel the loss. If you tend toward repression, this practice will help you go through more conscious and healthy grieving, with fewer side effects.

Sometimes it might take a few years to genuinely connect with your grief. I had to travel to Europe to teach a six-week meditation retreat course four days after my father died in New York, in late August of 1996. I didn't really get to grieve him until almost a year after his passing, due to my intense schedule; however, his death remained with me and felt always near. You can always do the real work when you feel ready, willing, and able to apply yourself to it.

Visualization and creative imagination can help us return to the experience of grief and go through it, to appreciate what we had, to feel the love and joy as well as the painful separation and anguish again, to cry, to re-parent ourselves, and eventually release the pain and move on to new relations of enhanced quality and depth with old karmic partners. Saying aloud what we need to say—even that which may have been left unsaid—serves as an excellent way to inter-meditate with someone even after they're gone. I have enjoyed some fruitful conversations with people others might not think are there.

9. **Breathe in and out.** Simple, right? And yet so difficult. Inhaling and exhaling, feeling our metabolism, our pulse, our heartbeat, helps us to equalize and rebalance harmony in body, mind, and spirit. We can take that further by practicing Tonglen and riding the breath, inhaling all the bad and releasing the good. Just breathing in and out, surfing the breath.

Use your in-breath to feel the pain, coming to know it through examination and equanimity, and then release it with each exhalation. Again, lucid present awareness is the key; stay attentive, conscious, and intentionally awake. You don't want to sleepwalk through adversity any more than you want to sleepwalk through joy. Don't miss the tragicomedy of it all—you've already bought your ticket and entered the door.

10. **Make space for empathy and compassion.** Put yourself in the other's place and try to see the situation through their eyes. Allow your pain and suffering to sensitize you to the suffering of others. Notice that they, too, experience travails, just like you, and find empathy and compassionate kinship with them as you realize there's no major difference between you and them. Though not recommended, being beaten upon, downtrodden, and bullied can help tenderize us; I know this from personal experience. Broken-heartedness can become openheartedness. Many say that we cannot (or will not) change our most ingrained habits, self-destructive behaviors, and addictions until we become truly desperate. Like failure and disappointment, grief and suffering can pointedly motivate us toward better things through renewed efforts, including refined thoughts and improved actions. I'm rarely as motivated and energized as when my heart instinctively responds to another's need and deepest desire, and our we-ness overrides most other obstacles, hesitations, limitations, or weariness.

Two Heads (and Hearts) Are Better than One

One of the great American Bodhisattvas as far as I'm concerned is the late Bill Wilson. He co-founded American Dharma, the Twelve-Step Program, and authored what I call its *sutra* or scripture—known as the "Big Book" and published as *Alcoholics Anonymous,* which he penned in the 1930s. It contains an important and fundamental insight: one cannot become free from alcoholic cravings, ingrained habits, and addictions by oneself. With a little help from a friend—Bob Smith—Bill Wilson found freedom from his alcoholism. Is this not the co-meditation principle, applied to one of life's most burdensome afflictions? We cannot do it alone, but can accomplish everything with the help of others. This American Dharma teaching, born and bred on this continent, brought freedom from craving and desire to millions and returned multitudes to health and sanity, including their family and friends.

The "Big Book" is based on the principle that we need completion to heal, recover our sanity, and come closer to something greater than ourselves (Wilson called it God or Higher Power). With or without the theistic overlay, there is a universal core of profound spirituality at the heart of the Twelve-Step programs. As Wilson puts it, we "may be suffering from an illness which only a spiritual experience will conquer." What some call God or Higher Power, Buddhist twelve-steppers might call the Triple Gem, their own true refuge and constant companion. Or we can call our Higher, Deeper Power *awareness* and rely on that rather than on our own thought, will, and ego alone.

Although counterintuitive, the fact that when it comes to adversity, two heads are better than one—even two alcoholic heads—twanged my bowstring at a frequency rarely heard in my familiar sacred symphony. This is a fundamental principle of inter-meditation or relational spirituality. We take this sacred and necessary journey together and unalone, remain healthy, and recover our sanity by passing it on, by carrying the message in the spirit of service, and paying it forward.

We're all just chickens clucking here in the cosmic courtyard, none better and none worse, none closer to God or the Divine than any other. This seems to me the pure and humble essence of the Bodhisattva Vow, and the original heart of Jesus' message, too. Let's help each other, surrender, and ask for help from something greater than our own will and our small and separatist selves. I don't know what other contemporary Western formulation says it better than the Twelve-Step Program—and let me assure you, I have searched, studied, travelled, and experienced most if not all of them.

Showing Up for Each Other's Hard Times

As a lama in the Tibetan Buddhist order, I am often called upon to attend sickbeds, deathbed vigils, after-death ceremonies, prayers, and other such spiritual occasions and gatherings. I have discovered, somewhat surprisingly, that—unlike performing weddings, which I no longer do—any priestly or pastoral time spent with someone who invites me to be with them while they're dying is time well spent, and often comes as the high point of my entire week. A few months ago a couple called upon me to pray for and help bury their tiny twins who had died just a few hours after being born. What a heartbreaker and heart-opener that was! Not to be morbid, but the authentic naked presence we often achieve in such moments puts to shame most other seemingly religious and spiritual activities we participate in. And I say this with humility and respect for the traditions I'm involved in.

I only pray and chant if people request it. The important thing seems to be to show up, as wanted, when needed, open and prepared for anything; and then just to be there for others rather than for oneself, disregarding as much as possible one's own agenda.

This principle applies well to the Bodhisattva's way of life. The level and quality of interbeing and inter-meditation we achieve in those situations is nothing less than awesome, miraculous even—I swear it. I wouldn't trade these precious and blessed moments, or this slightly unusual vocation, for anything. I feel infinitely grateful for these opportunities and challenges.

In 1973 I lived near Kangyur Rinpoche's monastery and orphanage on the outskirts of Darjeeling, in West Bengal, India. I received one-hour private lessons from the master's oldest son, the venerable Tulku Pema Wangyal, who remains my beloved teacher and mentor to this day. He lent me, from his own bookcase, my first copy of the Mahayana Buddhist classic on how to be a Bodhisattva, called the *Bodhicaryavatara—A Guide to the Bodhisattva's Way of Life*. In it, Shantideva writes:

> May I be the doctor and the medicine,
> And may I be the nurse
> For all sick beings in the world
> Until everyone is healed.

But Is Our Presence Actually Helping?

Can inter-meditation heal those we love as well as ourselves? Is there anything more going on here, or is it mainly the well-corroborated Placebo Effect coupled with a few other strands of positive thinking, loose research, and some psychosomatic symptomology? I try to keep an open mind, although I remain a bit skeptical. Innumerable miraculous healing stories exist in the anecdotal annals of religion and history, both East and West. I am not entirely without my own experiences of the mysterious and the marvelous, which even now I can hardly believe happened before my own eyes. However, today many of us seek more rational and even scientific corroboration for things we wish to invest ourselves in—our time, energy, and other resources. Though inter-meditation practice may not guarantee a miraculous uptick in a medical chart, it always plants seeds of Good.

Throughout the years people have told me stories about how Tonglen practice has had a healing effect on them and on others. My friend Resa Alboher, a cancer survivor and a true inter-meditator, says this beautifully:

> In doing Tonglen and other healing practices the thing
> that has helped me most—helped me to survive tough
> surgeries and live through the pain—is the sense that
> I am doing this not only for myself but for all beings.
> That having longevity gives me more chances in this
> one lifetime, in this human form, to do all I can to help
> others and realize the Buddha way. When you extend
> a healing meditation out there to all others, "out there"
> becomes relative, there is no out there, no others, just
> this oneness of healing itself.

Is this not the throbbing heart of inter-meditation, of healing the inner divide, of seeing through the illusion of separation?

Reaching Out in Prayer

Tara Brach, the Buddhist therapist, yoga instructor, and Insight Meditation teacher, when asked what Dharma teachers do when the going gets rough, replied: "When I'm feeling separate, I often reach out in prayer. It helps me realize an enlarged belonging." For me, separation and suffering are synonyms; that enlarged belonging Tara describes is the source of all compassion and the cure for suffering, alienation, and loneliness. It's what we see if we tear down the curtain between them and us, self and other.

Tara goes on to say, "I call on Prajnaparamita, the mother of all the Buddhas, the expression or personification of wisdom and love, that I visualize as radiating throughout all of creation. I call out, inhabiting longing and pain." Fellow ostrich-lineage-holders take note! She said *inhabiting*, not inhibiting, resisting, avoiding, or suppressing. Tara continues, "[I] allow myself to feel held in her infinite embrace. Gradually I realize that I am one with this boundless love and awareness, that I am both the holder and the held."[9] Inter-meditation is a way to get us to that place of being both holder and held.

I myself pray:

> Lord, Greater Power, inner power,
> Hold my hand
> Till I learn to uphold thee;
> Turn this way,
> Let me see your shining face;
> Let me be—
> Hold thee.

The Path of Wholeheartedness

Like I said, I don't necessarily come from the no-pain-no-gain school of hard knocks. I find it difficult to deal with adversity, even now, although I have to admit that as I grow up, slowly, I take things a lot more lightly than in my darker youth. It's hard to accept everything as a gift from above when it hurts, it sucks, it's disappointing, or even worse. But what's the alternative? "Just say no"? Try it, and see where it gets you, saying no to everything. I have learned that it's better to let go and let be, consent, accept and say "yes" to life, embrace it with passion and delight when possible. I often re-read and inter-meditate with Protestant theologian Reinhold Niebuhr's "Serenity Prayer," which I've already mentioned and have come to know by heart after keeping it in my wallet for years:

> God, grant me the serenity to accept the things
> I cannot change,
> The courage to change the things I can,
> And the wisdom to know the difference.

To accept the things I cannot change . . . How do we accept adversity or suffering as a path to enlightenment? How can we bow our strong, proud, and willful heads, and say thank you for whatever comes, whatever God sends us, as Judeo-Christian mystics suggest? I know now that my head is not the only neighborhood I want to live in; and I'm making the long journey from head to heart unalone. In fact, after all these years on the path and in the spirit, I feel that I am never by myself, no matter where I am, and everywhere is home.

One of my favorite poets—Emily Dickinson of Amherst, Massachusetts—once wrote a poem called "The Hour of Lead" that can teach us how to work with letting go:

> After great pain, a formal feeling comes—
> The Nerves sit ceremonious, like Tombs—
> The stiff Heart questions 'was it He, that bore,'
> And 'Yesterday, or Centuries before'?
>
> The Feet, mechanical, go round—
> A Wooden way
> Of Ground, or Air, or Ought—
> Regardless grown,
> A Quartz contentment, like a stone—
>
> This is the Hour of Lead—
> Remembered, if outlived,
> As Freezing persons, recollect the Snow—
> First—Chill—then Stupor—then the letting go—

I felt so inspired by these words that I based an inter-meditation on it:

INTER-MEDITATION PRACTICE

The Emily Dickinson Way

- First, go through that chill, the shock of the adverse event.
- Then accept that stupor, that frozenness.
- Hang with it long enough to experience a melting away, a letting go, which as we know is a letting come and go, morphing into a great letting-be.
- Surrender, trust, accept and allow, release (STAR).

Unfortunately, most of us just experience the chill, the frozen darkness, and get stuck in that place. That's the problem when we react unthinkingly from fear or panic. To inter-meditate with adversity we have to become willing to face all that comes our way, without over-reactivity or instability. Otherwise we will continually be forced to pay hidden costs—emotionally and physically—as if extorted by the demons of our own fears, insecurities, and anxieties. Fearlessness is difficult to aspire to, but I think necessary to work toward. Fearlessness doesn't mean getting rid of fear; it means facing fear and co-meditating and befriending it, unpleasant as it may be.

Adversity tears away all the veils between us and them, us and it. It cuts through the bullshit, stripping everything away, leaving us naked and exposed, yet somehow cleansed and purified at the same time—like a purging and renewing forest fire. But for that to happen, we need to stay patient and attentive. No hard and no easy. No obstacles and no obstacle-makers, and no one to be obstructed. Nothing to do and nothing to get rid of in the naked state of numinous and fresh nowness-awareness, free of past and future. *Emaho!* Wondrous. The great healing doesn't depend on whether you live or die, whether you become cured of the malady or not. Inter-meditation brings healing on the soul level—freedom from dis-ease, unease, and what truly ails and afflicts us. Then we're free to be sick. Or die. No problem. Not at all.

When my time has come
and impermanence and death
have caught up with me,
When the breath ceases,
and the body and mind
go their separate ways,

May I not experience delusion,
attachment, and clinging,

But remain in the natural
state of ultimate reality.[1]
DZOGCHEN MASTER LONGCHENPA

8

No Cure for Old Age and Death

Seeing through the Veil of Mortality

Why Death?

The Buddha didn't have a human name for his teacher. He said death itself was his guru; moreover, the Buddha claimed that death and mortality are the most influential and far-reaching subjects of meditation. That's what inspired him to seek enlightenment, the merging beyond dualism, beyond life *and* death. For this reason, I stress the importance of inter-meditating with death.

Death—our own and that of everyone we've ever known and loved—is the only thing we can be certain of, and when it comes to dying, inter-meditation is one of the most powerful and profound tools to help us. In the previous chapter I wrote about grief, suffering, and loss, but there's more to it, especially when it comes to helping others have a good death and preparing for our own. Death can be painfully intimate—gut-level personal when someone close to us dies—and simultaneously much larger than we can conceive, universal in its scope and illuminating in providing us perspective we might otherwise not achieve.

Even though I have contemplated the matter of life and death for decades, I still find it unbelievable that I will die someday. I know it's true; it is going happen. I don't know exactly when, where, or how. Still, I can hardly believe it. The small ego-mind cannot comprehend it! None of us have ever known—or at least can remember having known—a world existing without us as we currently know ourselves. *My* world? The *end* of my world? *My!* It's all ultimately incomprehensible. The words *life* and *death* are merely placeholders, sticky notes to remind us of the irrefutable truths beyond our minds, beyond our understanding.

Being with Dying

My mother, Joyce Miller, had a delightful sense of humor, which she inherited from her Jewish immigrant parents and Old World Yiddish-speaking grandparents, and especially from her Tilden High School Spanish teacher, Sam Levinson, who later became a famous Borscht Belt Catskills comedian. Mom spoke Spanish and French fluently, and she skipped two grades in school—no small feat in her competitive and achievement-oriented community in Brooklyn in the 1930s and 40s.

During the last days of my mother's life, in 2008, I spent a lot of time visiting and inter-meditating with her as she lay in a hospital bed in Long Island. We understood each other; we spoke the same inner as well as outer language. How could it be otherwise? She'd been my mother for fifty-seven years in this present incarnation, and was perhaps with me in some way long before that. She gave me life, my first nourishment, taught me how to talk, and how to read when I was four years old. (She wanted me to have a running start in kindergarten. No wonder that I'm still running!)

Eventually I had to leave the hospital to head north to lead our annual Dzogchen Center nine-day summer meditation retreat at the Garrison Institute in upstate New York. When I arrived that Friday afternoon, while the staff was setting up, I received a call from my sister, Carol. "Mom has just died," she told me. Our brother, Michael, got on the line and asked, "When can you come?" So I gave my opening evening talk to the hundred or so retreat attendees, left them in the care of my assistant teachers, and drove back to Long Island early the next morning to be with my family.

I met Carol at the Jewish funeral home my mom had chosen long ago, where my dear grandmother Anne—Mom's mother—had also been laid out over twenty-five years before. They brought my sister and me into a room to view the body. Family came and left as I stayed with my mom, meditating and praying for and *with* her. I could sense that she was still around. Every cell of my body—which had come from hers—was connected to her and continued to receive her special Jewish Mother transmission. The feeling that unfolded as I inter-meditated with her gradually expanded to encompass all those souls who'd gone before so we could come (and eventually go) in the grand and mysterious waterwheel of life and death, the endless shining surge of change and continuity.

My mother lay on a table, under a clean white sheet. Her folded hands and bare feet stuck out slightly. She liked to wear jewelry, but had given all of it—including her watch, wedding band, and engagement ring—to my sister during those last weeks in the hospital. There was one noticeable exception—on her ankle were the sandalwood Buddhist prayer beads I'd brought her from Nepal, carved in the shapes of tiny skulls. The small skull-bone wrist *mala* is intended to remind the wearer of impermanence and death, and to cherish life and love while we still have them. Those beads were all she had kept, all she had taken along for the journey. That was her lifeline, as well as her sign to our family and to me, her first son, the family's Buddhist "rabbi"—Lama Surya Das. I knew it then and I know it now. Tears fall even as I write this.

After an hour or so of our inter-meditation at her side, I left the funeral home and met up with Carol, her kids, and my brother across the street at a diner. I found them around a table sharing the ritual most families do best—fooding. My twenty-eight-year-old nephew Lonnie was there. I can't remember what he ate, but I guarantee it involved animal protein. We have a lively and deep relationship. Mensch that he is, he asked me how I was doing, how it went for me at the hospital?

I told him, "Your grandma gave me a message for you."

Without missing a beat, Lonnie asked, "What did she say?"

Everyone listened, quiet for once. No mean achievement for our family on that occasion, or any when we all gather in one place.

I told Lonnie, "She said I should tell you her important message only as needed. So stay tuned."

There was another moment of silence. Then everyone laughed that kind of cathartic laugh that only people who really love, trust, and inter-are with each other can share. My mother was right there with us. Joyce Miller—smart and funny as hell. There was no other shoe to drop. Now I had the license to tell Lonnie whatever I wanted, whenever I wanted, and even say it came straight from his grandma!

A few days later we memorialized and buried my beloved mother, but that doesn't mean that I stopped inter-meditating with her. Whenever I miss her or need her I look at a photo or visualize her unforgettable face—*my* face, and yet not mine. I sit still and I wait until I feel her presence. Then I commune with her, hang out, and even talk to and with her (in my head, mainly). Sometimes I just go deep and sit with her as if we're meditating together, as if eye-gazing or facing each other in partnered spirituality, just being and commingling, merging, flowing, and knowing. Mom speaks to me in her inimitable Jewish Mother Long-Island-by-way-of-Brooklyn voice, "I might know more about that than you think. Let me tell you something, Jeffrey . . . " as she always put it. And tell me she does.

It makes me think of that charming movie *Oh, God!* At the end, the naïve young supermarket manager played by John Denver asks God, played by centenarian George Burns, "How will I talk to you after you're gone?" God replies, "From now on you talk, I listen. I'll be here. You'll know." That'd be my mother. She's there. I know. Perhaps you too feel this about someone you've lost.

Benares

In several ways, my mother's death prepared me for another experience. When I was in Benares recently, visiting the Ganges River—one of the Earth's most sacred places, for Hinduism as well as other religions—I spent hours sitting on the ghats, the old stone steps leading down to the river. I meditated there in what is essentially an open-air crematorium, as corpses around me burned on open funeral pyres.

In this ancient holy city jam-packed with souls living and dead, I reached a place in my meditation where it became inter-meditation—I began to feel as if my self, my body, and all of my history were being devoured by fire as well. It takes hours and hours for a human body, which is dense and meaty, to be ritually ignited and completely consumed by flames. The sounds, smells, smoke, and ashes are intense as sinews dry up, dead limbs jerk, fatty flesh sizzles, and joints pop. Everything around me felt like part of me—the crows, vultures, insects, and people in hand-hewn rowboats and pole rafts. All of us—the people both living and dead, the animals, the river—went in and out of the jaws of the universe like the myriad things pouring in and out of Lord Vishnu's gargantuan mouth, the source of all things. As it says in Hinduism's primary sacred text, the Bhagavad Gita, or "Song of God":

As the rivers' many
currents of water
Rush forward
toward the sea alone,
So, over there,
those heroes
of the world of men
Enter into your
wildly flaming mouths.

As moths,
with great velocity,
Enter a blazing fire
unto their destruction,

Similarly,
the worlds also
Enter your mouths
with great velocity,
unto their destruction.

Devouring them
from every side,
you lick up
All the worlds with
your flaming mouths.
Filling the entire
universe with splendor
Your fierce rays burn,
O Vishnu.[2]

Graveyard Sauntering

You don't have to visit the funeral pyres along the Ganges River to experience this crucible of inter-meditation.

One of my favorite American Buddhist meditations is something I call "graveyard sauntering" or "cemetery contemplation." Nowadays, in the West at least, graveyards are often as beautiful as parks. They don't look anything like scary cremation grounds with crows and vultures, they don't smell like smoke and cooked flesh, and they don't issue flying sparks and ashes. In American cemeteries we can walk or sit, read the tombstones, and think about people who lived, who had families, who made dinner, who loved their dogs in the 1700s, 1800s, 1900s, or even last week. Where are they now? Where are their stories? Where are those who loved them? Where is their "rare and precious life" now?

If we don't have time for a walk, we can just drive past a cemetery. We can practice staying present as we pass, conscious that this place represents a huge repository of lives and deaths, a collection of dreams and ambitions, fears and disappointments—the tangled growth of unexpurgated lives. Or we can go to other places that don't look like parks, where death smacks us across the face and sorrow seeps into our hearts—places where we can't turn away from death's reality, places like a funeral parlor, morgue, battlefield, cancer ward, nursing home, bone-pile behind a butcher's shop, or slaughterhouse. Zen Buddhist teacher Tetsugen Bernie Glassman leads annual meditation retreats on the site of the Auschwitz-Birkenau death camps, so people can pray and co-meditate with those that went before, bear witness, and inter-meditate with all the horrors of the Holocaust.

Cemetery contemplation in any form is an invaluable meditation. By connecting to the deceased—their lives, their deaths—we can learn to inter-meditate with them. It takes a little creativity to put ourselves in that state of mind where we are face-to-face and heart-to-heart with death, but it's crucial, especially in our sanitized culture where old people, sick people, and the dying and dead are hidden away from our sight.

As we inter-meditate, we need to take it beyond the merely conceptual mental level. We need to reach into the heartfelt, emotional, intuitive sense of things, and then go beyond even that. If we don't have time to visit a cemetery or someplace where death manifests vividly, we can keep flowers around a little longer than we usually do and watch them die and shrivel up, or take some autumn leaves and contemplate their impermanence, or watch a candle burn down. Even something as seemingly mundane as visiting the town dump gives me a keen feeling for all the lives and hopes and dreams and losses inherent there. When I see a double-bed mattress, or broken stroller, or moldy books, or broken couches—all once so new and shiny and desirable—it has a profound effect on me. All these things now heaped like driftwood on the shore of life with its storms and currents, mysteries and promises, exigencies and uncertainties.

When we start to contemplate mortality, we might feel a little more urgency for life, to live and love and be loved. We might well reconsider our priorities—how we spend our days, and with whom. Do we enjoy time with our loved ones, or are we perhaps working and saving away to spend time with them *later?* This is a pretty fiction.

The Buddha said if we truly felt, without covering up the pain, insecurity, anxiety, and fear of unenlightened existence, we would meditate and strive for deliverance as if our hair were on fire. Think about it. If your hair were on fire, you'd stop futzing around, drop what you were doing no matter how "important," and put the fire out. You would immediately attend to the matter at hand. The Buddha also said all his teachings were just expedient means to lure the children out of the burning house of samsara and onto the way of freedom, peace, and bliss.

Inter-meditating with those who were once alive as we are now reminds us to always keep death and mortality in the forefront of consciousness—at the top of our minds, the tip of our tongues—in order to better live and appreciate the here and now, just as it is. This contemplation helps me love the ones I'm with, and not become distracted by other fantasies and imaginations.

I find myself cherishing life in all its forms, and I feel thankful for every single day, almost from the moment I awaken. Inter-meditating with death makes us better inter-meditators with life. Life is tenuous and fragile, fleeting and contingent—we need to rejoice in and protect our precious life, as well as all the lives connected to and around us. That's why I love to inter-meditate with death!

No Words, No Doubt

In August of 1999 my wife, Kathy Peterson, and I went to visit Nyoshul Khenpo Rinpoche on his deathbed at our Nyingma Center where he'd long resided—in Dordogne, southern France, in the forested wilds between Bordeaux and Aix-en-Provence. I spent my days meditating with my teacher, chanting to him, and sometimes, when he felt up to it, talking about all sorts of things outer, inner, and secret. Although almost bedridden during that last month, Khenpo Rinpoche perked up one morning and asked to go outside for a walk. While I pushed his wheel-chair along the dirt driveway and country path, Khenpo's lovely Bhutanese wife, Damcho-la, and the monastery's retreat master, Tulku Pema Wangyal, joined us. People popped up as if from nowhere and came out to see Rinpoche and receive his blessing. We all knew these were to be his last days in this incarnation. It was a bittersweet moment, shining bright in the memory-theatre of my mind.

Near the very end of his life, as his brain tumor took hold, Khenpo Rinpoche reached up to me from his deathbed, took my hands in his, and placed them on his heart. We were as one—no separation, no words, no doubt. In this simple gesture—an inter-meditation in its purest form—I understood that it was time for him to go, and I also knew that he would always be with me and in me, and I in him. The Buddha, the teacher, and the disciple became one.

I still have Khenpo Rinpoche's copy of his favorite book, the *Treasury of the Vast Nature of Reality*, one of seven vital works by the seminal fourteenth-century Dzogchen master Longchenpa. We used to chant it together for forty-five minutes almost every morning. Rinpoche carried on Longchenpa's lineage and passed it on to countless disciples, including the Dalai Lama. Khenpo left that silk-wrapped rice paper Dzogchen text to me. His wife gave it to me after he passed away, along with a Buddha statue, a yellow silk monk's shirt, a *dorje* and bell, his spectacles, a mala, and some other personal items. These simple possessions remind me of all the wisdom that our noble Buddhist tradition has preserved over the millennia—all of the essential instructions that countless masters have preserved, practiced, realized, embodied, and passed on to us. These items also remind me that it is now my sacred responsibility to keep Khenpo Rinpoche's teaching alive, and pass it on to the next generations, including the one-to-one secret whispered Dzogchen pith-instruction lineage he vouchsafed to me. My inter-meditation with you becomes your inter-meditation with me *and* with him. This is a personal example of how inter-meditation can help us, and we can help bring each other along the Great Way, through conscientiously practicing the loving and altruistic Bodhisattva spirit in action together. That's why I was born. That's why I must prepare for the end in a proper manner, when my time comes. This is the legacy we have inherited, our royal spiritual birthright and inheritance.

If You Leave Me, Can I Come Too?

On the day of his actual death, or *parinirvana* (as Tibetan Buddhists call it)—January 24, 1364—Master Longchenpa wrote:

> This life is finished, Karma is exhausted, what
> supplication could achieve has ended;
> Worldliness is done with; this life's show is over.
> Having realized, in one moment, the
> very nature of self-manifestation
> Through the vast realms in the bardo,
> I am close to taking up my seat at the
> beginning of all and everything.
> The riches found in myself have made
> the minds of others happy,
> Through this magic existence the opulence of
> the island of deliverance has been realized.
> Having been with you, my excellent
> disciples, during this time,
> I have been satiated with the joy of dharma.
> Now that the connection with this
> life has lost its karmic power,
> Do not lament about this beggar who
> died happily and unattached,
> But constantly pray (that we be together in spirit).[3]

I still inter-meditate with my teachers every morning and evening. I keep their pictures on my altars at home as blessings, encouragement, and inspiration, and in gratitude for all they have done for me and passed down to us through their decades and lifetimes of dedicated Bodhisattva practice. I sit with them and view their beloved faces; I look into their clear eyes, and it seems as if they're doing the same—looking back at me and reciprocating as we inter-meditate together. This is part of what we call Guru Yoga practice in Vajrayana Buddhism. If I don't have a picture on hand, I visualize my teachers and go through the same steps and stages, with the same results. My Buddha-gurus are always with me and in me, in reality, in memory, and in my psyche. Just as yours will be with you.

Here's the bottom line: my parents and gurus guide, protect, bless, and support me. Alive or dead, or reborn as new recognized reincarnate lamas (*tulkus*) by the Tibetan lineage hierarchy, they are like my own conscience, or my inner guru, which is an internalized version of all that they believed, taught, and embodied. My teachers constantly remind me of our relationship far beyond death, the gossamer borders and boundaries of self and other, this life and the next.

> Rejoice in and protect our precious life, as well as all the lives connected to and around us.

INTER-MEDITATION
PRACTICE

Nine-Part Tibetan Death Convergitation Technique

Sometimes I use one of my Buddhist texts, like the *Treasury of the Vast Nature of Reality,* to begin an inter-meditation that reflects on the impermanence and fragility of life. Sometimes I use a poem, a mystical song, or a sacred teaching from another religion. I read and reread each line, each word, intentionally, and I reflect on how everyone who is born dies—the powerful and impoverished, celebrated and obscure, venerated and maligned. These texts help me remember the extraordinarily mysterious, infinitely variegated, persistent yet frangible nature of life. I contemplate lifetimes, human and otherwise, from atoms to the universe, from fruit flies to the ancient Galapagos tortoises whose slow metabolisms allow them to outlive us by so many years. These creatures give "lifespan" a more elastic meaning, not unlike the divine and semi-divine beings of other-than-human realms in Buddhist, Hindu, and other cosmologies. Looking up at the stars and extending laterally to embrace the myriad beings, my own existence and current preoccupations seem dwarfed in comparison and I feel less self-centered, central, and indispensable.

I like to ponder how many beings there are on Earth—over seven billion humans, not to mention the quadrillions of insects, birds, fish, bacteria, flora, and other forms of life seen and unseen in our biosphere. I think about all the hives and swarms, groups and gatherings, cultures and civilizations, that have grown, flourished, and disappeared over the centuries and millennia. Considering the scope of all that impermanent flotsam and jetsam helps me keep my own thoughts, feelings, and physical sensations in perspective. Everything rises and falls, appears and disappears, simultaneously co-emerging in a whirling of mind-states that coalesces into the nature of reality and how I presently happen to experience it.

Once I've connected with both sides of my brain, once I've calmed down and quieted my mind, and once I've gentled my heart and breath and energy, I can return to the natural state of harmonious flow and simply feel and heal any lingering imbalances or restlessness. After enjoying a few deep breaths, I contemplate the following nine steps to inter-meditate with death and mortality. I consider each of them conceptually and then breathe into and out of them—making the steps part of my own experience and memory rather than something merely two-dimensional, abstract, or conceptual. Eventually I grok or merge into a place of interbeing, intimacy, and non-separation—an excellent inter-meditation, which I call *convergitation.*

1. We all die. Nobody gets out alive. Life is chronic, but death is not necessarily final or even fatal.

2. Our inevitable dying begins at the moment of our birth.

3. Death is imminent. We don't know when. Life is frangible, contingent, tenuous, and fleeting.

4. Death is all but random. It strikes like lightning.

5. Far more circumstances lead to death than to life.

6. Our bodies weren't made to last forever. Meditating or some type of genuine spiritual practice *now* is the only thing that will help us *then*, the moment of death.

7. When our time comes, no amount of money, social status, bodyguards, or expensive legal teams can change the schedule.

8. Neither can our friends or family, much as they may wish to.

9. None of us can withstand death. All of us, at this very moment, approach our inevitable departure, and everything comes to ruin. Remember "Ozymandias," Percy Bysshe Shelley's well-known poem:

I met a traveller from an antique land
Who said: "Two vast and trunkless legs of stone
Stand in the desert. Near them, on the sand,
Half sunk, a shattered visage lies, whose frown,
And wrinkled lip, and sneer of cold command,
Tell that its sculptor well those passions read
Which yet survive, stamped on these lifeless things,
The hand that mocked them and the heart that fed:
And on the pedestal these words appear:
My name is Ozymandias, king of kings:
Look on my works, ye Mighty, and despair!'
Nothing beside remains. Round the decay
Of that colossal wreck, boundless and bare
The lone and level sands stretch far away.

Everything passes, and nothing remains, not even the mountains and the seas. Yet all is not lost—not really, and not forever. Countless people throughout history in the East and West have believed in some form of the afterlife, or of reincarnation, rebirth, and the like; many still do. Perhaps modern scientific findings like the continuance of genes and chromosomes to offspring actually track back to more primitive beliefs in how things continue from one generation to another. Science tells us that energy is never created nor destroyed; it merely cycles around in our vast cosmic ecosystem, in the greater ecology of being. Is not conscious aliveness a form of energy?

If we re-envision our relationship to all things so that we no longer strive fruitlessly to control, dominate, and manipulate—if and when we embrace our incredible, inter-woven interconnection—we come to see through the illusion of separateness and solidity. Doing so, we can experience the contingency and insubstantiality of material things, and settle into our fundamental interconnectedness and interdependence. Feeling fully connected to ourselves and all aspects of our own experience, excluding nothing, we naturally flow into and with our undeniable interconnectedness to all beings. We are never alone, neither in joy nor in sorrow—not really. As we loosen our death-grip on events and people, we gradually learn to experience little or no separation, little impermeable solidity or rigidity. We flow with the go, and don't feel that there's much more that we have to know. This leads to trust and conviction (and not mere belief), safety and security (not mere dependence), and faith in our own wisdom and experience. This is more like a worldview or viewpoint, a perspective or gestalt (bigger picture), than a mere feeling; it arises out of the penetrating perception of complete and utter interconnectedness and dependent origination. We all belong to each other and are responsible for each other. We may sometimes feel alone, but at least we are alone together. My major might stay *me* and my minor remain *you* (and others)—in the relative sense of things—but we're not alone.

A Good Death: The Process of Dying

I'm planning to die sitting up in the light, be cremated in the Buddhist way, and have my ashes spread in the river and the fields at Dzogchen Osel Ling, our ranch retreat center outside Austin, Texas. In that way I intend to continue co-meditating symbolically and in spirit with my students, followers, friends, and colleagues there, and wherever they choose to find me. Death is nothing to be feared, simply one part of the life cycle. We have been given so much; I want to match and enhance it!

Inter-meditation can undeniably help those about to pass on with a "good" death—be they friends, family members, or victims of a disaster on the other side of the planet. One of the early visionaries of the hospice movement, Ira Byock of Dartmouth College, is a proponent of dying well: "I don't want to romanticize it. Nobody looks forward to it. But we shouldn't assume that it's only about suffering and its avoidance or its suppression. That in addition to, concurrent with the unwanted difficult physical and emotional social strains that illness and dying impose, there are also experiences, interactions, opportunities that are of profound value for individuals and all who love them."[4]

Pa-Dampa Sangye was an eleventh-century spiritual adept, a renowned yogi and *siddha* with extraordinary psychic and spiritual powers. He traveled a lot: ten years in Tibet, twelve years in China, and he finally returned to the Everest regions village of Tingri to die. As Pa-Dampa Sangye lay dying, he articulated his last teaching, his final inter-meditation: "My mind has blended with all things." Then he fixed his gaze on the open sky, exhaled forcefully, and passed away.

In the Buddhist tradition, as with any religion, preparing for the moment of death is of utmost importance: our whole lives lead up to this grand finale! (Or, at least, this grand repurposing.) We could call the classic Tibetan Book of the Dead the "Big Tibetan Book of Inter-Meditating with Death," as it sublimely instructs all about the teachings of death and the process of dying, and how to live up to death in the most authentically conscious way and reap the ultimate rewards of doing so. These profound teachings were commonly used to explicitly and even loudly instruct the dying person:

> My mind has blended with all things.

> O, Child of Buddha Nature, that which is called death has now arrived. Therefore you should adopt an altruistic motivation and concentrate your thinking as follows: I have arrived at the time of death, so now, relying on the process of death, I will single-mindedly cultivate a Bodhisattva's altruistic intention. I will meditate on the generation of loving-kindness, compassion, and an altruistic Bodhicitta intention to attain enlightenment. For the benefit of all sentient beings who are as limitless as space, I must attain perfect Buddhahood.[5]

Note that at the penultimate moment, the instructions don't tell the dying person to focus on themselves and to hell with everyone else. Rather, the Tibetan Book of the Dead encourages us in our final moments to altruistically pull a few more people into our lifeboat as we release self-centered preoccupations and open our hearts to larger and more spacious aims and goals—noble Bodhichitta.

I could write a whole book commenting on everything included in the Tibetan Book of the Dead, but I mostly want to focus on one particular practice especially relevant to inter-meditation: the recondite practice of *phowa* (consciousness transference). Phowa—a crucially helpful Tibetan deathbed aid—occurs when a lama or spiritual friend guides a person into the death process and through the subsequent passage of transition (called *bardo,* or the intermediate stage) toward their next rebirth. According to the teachings of Tibetan Buddhism, phowa entails the purposeful boost and transference of consciousness to a higher plane. The lama helps the dying person perform this in practical ways, and together they commingle, mix minds, and—in more ordinary spiritual English—combine soulful energies.

Tibetan lamas like Ayang Rinpoche (the "Phowa Lama") and Sogyal Rinpoche (author of the highly recommended *Tibetan Book of Living and Dying*) teach that for about twenty-one days after a person dies, they remain more connected to the life they have just departed than to the one they will soon be reborn in. For these three weeks, the teachings encourage loved ones to continue their (mostly silent) communication with the deceased person—to say their goodbyes, finish any unfinished business, reassure the dead person, and encourage them to let go of their old life and move on to the next one. Those left behind can offer up prayers, food and drink, candles, and good deeds to help feed and guide the departed and those accompanying them through the difficult transitions of the bardo. Just talking to the dead person can be reassuring to the bereaved. Those left behind can benefit by feeling that the bardo traveler receives the message and feels eased by all of the pure-hearted efforts, offerings, prayers, and aspirations. The spiritual mind of the deceased person at this stage—the "mental body," as the Dalai Lama's tradition likes to call it—can still be subtle and receptive, not unlike someone alive yet in a deep coma—someone who may hear but can't respond.

Some Western scientists have come around to this Tibetan way of seeing things. About his own near-death experience, Christian neurosurgeon Eben Alexander writes:

> Modern physics tells us that the universe is a unity— that it is undivided. Though we seem to live in a world of separation and difference, physics tells us that beneath the surface, every object and event in the universe is completely woven up with every other object and event. There is no true separation.
>
> Before my experience these ideas were abstractions. Today they are realities. Not only is the universe defined by unity, it is also—I now know—defined by love. The universe as I experienced it in my coma is— I have come to see with both shock and joy—the same one that both Einstein and Jesus were speaking of in their (very) different ways.

Sounds like an inter-meditator to me. Alexander continues:

> I've spent decades as a neurosurgeon at some of the most prestigious medical institutions in our country. I know that many of my peers hold—as I myself did—to the theory that the brain, and in particular the cortex, generates consciousness and that we live in

a universe devoid of any kind of emotion, much less
the unconditional love that I now know God and the
universe have toward us. But that belief, that theory,
now lies broken at our feet. What happened to me
destroyed it.[6]

I have experienced several out-of-body experiences, but I haven't
yet benefited from a near-death experience. In my heart, however,
I know the unconditional love that Alexander speaks of—and I
know without a doubt that I'm never alone. I can tune in to my
invisible array, those who've gone before—parents and forefa-
thers, my spiritual lineage, teachers, benefactors, Dharma friends,
and even Buddhas and Bodhisattvas. Or as America's early philosopher Ralph Waldo Emerson puts it:

We return to reason and faith. There I feel that nothing
can befall me in life,—no disgrace, no calamity, (leaving
me my eyes,) which nature cannot repair. Standing on
the bare ground,—my head bathed by the blithe air, and
uplifted into infinite spaces—all mean egotism vanishes.
I become a transparent eye-ball; I am nothing; I see all;
the currents of the Universal Being circulate through
me; I am part or particle of God.[7]

Facing Death

Fear of death is deadening; it steals our vitality. By contrast, fearlessness enlivens us, protects us, and powerfully enhances our
lives. To gain the secret of life, we must face death, and thoroughly; we must chew death up, digest it, and even evacuate

it. When we realize our unborn and undying essence, death can do us no harm. "Die before you die, and you will never die," proclaim the Sufis, doubtless referring to ego-death and surrendering self-will to the Higher Power. We are all going to die, but who among us is going to really live?

As I've mentioned before, as a lama I work extensively in consoling and counseling people facing death through illness, age, or other crises—either their own or the death of someone they love. Inter-meditating with people near the time of their death is incredibly important, but there are more ways we can face death and inter-meditate with others. In the early 1970s I lived in Calcutta during the Indo-Pakistan War, when Mrs. Indira Gandhi—the Prime Minister of India—imposed martial law. We experienced air raids and blackouts at night. The state-ordered rationing created long lines in the streets to get basic necessities like gasoline, milk, bread, rice, butter, sugar, and yogurt. It was a difficult and frightening time, and yet I have rarely felt so attentive, enlivened, alert, and even wired—though not strained as if stressed-out or over-caffeinated. We didn't experience day-to-day danger necessarily, but the Sword-of-Damocles-like specter of air strikes made every night an adventure as well as a bonding experience. Both Indians and foreigners felt a pervading sense of camaraderie almost like the World War II stories I read as a boy that connected strangers and brought friends closer in the London Underground during air raids or in the foxholes on the Front. This type of spontaneous collective cooperation and unmasking through the naked immediacy of necessary connection is a natural inter-meditation.

Years later, back from my India sojourn in the 1990s, I read *The Things They Carried*, Tim O'Brien's now-classic collection of

predator. Communication, connection, and mutual concern took place beyond words. Everyone co-merged. This is true inter-meditation—*shared spirituality beyond the polarities and dichotomies of self and other.*

Of course, we don't want to endure war or face a terrible disaster to become inter-meditators. However, understanding these kinds of experiences can help us recognize the sensation, the Bodhichitta of inter-meditation, and usefully apply it in our more quotidian lives, opening our hearts as wide as the world.

INTER-MEDITATION PRACTICE

Perspectivising—With Every Breath a Little Death

Much of being with death and fear is a matter of understanding our place and function in the universe. To do so, I recommend one extremely helpful practice I call *perspectivising*—inter-meditating with the infinitely large and the infinitely minute.

- Start by considering the biggest event in the news or your life this week. Then zoom out and consider the past hundred years, the past millennium, back to the Magna Carta and Charlemagne's time, then back to the Axial Age, when the present world religions arose, around the time of the births of Zoroaster, Buddha, Christ, and then Mohammed. Then travel back to prehistoric times and even further, to the emergence of mammals out of the oceans, the dinosaurs, the birth of the oceans on the cooling planet Earth, then all the way back to the Big Bang and whatever you imagine may have preceded it. Mingle your mind with a past beyond imagining.

- Now reverse the film in your mind. Start at the beginning of time and travel forward, to dinosaurs, to the Crusades and to Columbus and the other European explorers, to the Civil War and the Great Depression, to the past century and your grandparents' and parents' youth and upbringing, and then to your own birth, and right back up through Y2K and 9/11 and into the present moment in the good old US of A (or wherever you are right now). Focus all of your awareness now on your body and its physical sensations in this present moment. Ground yourself through collected attention—a focused, concentrated mindfulness— in the most prominent feeling or sensation right now. Feel the somatic feelings and sensations. Think about your vital internal organs—heart, lungs, kidneys, bladder, stomach, spleen, and liver—all working quietly away, pumping and processing, digesting, filtering, and reabsorbing—and your blood and other bodily fluids, all flowing like the ocean tides. Now, contemplate things you can't directly feel like cells splitting or the trillions of microbes and bacteria thriving and dying within you. Consider yourself, just for now, as a lovely, well-socialized skeleton, a corpse in the making, as you sit with the specter of death and impermanence and put yourself through these inter- meditative paces. For what are we anyhow but living corpses—"meat-sacks" as a doctor friend so coolly puts it—fuel for the internal combustion engine of the mulch and compost piles of this grand, over-exploited organic garden called Earth?

- Go deeper into this ever-present here-and-now moment as you breathe in and out. Remember, with every breath a little death, a little relinquishment. Breathing in, calm the mind; breathing out, relax, release, and smile. With every breath a little birth. It's a ceaseless tide, like a waterwheel turning, emptying and filling its buckets again and again. This is the ancient Indian image of the cycle of rebirth.

- Once you've practiced this for a while, try doing it with someone else—your partner, a sleeping child, or a sick or dying friend or family member. Celebrate the life you live by embracing and preparing for your own death. This is a universal relational meditation, found across the globe in Native American teachings and European texts from the Middle Ages such as *Ars Moriendi*.

Death Is a Real Illusion

Inter-meditating with death is such an important way of nurturing and nourishing our best and deepest selves, integrating everything along the path toward growth and awakening. It's a way of being with and *one with*, inseparable from. Slowly read that sentence again, please. This is the essence of inter-meditation: it's a way of being with and *one with*, inseparable from.

Inter-meditation maintains that edgeless vulnerability and permeability, an interpenetrating awareness in which all things and experiences appear and mutate. What's the alternative, anyway? Separating ourselves behind a moat in the castle of our own egotism, or being only partly present for our lives, constantly wishing and fantasizing that we were elsewhere? Diverting ourselves through an infinite variety of entertainments, sleepwalking through life? That's the opposite of inter-meditation. That's walking with death, not dancing with life.

Genuinely encountering death resembles a high-wire act. We try to maintain some balance amid the ups and downs, the shocks and unknowns, in both the inner and outer dimensions, all while keeping our hearts and minds open. Interactions with others and their desires and confusion, fear and anxieties can pose some significant challenges. But this suffering interconnects us with all suffering, with universal suffering, and makes us more empathetic. In his book *Meetings at the Edge: Dialogues with the Grieving and the Dying, the Healing and the Healed*, Stephen Levine writes, "This is the 'cosmic suffering' that opens us into the universal and allows us to go beyond 'the separate self,' to touch the deathless within us all. . . . We have within us all that it takes to face the immensity of this pain, to let it soak in, to learn to breathe it into the heart, to let it burn its way to completion." As the first Jamgon Kontrul of Tibet says, illness works like a broom to sweep away obscurations and defilements, a precipitant clearing out the way for enlightenment.

"Is death real or an illusion?" When asked this question, Dudjom Rinpoche, one of the legendary masters of modern Tibetan Buddhism in exile, replied: "Death is a real illusion." That bears repeating: *Death is a real illusion*. As far as we are able, we should become comfortable with the illusion-like phenomenon of death. Inter-meditating with the dying works as preparation for our own deaths, as well; the practice is a two-way street, like all co-meditations. This familiarity allows us to become more fully conscious of our own mortality—ideally, we become aware that each day, hour, or minute could be our last, and that life is tenuous and fleeting, and thus live accordingly, savoring it moment by moment.

As thirteenth-century Tibetan master Thogmé Zangpo says:

> This life is transient and impermanent.
> All the goods we've accumulated
> and relationships we've enjoyed
> will change or come to an end.
> The mind is like a temporary
> guest in our bodily house; it will
> someday pass beyond. Learn to think of
> the larger picture beyond this one lifetime.[9]

Death is a real illusion.

Another of my favorite writers, John Muir, puts it poetically: "Let children walk with Nature, let them see the beautiful blending and communions of death and life, their joyous inseparable unity, as taught in woods and meadows, plains and mountains and streams of our blessed star, and they will learn that death is sting-less indeed, and as beautiful as life."[10] Once we begin to realize that death and separation are an illusion—"no old age and death, no end to old age and death," as the Heart Sutra affirms—and see the complete interconnection of all beings, once we actualize that *no-separation*—then we're ready to paint on a bigger canvas—the world itself and all of its inhabitants.

The Buddha, Shakyamuni, our teacher, predicted that the next Buddha would be Maitreya, the Buddha of love. . . . It is possible that the next Buddha will not take the form of an individual. The next Buddha may take the form of a community, a community practicing understanding and loving-kindness, a community practicing mindful living. And the practice can be carried out as a group, as a city, as a nation.[1]

THICH NHAT HANH

9

To Save One Soul Is
to Save the Universe

Becoming One with the World

I recently spent time in Nepal at my dear lama friend's beautiful mountaintop monastery, Druk Amitabha Gompa, overlooking the Kathmandu Valley. His Holiness the Gyalwang Drukpa Rinpoche gave a series of teachings interspersed with special prayers and *pujas,* chants and rituals, including ones for the recently deceased. In front near the nuns and monks sat, among over eight hundred attendees, dozens of people whose parents or other family members had recently died. Incense smoke curled upwards in long, sinuous clouds. Monks poured water over the shiny silver faces of spherical ritual mirrors, cleansing and purifying departed spirits and their karmic accumulations. Attendees reverentially placed slips of paper with names written in Tibetan, Chinese, Japanese, Vietnamese, English, French, German, and Russian into a brazier; the slips became flames—smoke wafting up into smoke. Deep drum beats and sonorous chanting reverberated between the walls and also in my diaphragm; splendid symphonies of sound filled the elaborate canopy of the altar mandala and protection tent overhead, the sacred circle around us, the entire room, and monastery precincts. Prayer flags flapped on high poles, singing in the wind, spreading prayers and loving-kindness vibrations further into the atmosphere and reaching all the beings in nature and the five elements too.

I sat onstage near His Holiness Drukpa, the Dragon Master, in a row of red-robed lamas—amid the ceremony and ritual, the thud of the giant drum, the Tibetan long horns, the rattle of hand *damarus*, and the sacred cacophony of eight hundred people chanting—when suddenly, astonishingly, I was no longer there. I found myself alone in a crystal cave, a light beam emanating from His Holiness's central sun, moving out into the great wide world. I intuited, felt, grokked, and appreciated right then and there that there is no separation between God and soul and human—no me, no you; we're all one continuum of numinous, luminous energy-flow and splendid presence. All I had to do was to relax and align myself totally with the present moment and relinquish dichotomous subject-object fixation, surrender my will and ego-mind, and settle down into the flux and flow of all and everything—not a small matter, indeed. So I did! Suddenly Surya Das *was* the Buddha and BuddhaMind, the grand lama Rinpoche conducting the ceremonies and the entire gathering too, the prayers and the music, incense, wind, and sky. I was all souls—in the monastery and outside, in the Himalayan sun, with the fluttering prayer flags, the soaring hawks—the sum of all beings.

Imagine if world leaders could experience that? Politicians? Democrats grokking Republicans? Refugees interbeing with oligarchs? Oppressors with oppressed? White police officers with young black men? Rich with poor? And we with all of them? Wouldn't this level of inter-meditation bring us back into balance and harmony, as our interests, values, and ability to connect further developed and evolved as empathic resonance deepened?

I'd like to send plenty of government officials (not to mention doctors, lawyers, teachers, and military leaders) to Nepal or Bhutan for some serious Buddhist mind-training, Lojong, and inter-meditation study. But we can all meditate *with* instead of *on*, wherever and whenever we are, right here; that's the essence of co-meditation. The ancient scriptures of India say that we are all part of a universal web of light, each of us reflecting the illumination of the whole.

That web reaches everywhere. When I walk near my home in the countryside, I am often struck by the way drivers wave and smile rather than zipping by me anonymously. I wave and smile back. This simple, little practice builds community and spiritual connections, acknowledging that we're all together in this web. It's a quick and un-self-conscious inter-meditation. I love it.

Simple practices like these—in addition to the formal, carefully orchestrated ones—can allow the world into our hearts and allow our hearts to embrace and fill the world. They're a way to resolve the conundrum between us and them, national pride and global compassion. The future of humankind and our planet depends on us, on our understanding of our relationships—human and otherwise—in the world in its entirety. Inter-meditation helps us become responsible stewards and citizens.

In an interview with British journalist and meditation teacher Christopher Titmuss in *Spirit of Change,* Vimala Thakar puts it like this:

We are the weavers of the fabric of modern society.
We can weave love, truthfulness, and peace
or we can weave hatred, mistrust, and war.
We will have to wear whatever fabric we weave.[2]

Or as I like to say: Transform yourself; transform the world.

Do you remember the days after September 11, 2001, when we all came together? Or after the Indian Ocean tsunami and earthquake in 2004? After Hurricane Katrina? Hurricane Sandy? That beautiful coalescence—that exquisite unity—felt visceral; it gave new meaning to the word *heartfelt*. Now, imagine sustaining that.

For the Benefit of One and All

When dealing with crises, especially the ones that feel too enormous to comprehend, I return to the Buddhist scriptures for answers. My Zen friends chant: "Sentient beings are numberless, I vow to save them." Tibetan Buddhists put it this way: "I take refuge in the Three Jewels—the Buddha, the Dharma, the Sangha—from now until all beings are enlightened I shall practice the six Paramitas, the perfections—*generosity, moral self-discipline, patience, enthusiastic effort, mindful awareness*, and *transcendental wisdom*—for the benefit of one and all."

That's the gist of it—*for the benefit of one and all*. We don't seek liberation and enlightenment just for ourselves; we focus our aspiration toward others and assume universal responsibility for striving toward collective awakening. We think less of self-growth and personal (perhaps selfish) aims, while broadening our scope to include the welfare, well-being, happiness, and fulfillment of all. Most others are just like us—they want and need the very same things for themselves and their families, loved ones, and communities; they also encounter similar dangers, hindrances, and difficulties.

When we talk about awakening, we can't just rely on the teacher, the teachings, and our practice; we have to remember the Sangha, too—the community of kindred spirits and helpmates. One of the original meanings of Sangha is *contact*. It means making warm, meaningful contact—it's the *inter* in inter-meditation. In the Buddha's time, Sangha specifically meant ordained monks and nuns; later the meaning expanded to include practitioners of all kinds, not just monastics. I think we can expand it even more to include the Sangha of all beings. In Burmese, people use the expression *yezed sounde* for sacred spiritual connection or spiritual friendship—a gorgeous little phrase that literally means "water-drop connection" or the natural adhesion and cohesion that brings and keeps kindred spirits together.

We can cultivate precious Bodhichitta, the awakened heart/ mind, with loving, gentle inter-meditation practices, starting small—with ourselves, those we love, those we know, those we like—and ultimately radiating that loving-kindness, compassion, and joy to the entire universe.

This inter-meditation can take the form of formal, seated meditation, prayers, chants, advocacy, social action, or simply feeding and loving others, as my first guru, Neem Karoli Baba, urged us to do. The whole path of enlightenment is not as far away as we may think. All of the inter-meditation practices in this book—and all of the ones you might develop on your own—send us in this direction, toward Bodhichitta, toward cohesion and coherence, the widening embrace of loving compassion and unselfishness.

Here's something I wrote one spring while living in Sonada Monastery in West Bengal, India, decades ago, which applied then and applies now:

> Wisdom is the ultimate virtue;
> selfless love and compassion in action are the
> ultimate benefit.
> Wisdom is like an inner sun;
> compassion and unselfish service and generosity
> are some of its many rays.
> Spiritual life is the ultimate career and lifestyle.
> Connection is the ultimate skill/talent.
> Contentment is the ultimate wealth.
> Faithful devotion is the hardest thing to fabricate.
> Humility is my own greatest challenge.
> Healing is the finest gift.
> Unselfishness is the central virtue.
> Peacemaking is the ultimate art.
> Selfless love is the supreme miracle.
> Generosity is the ultimate career.
> Moral self-discipline is the ultimate way of life.
> Patient forbearance and acceptance is the hardest practice.
> Constant enthusiastic effort is the greatest
> challenge to maintain.
> Mindful awareness and alert presence of mind
> is the main thing to be cultivated.
> Discriminating wisdom and selfless
> love are the ultimate fruits.

9/11

On September 11, 2001, I was at my farmhouse home in Concord, Massachusetts, working on a Tibetan translation project, when my wife called from work and said, "Turn on the news! A plane hit the World Trade Towers."

I rushed to turn on the TV, just in time to see a plane hit the second Tower and the ensuing fires, people pouring from the building and jumping out of windows, and yellow-clad first responders rushing into the billowing clouds and chaos—images that remain forever seared into my brain. I feel tears welling up, replaying these horrendous scenes in my mind's eye right now.

And then there was the eventual crumbling of one gargantuan tower after another. What a shock! How unreal it all was. At first it seemed like special effects from an action movie. It was so hard to comprehend. *How could this happen*? Was it for real?

I called my wife back. She was worried about our neighbor Diana who worked as a flight attendant and had a six-year-old son in school; we wondered where she was. As it turned out, she was in a plane on the runway at La Guardia that morning, and saw what happened from a distance. We prayed together on the phone, both with words and then in shared silence. I chanted some Tibetan prayers and mantras. We stayed on the line together, finding refuge in our small Sangha of two, inter-meditating for several minutes while observing the chaos in downtown New York City on the television screen. Our shared time across the telephone lines in that sacred manner gave us both solace and refuge, the strength to hang up and try to call loved ones in the Northeast in order to make sure everyone was okay, or as okay as they could be.

I tried to phone New York City, where my family of origin lives. The lines were jammed. My sister the accountant was supposed to be at a financial meeting at 9 a.m. in one of the Trade Towers. She was late commuting from Long Island, so went directly to her office instead; the fortuitous accident of a delayed railway train kept her from tragedy.

Meanwhile, a report came in of another flight hitting the Pentagon. My brother the scientist had been consulting in Washington, DC, that week. I'd later find out he was locked down overnight in a building across the street from the Pentagon immediately after it was hit.

My niece's friend called her from one of the Towers and left a message—the last anyone ever heard from her. Alison talked about that traumatic memory for years. My father worked on Chambers Street for a number of years. I thought about how often I'd visited his office in the Financial District near where the giant Towers fell.

One of my long-term meditation students, Martha, an investment banker, works for one of the large investment firms and lives with her family across the river in New Jersey in a small suburb. Half the men in her town didn't come home that night; too many people around New York City experienced this heart-cracking fact of life. Months later, with tears in her eyes, Martha told me that she'd attended more young men's funerals, every day for weeks, than anyone should have to in an entire lifetime.

My mother told me that the firehouse in her old Long Beach neighborhood stayed virtually empty during the following months. Every single truck and emergency vehicle had raced to Manhattan, and almost none returned. I tell you, since that dreadful day I've had quite a renewed feeling of respect for first responders and all who wear those hats and coats in emergency situations.

So much suffering. It felt like a body blow, an assault to my sensibilities. I've lived all over the world, but I still, like Billy Joel, have a New York state of mind. And I'm just one person, someone who's never lived in the City. Think of the web of suffering that wove its way and rippled across the world that day when those four planes struck. I can still see, branded in my memory, the enormous storm cloud of dust rolling away from the burning Twin Towers, and crowds of all kinds of people who ran away while the yellow jackets ran directly into the heart of the disaster. They plunged in, quickly climbed eighty stories carrying heavy equipment loads, and ultimately died up there—while desperate people leaped out of windows "like birds on fire," as one child said. I remember all of this. How could I forget?

Later that autumn I traveled with His Holiness the Gyalwang Drukpa, who had come from his monastery in Nepal to New York City to teach and receive a humanitarian award from the United Nations. He told me that he wished to visit Ground Zero. When we arrived there, His Holiness immediately entered an intensely spiritual state. We walked slowly, circumambulating the entire holy charnel ground with him leading the way, wrapped up in his maroon and gold robes, fingering his Bodhi seed mala beads. It took hours, covered several large city blocks, and he never spoke the entire time. Later His Holiness told me he felt the numerous spirits thronging there; he was able to liberate some of them.

September 11 was a turning point in American history. It opened the door to a genuine teaching moment—remember the flags, the songs, waving at firemen, the sense of unity? Yet what have we learned? How much has actually changed for the better since then? The Dalai Lama told President Clinton, in a private meeting at the White House in the early 90s, "You are the most powerful man in the world. Every decision you make should be motivated by compassion." *In reality, each of us is the most powerful person in our own world.* We would do well to follow this audacious advice. Like the Talmud teaches, "To save one soul is to save the world."

I think we need to clear our minds and hearts rather than remain stuck on the treadmill of events, unable to move freely under the burden of old, semiconscious habits and conditioning. Each of us can make a significant difference, especially if we pull together. People seem to avoid facing problems they feel they have no idea how to solve. But is there any other thing to do, given what we face today and the world we will ultimately leave to our children and grandchildren? The fate of the world rests in our hands. We would do well to consciously move from shock and trauma to transcendence, along the broad and welcoming avenue of cooperation and collaboration, remaining calm, resolute, resilient, and balanced. Carl Jung once asked, "Does the individual know that he is the makeweight that tips the scales?" I do.

War and Peace

> Peace is not an idea. Peace is not a political movement, not a theory or a dogma. Peace is a way of life: living mindfully in the present moment. . . . It is not a question of politics, but of actions. It is not a matter of improving a political system or even taking care of

homeless people alone. These are valuable but will not alone end war and suffering. We must simply stop the endless wars that rage within. . . . Imagine, if everyone stopped the war in themselves—there would be no seeds from which war could grow.[3]

CLAUDE ANSHIN THOMAS

America has remained at war most of the last sixty years. As I write this sentence, wars rage in more than forty-two countries of the world. The question is not war or peace—a choice we can easily make—but living with war *and* in peace, a far more complicated equation. The military industrial complex and arms industry is certainly complicit in this thorny tangle, which is far more complex than a seeming battle between the forces of good and evil, or for freedom and democracy, as some have put it. "War is a crime. Ask the infantry and ask the dead," said Ernest Hemingway, who had firsthand battlefield experience, was seriously wounded, and was no patsy. If we agree that war is outmoded as a means of resolving conflict in our shrinking yet increasingly complex, pluralistic, post-modern world, we must ask ourselves: What shall we find to replace it? How can we help make this new century one of dialogue rather than one of bloodshed?

My inter-meditating neighbors in Cambridge at Harvard Law School's Project on Negotiation have studied and documented how we can find common ground through putting ourselves in the place of the other and seeing things through their eyes. Their studies in negotiation and conflict resolution tell us to look and listen for what the other side needs and wants, and then look and listen harder—try to learn their story. I apply this all the time. Almost all fears are fears of the unknown; accurate information and familiarization acts as a potent antidote.

The Project on Negotiation suggests that, after striving to understand the other side, we examine our own contribution in maintaining the conflict, no matter what is going on. This is the part we can immediately control. It's an approach that's applicable to situations large and small—from not pushing your partner's buttons to not ignoring what's happening on the other side of the world. It's inter-meditative in that the action of altering our behavior can change the circumstances of others. We must do all that we can, especially since we never truly know what will ultimately make the most difference to create positive change and transformation. All that we can do is to do all that we can.

I am definitely becoming more mellow as the years advance, but will never give up no matter how discouraging corporate corruption, political self-interest, environmental destruction, social injustice, and international terrorism and bloodletting become. I don't see any other way but to continue the good fight, and to make it a peaceful one if possible, throughout all my lifetimes, for the benefit of all that lives and breathes—beyond humanity and its discontents, and including all beings seen and unseen. This requires re-prioritization, inner strength, fortitude, and inter-meditation without ceasing. I believe that together we are up to this vital task.

Kalachakra: The Infinite Wheel of Time

Tibetan Buddhist lamas have a practice to get to this place—of changing and transforming themselves for the betterment of the world. The Kalachakra is an esoteric tantric Buddhist teaching, an empowering initiation, and it links directly to the dichotomy of war and peace and the ancient myth of Shambhala warriors, tantric Bodhisattvas who are like Mahatma Gandhi, a self-described "soldier for peace." Perhaps you've heard of the Dalai Lama giving Kalachakra empowerments—elaborate ritualistic ceremonies for several days, including initiatory rites, chanting, group meditation, and teachings, in large public venues around the world. Kalachakra means "The Infinite Wheel of Time," and the Dalai Lama offers these blessings and teachings, he says, in order to further world peace, tolerance, and harmony. It is extraordinarily efficacious for developing the wisdom of enlightenment and fearless compassion in action necessary in our era.

Such advanced tantric empowerments and consecrations were traditionally given only to smaller groups of carefully trained, prepared, and devoted disciples, although the Kalachakra has sometimes been an exception to that rule. But now most Tibetan lamas have become more open regarding these transmission ceremonies and teachings, and occasionally offer them to large groups of people—Sanghas, congregations, and communities—sometimes as large as two hundred thousand people at once, especially in Asia. Quite an inter-meditation!

The Dalai Lama has helped open the mystic's gate, allowing people to participate just for a blessing or a co-meditative experience, even if they're not advanced Buddhist practitioners. He reiterated this point standing alongside Cardinal Theodore McCarrick, the former Archbishop of Washington, at the 2011 Kalachakra for World Peace in Washington, DC, which I happened to attend. The Dalai Lama often says, perhaps only slightly in jest, that he offers these advanced initiations publicly as a pretext, so people will come and hear the basic Buddhist teachings we all need to take to heart, including the Four Noble Truths and the Eightfold Path to enlightenment. He also speaks of the union of wisdom and compassionate action; he stresses the importance of honesty and kindness over mere external religiosity or parroting prayers and mouthing platitudes. When I attended his thirty-first Kalachakra empowerment, the Dalai Lama told the crowd of over eight thousand:

> We must be twenty-first-century Buddhists, not just ritual faith and belief Buddhists—and live our values in our daily lives, combining the development of modern scientific knowledge with timeless wisdom understanding. Self-discipline is the real answer to bringing about a better society and more peaceful world. Hypocrisy and corruption have nothing to do with religion or the lives of we who strive to practice according to our own traditions.

In other words, he encouraged the crowd, no matter what their faith, to not just talk about inter-meditation but to actually practice it! Again, we are encouraged and even exhorted to go beyond the limits of self-concern and open ourselves up to others and the world. I wrote a prayer for peace on this topic that you might find useful; try it as an inter-meditation in your own practice:

> May wisdom blessings and Buddha nature
> pour through us,
> to the limitless benefit of everybody everywhere.
> May we open to the sufferings of this world,

feeling what others feel, empathizing with
the pain of others and ourselves;
Learning to listen better, to tune in, to sense the subtle
movements and connections and patterns of things,
To open up to sufferings and difficulties of the world,
to be able to better experience them without
suppressing, avoiding or ignoring them,
To better analyze them, understand them, and to
see our way through them, whatever they are,
And assimilate these sufferings, difficulties, tragedies,
and travails as steps on the path,
making even stumbling blocks into stepping stones,
making even shit into fertilizer
on the fields of spiritual awakening and universal unity.
Emaho!—so be it!

INTER-MEDITATION PRACTICE

Voting as an Inter-Meditation Practice

> We are on dangerous ground if we believe that any
> individual, any nation, or any ideology has a monopoly
> on rightness, liberty, and human dignity.
>
> DAG HAMMARSKJÖLD

If the world is the Diamond Net of Indra, then each country
represents an individual jewel in the larger fabric. America
has always seemed a deeply divided nation to me; I've found
that it seems to get worse around election time. For this
reason, I developed an inter-meditation practice specifically
for elections; you can use it during your local or national

elections, or while watching the process of voting in a country across the world:

- First, whoever you vote for, whatever your opinion, take a reflective breath during the act of voting.
- Keep breathing. Breathe through your hopes and fears. Whatever the result, there will be other elections, candidates, and issues to concern yourself with, become informed about, and actively engage in.
- Second, consider and reflect upon things as they are—not just how you think they should be or how they used to be.
- Third, detach yourself from the momentary emotions clouding your thoughts and perceptions, and try to consider historical origins and causes of the issues at hand, as well as the longer-term implications.
- Fourth, remember to devote yourself to healing body and spirit, individually and collectively. To transform the world, you must first transform yourself.
- Occupy the spirit! Don't leave it to the 1%—the lamas, swamis, bishops, and popes.
- Remember to be joyful while you're at it. Life ain't much fun if you take yourself too seriously.

Start by looking and listening while you breathe; become calm and clear, and stay aware. Awareness is curative. For example, if you feel the damaging influence of religious intolerance and partisanship on a larger scale, you should direct your awareness to any evidence of dogmatism and fanaticism in yourself—not just in your own heart, but also in your home, neighborhood, office, schools, and place of worship as well. Wishing for these forms of bias to merely vanish won't do the trick; you have to work to dispel your own prejudices and narrow-minded ways of thinking; then you can change the world around you. There is an "us," but there isn't really a "them." United we sit, divided we fall, as an inter-meditator might say.

We Are the Ancestors of Generations to Come

We live in volatile, complicated times, yet we can find middle ground amid the welter of candidates, information, and opinions. To loosen my own attachment to opinions, I work on becoming less judgmental and invested in my particular views, although I certainly do have them. The Buddhist teaching on the dream-like, changeable, and contingent nature of reality comes in handy here.

But if it's all like an illusion or dream, why should we care at all? Because there's a qualitative difference between a good dream and a nightmare. Even if you know your child is dreaming, don't you wake her up and comfort her from a nightmare? It helps to remember the illusion-like nature of life, but its painful disappointments feel real enough.

We need to recognize that we're all interwoven. We need to get more involved, educate ourselves, talk to our friends and teachers, and *then* vote. Then you can participate in the election with your conscious inter-meditation—your intentional action can then contribute to impacting the lives of hundreds, maybe millions. There's no point in complaining about politics if one doesn't take the trouble to vote. I myself am lobbying full time for enlightenment.

Inevitably, the best candidate (according to your view) sometimes won't win. When that happens, please don't just give up and check out, sit back, and resolve to watch the world go off course. Get back into it the best way you can. We are the ancestors of the generations to come; it is up to us what they shall inherit, and we must do our damnedest not to make it harder for them through our blindness, apathy, and selfishness.

When all else fails, why not repeat my prayer penned on the cusp of the new millennium, which many of my Dharma students use every day:

Millennium Prayer
May all beings everywhere,
with whom we are inseparably interconnected,
and who want and need the same as we do;
May all be awakened, enlightened, healed
and comforted, fulfilled, and free.
May there be peace in this world,
and an end to war, violence, poverty,
injustice and oppression,
And may we all together complete the spiritual journey.
Homage to the innate Great Perfection,
the Buddha within each of us;
May all realize and actualize that.

Extra! Extra! Inter-Meditating with the News

As a citizen of this planet, especially during election times, I feel obliged and motivated to tune in to the news. I'm not a hermit, after all—I'm a lama, teacher, poet, and spiritual leader. I usually find the news so repetitive or mindless that I just skim the headlines, wishing I could find a "Good News Newspaper" somewhere. It seems that modern media focuses so much on suffering, greed, corruption, and tragedy—we can easily become discouraged or even depressed by it all. Also, the biased slant of each of the media outlets is often so obvious it can tarnish our trust-factor.

Sometimes a "news fast" is in order. I occasionally prescribe a few days of "no news is good news" to myself or people who are too addicted to being tuned in every hour to all that media noise. We need not become news junkies or experts to stay informed. I didn't invent this practice, of course. Shortly before his death, Joseph Campbell, the world's foremost authority on mythology, told Bill Moyers in an interview,

> You must have a room or a certain hour or so a day
> when you don't know what was in the newspapers that
> morning, you don't know who your friends are, you
> don't know what you owe anybody, you don't know
> what anybody owes to you. This is a place where you
> can experience and bring forth what you are and what
> you might be. This is the place of creative incubation.
> At first you may find that nothing happens there. But
> if you have (such) a sacred place and use it, something
> eventually will happen.[4]

Remember what seventeenth-century French mathematician, physicist, inventor, and philosopher Blaise Pascal said: "All man's troubles come from not knowing how to sit still in one room."

Because we can't always take a break from media or other electronic distractions, we can remember to breathe, summon pure intent, and meditate with the world *using* our newspapers, televisions, and handheld devices. We can actually become fully present with the grief and suffering that we see, just sitting with it, prayerfully, reverently, soulfully—open to responding and even taking action, when appropriate. As you watch the news, try this mantra: "Things are not what they seem to be; nor are they otherwise." This mindbender comes from the third-century Buddhist Lankavatara Sutra, but it's as pertinent today as it was millennia ago. Chewing on such a conundrum can help us break out of our habitual thinking and dualistic, conceptual framework. When it comes to the news, this mantra reminds us to think outside of the box, and that everything that seems certain can be questioned. It's also subject to change.

As you cheer or rant at the talking heads, remember that all assertions can be logically undermined—even the one I've just made. Once we realize this, we have the opportunity to loosen our tight grip on our own precious opinions, which, we must remember, arise mainly from our own picture of things. Everything we think is derived from the story we have concocted for ourselves or have been told by others.

It would behoove all of us to remember the ancient, yet timeless, spiritual adage: *If we know the whole story, there's a lot less to be angry about.* In fact, this approach has become one of my favorite practices in any situation, not just when encountering upsetting news. Essentially, we need to learn to love more genuinely, unselfishly, soulfully, and with warm compassion in our hearts—for that is why we're here.

If I watch too much mainstream news and world reporting, I often feel down and even despondent. Yet, whenever I meet a young person, I begin to feel great hope and optimism, as their enthusiasm and idealism tweaks mine and, as it were, *phowas* me into a higher level of Bodhisattva consciousness and service-oriented activity. It works both ways, you see; the more we give, the more we get, as everyone says but few truly comprehend. The more I ask for help from the younger generations, the more help they seem to receive themselves. This is truly a reciprocal inter-meditation that comes from mutual need, supply and demand. On my part, just being able to ask helps level the field and get me out of my own way, regardless of how my request is answered. It's like praying: the benefit is already there from the get-go; what happens later is secondary. A Bodhisattva can't maintain and further his or her practice without sharing and passing it on to others, as wanted and needed, without proselytizing. I receive significant infusions of hope, energy, and strength in return for whatever little I can contribute.

Enlightened Citizenship

So when we vote, when we watch the news, what qualities do we look for in our leaders? How do we want to behave as citizens ourselves? The pioneer in the field of leadership studies Warren Bennis writes:

> Today the people who can afford to are increasingly retreating into their own electronic castles, working at home and communicating with the world via computers, screening their calls on answering machines, ordering in movies for their VCRs, food for their microwave ovens, and trainers for their bodies, keeping the world at bay with advanced

security systems. They refuse to acknowledge what is happening—and the costs to our whole society of what is happening—to those who lack their resources. Trend spotters call this cocooning but it looks more like terminal egocentricity.[5]

Terminal egocentricity is the opposite of inter-meditation. When people become stressed and traumatized, they withdraw. They hunker down in solitude or within their family-cocoons. The crazy busy times we live in cause us to lose touch with others, except in superficial ways like via social media. This isn't inter-meditation. If we become fearful isolationists we lose our sense of community—just when we need it the very most, for the sake of ourselves and the world. This is true of individuals and nations alike—isolation is a terrible thing, and isolationists generally make poor citizens.

We need each other in order to make spiritual connections and consciously evolve. In Judaism, we gather *minyans* (groups of ten or more) to increase the power of prayer. Jesus said, "Whenever two or more are gathered in my name, I am there also," affirming the transformative power of collective spiritual energy. This means losing one's own selfish preoccupations and taking up the occupations and concerns of the world, like Albert Schweitzer and Mother Teresa's joy in service.

And it's not just spiritual teachers who hold this opinion. Numerous political leaders assert this, as well. Take Václav Havel, leader of Czechoslovakia's Velvet Revolution, which proved to be the most nonviolent overthrow of a totalitarian government in centuries. He writes:

We seem to have lost our certainty that the universe, nature, existence, our own lives, are works of creation that have meaning and purpose. I am not an expert on religion, but it seems to me that the major faiths have much more in common than they are willing to admit. They share a basic point of departure—that this world and our existence are not freaks of chance but rather part of a mysterious, yet integral act. And they share a kind of catalogue of moral imperatives that this mysterious act implies.

Perhaps a way out of our current bleak situation could be found by searching for what unites the various religions—a purposeful search for common moral principles. With these we might cultivate human inter-existence while cultivating the planet on which we live, suffusing it with the spirit of this ethical common ground, what I would call the common spiritual and minimal condition.[6]

Consider the Vimalakirti Sutra, a Buddhist teaching about Vimala, an enlightened businessman who lived during the time of Buddha. Although he worked as a businessman, Vimala was wiser than all the monks and nuns of the time. *They* came to *him* for guidance, as he had the final word on ultimate wisdom even though he was "just a layman." In those days, "just a layman" meant something particular. Laypeople—householders—were expected to support the monks and nuns—the "real" practitioners. I don't think we can think that way anymore; we each must undertake this journey, if and when we feel called. We ourselves must become the genuine practitioners and citizens—not just monks and nuns, government officials and law officers, schoolteachers, or people who protect our country and even fight wars for us. And if we look around we see this idea manifesting in everything from soup kitchens and grassroots organizations to crowd-funding, Occupy Wall Street, and even Wisdom 2.0, a community that utilizes the Internet for connection, not isolation.

Om Mani Padme Hung

Om Mani Padme Hung is probably the mantra most often associated with Tibetan Buddhism. It is the mantra of the compassionate Buddha—the archetype or embodiment of loving compassion, wisdom, and unconditional love. Essentially it means "the jewel is in the lotus" or "the Buddha is within us." Chanting this mantra, we practice transforming our attitude, cultivating unconditional empathic love and compassion, and ultimately awakening our enlightened mind.

My own root guru Kalu Rinpoche constantly chanted *Om Mani Padme Hung*. Wherever he went, inside his Sonada Monastery in Darjeeling or when traveling, day or night, Rinpoche always had his mala beads in hand, fingers counting off the Mani mantras one at a time, accumulating them by the millions, year after year. People around him say that, over time, he mindfully recited more than three trillion Mani mantras—but who's counting? The Buddha of Compassion, Avalokita (also called Chenrayzig), was his *istadevata*, his *yidam* (indwelling deity/sublime archetype) or divine identity, and his actions were entirely congruent with that sacred ideal image and grand Bodhisattva value system.

Rinpoche seemed to have a heart-shaped face, wrinkled and lined like a roadmap. Although he suffered from tuberculosis,

Rinpoche seemed the embodiment of loving-kindness and compassion, patience and humility, generosity and kindness, every single day—just like Avalokitesvara Bodhisattva. Rinpoche and countless other Tibetan Buddhist teachers always emphasize this fundamental virtue of warmhearted compassion; no matter what mystical and profound teaching there may be, we still have to walk the Earth with each other, respect each other, and get along. That's why we chant *Om Mani Padme Hung;* repeating the mantra brings us closer to unconditional love and compassion. We desperately need this compassion-generating beam or healing wavelength in our violent and competitive times—for our personal development as well as for universal evolution. It is the core of my own practice and path.

Chanting is such a powerful practice because it involves the body, mind, and spirit; it utilizes intention, concentration, breath, heartbeat, chest, lungs, voice, tongue, and mouth—our entire being. And when we chant together, the resonance, blending, and synergy are quite powerful. So as we practice chanting, our voice becomes the voice of the Divine, the Buddha, Avalokita—the manifest expression of unconditional love and universal compassion.

Try it. Do it with a friend. Or better yet, an adversary!

INTER-MEDITATION PRACTICE
Entering the Sacred Dimension of Buddha Avalokita

As you chant *Om Mani Padme Hung:*

- Visualize all beings as one body—receptive, gentle, nonviolent, harmonious, and balanced.

- As if your mind were made of light rays, infuse that one body with blessings.
- Radiate loving-kindness and benevolence, and allow it to come up, come in, come out, and flow through.
- Radiate compassion, feeling what others feel and being moved to help, and allow it to come through.
- Radiate empathy and sympathetic joy, and allow it to well up and come through.
- Radiate equanimity and dispassionate objectivity, and allow it to come in, to come out, and to enrich itself at and around your inner center, your character core.
- As you do this, the barrier between self and others will dissolve as you enter into the sacred dimension of Buddha Avalokita, great compassion, who naturally sees others as just like himself and treats them so, just like he would his own cherished children.

We can study chants, prayers, scriptures, and sutras. We can talk about, memorize, appreciate, and recite them. But it won't amount to much if we don't internalize, embody, manifest, and actually live it. Essentially, we need to learn to love more genuinely, unselfishly. When asked the purpose of life, I've heard the Dalai Lama say: "To be happy and help others be happy." I'm good with that.

The purpose of life:
To be happy and
help others be happy.

When I am alone meditating in the mountain wilderness, I am never alone. All my gurus and the Buddhas and Bodhisattvas are with me, blessing, inspiring, guiding, and protecting.

JETSUN MILAREPA

10

Neither Within nor Without

One-ing—Realizing our Inseparability
from Nature and Our Higher Selves

Walking

Sometimes we go for a walk in the rain just to go for a walk in
the rain. And sometimes we experience an epiphany. All of a
sudden, as if out of the blue, it suddenly feels as if we're one
with everything, directly sensing nature—every sound, scent,
and fresh crystalline raindrop. Imagine if we could experience
that kind of heart opening and rapture permeating our entire
life and the lives of everyone around us, in every moment?
That's what inter-meditating with nature can do for us—utterly
uniting the inner with the outer while awakening the Buddhaness within.

One of my favorite inter-meditations is my morning walk with
my dog. I inter-meditate with her and we inter-meditate with nature,
spontaneously engaging in what I lovingly call "conscious drifting as
co-meditation." I relish the fallow-mind time, when I'm free to allow
all of my plans and preoccupations, defenses and barriers, to fall

away. The Italians have a wonderful phrase for it—*dolce far niente*, meaning "sweet doing nothing." Henry David Thoreau described his four-hour walks through the woods near Walden Pond like this:

> So we saunter toward the Holy Land, till one day the sun shall shine more brightly than ever he has done, shall perchance shine into our minds and hearts, and light up our whole lives with a great awakening light, as warm and serene and golden as on a bankside in autumn.[1]

I think of Thoreau as I try to make my daily dog pilgrimages journeys without goal, as the Tibetans say. Often I stumble upon a treasure, perhaps a hawk feather or entire bird's nest, or special shells on the beaches I haunt. I might bring home that gift and put it on my home altar or in our garden. Sometimes the treasure knows just who it's meant for, and I'm just the messenger and delivery boy on its way to that third person—a friend or student. What a delight!

Nature worship is one of the oldest and original forms of spirituality, including pantheism, shamanism, and sun worship. We are indubitably part and parcel of nature, and nature is part of us. Who can intelligently argue with that? My kind of sauntering through the holy land of my own neighborhood, communing with other dog people and their fine furry companions along the way—seemingly at random but doubtlessly in tune with some higher, dog-deity-like purpose—allows me to journey from my head to my heart and beyond. This relational inter-meditation naturally leads to love and local stewardship. Moreover, it can create a sacred awareness to help us find our true center, being temporarily upstream from mere doing and the social roles we play and titles we wear—a genuine spiritual presence.

We return to nature—solid, reliable, and welcoming—as we commune with the changing seasons, trees, animals, oceans, and sky. Inter-meditating with the good earth, we experience precious and poignant poetry, mystery, elusiveness, sorrow, and the raw impermanence of this gritty, ephemeral, and dream-like world.

The Neuroscience of Conscious Drifting

It turns out that neuroscientists and psychologists are picking up on the idea of conscious drifting as well. "Well-Being Trails" have sprung up all over Luxemburg, Sweden, France, and Finland; sponsored by mental health services, the trails include signposts with psychological prompts to enhance relaxation.

According to Kalevi Korpela, a psychology professor at the University of Tampere,

> When people recover from stress, the first things to change are physiological: less muscle tension, lower blood pressure, and slower pulse. The first exercises in the Well-Being Trail, which the walkers can engage in guided by the signposts, boost physical recovery. The exercises are about relaxation techniques and observing the natural environment . . . the signposts ask the walkers to identify their mood and to talk about it aloud to the surrounding nature. After the body and the emotions have changed, the walker's ability to concentrate and attention improve.[2]

Body-mind-spirit masters have employed these integrative inner-sciences and sacred techniques throughout the ages, usually focusing on the breath. Tibetan energy yoga has helped me to loosen the knots in my psyche and unfreeze some of my defense mechanisms, rendering me much more open and permeable to feelings of all kinds, especially empathic compassion.

Some modern scientists also encourage these type of walks. In her book *A Mind for Numbers*, industrial and systems engineer Barbara Oakley asserts that taking walks can help us open up to what she terms the "diffuse mode"—the opposite of problem-solving focus. It's what we might call an open mind—a readiness for inspiration and connection:

> Walking spurs creativity in many fields; a number of famous writers, for example, including Jane Austen, Carl Sandburg, and Charles Dickens, found inspiration during their frequent long walks.
>
> Once you are distracted from the problem at hand, the diffuse mode has access and can begin pinging about in its big-picture way to settle on a solution. After your break, when you return to the problem at hand, you will often be surprised at how easily the solution pops into place. Even if the solution doesn't appear, you will often be further along in your understanding. It can take a lot of hard, focused mode work beforehand, but the sudden, unexpected solution that emerges from the diffuse mode can make it feel almost like the "Ah-hah!" mode.[3]

Writing for the *New York Times,* Gretchen Reynolds reports on a study by the Heriot-Watt University in Edinburgh and the University of Edinburgh in which portable EEGs were attached to the heads of twelve young adults who were then sent to walk through the city and a park:

> When the volunteers made their way through the urbanized, busy areas, particularly the heavily trafficked commercial district at the end of their walk, their brain-wave patterns consistently showed that they were more aroused and frustrated than when they walked through the parkland, where brain-wave readings became more meditative.
>
> While traveling through the park, the walkers were mentally quieter.
>
> Which is not to say that they weren't paying attention, said Jenny Roe, a lecturer at Heriot-Watt's School of the Built Environment, who oversaw the study. "Natural environments still engage" the brain, she said, but the attention demanded "is effortless. It's called involuntary attention in psychology. It holds our attention while at the same time allowing scope for reflection," and providing a palliative to the nonstop attentional demands of typical, city streets.[4]

So once we reach that place of mental quiet—of letting go, of relaxed openness and clarity—how do we turn it into an inter-meditation and "flow with the go," as I like to say?

Natural Meditation: Sky-gazing, Cloud Watching, Fog Collecting

My former English pupil, the enlightened master Gyalwang Drukpa XII, once told me, "Everything must be meditated. Everything can be appreciated and even enjoyed, as it is, beyond judgment of good and bad."

These practices don't have to be formal or difficult or exotic; bird-watching is an excellent secular example of natural mindfulness inter-meditation in action. You can just look at and label a bird, "Oh my! There's an ivory-billed woodpecker!" or you can mindfully arrive at a meditative place *with* the bird—no separation between you and it. Just breathing the bird in through all the senses and mind-gates, and breathing it out until flow overtakes your habitual consciousness. People have inter-meditated like this for ages—notable examples include haiku poet Basho, St. Francis of Assisi, John Muir, John Cage, and Annie Dillard. You can do it, too.

Or maybe birds aren't your thing? My friend Susan calls her garden her church. Kneeling in the sun, beneath the vast cathedral of the trees, clouds, and sky: what could be more sublime, more sacrosanct, all-embracing, and worth surrendering into? I myself like to simply visit gardens and inter-meditate with them. Try it yourself sometime: inhale; inter-meditate with the flowers, vegetables, sunlight, loamy earth, birdsong, and bugs; pay attention to your relationship and connection with each of these things. Feel it growing up around us and through us. Ultimately, we'll all end up as compost.

Where's the separation? When you bite into a freshly picked tomato still warm from the sunshine, where does the tomato end and you begin? This is one-ing—incandescent being while seeing through separateness.

I Speak for the Trees

I'm not much of a green thumb, but I consider this world my garden. How gorgeous it is! How homey and delightful. Maharajji Neem Karoli Baba once said, "You are all like flowers in God's garden, blossoming in their own time and various ways." The giant weeping willow outside my bedroom window always takes me beyond the boundaries of my small self into the essence of Big Self, of inter-meditation. Its swaying arms and trailing, tangled branches remind me of multi-armed Himalayan goddesses, guardians and dakinis, while the North Atlantic winds and other seasonal elements naturally awaken all sorts of wild dance and natural theatrics.

Everything must be meditated.

As a boy, I loved to read about the Ents, the wise tree-elders of Middle Earth, in J.R.R. Tolkien's fabulous *Lord of the Rings*. Trees carry an immense and intensely spiritual energy as any shaman will tell you and any meditator should know. There are the dryads, or tree nymphs, of Greek antiquity, the Druids who sought out oak groves as places of worship, and the willow tree sacred to the Egyptian god Osiris. Throughout history we have been tree-worshippers, tree-huggers, and tree-sitters like the activist Julia "Butterfly" Hill who lived in a fifteen-hundred-year-old redwood to prevent loggers from cutting it down. And of course, the Buddha achieved enlightenment beneath the sacred fig tree we know as the Bodhi Tree, which sheltered and shaded him from rain and sun.

I mentioned my fascination with trees to one of my Dharma friends, a learned Catholic and a Zen master named Father Michael Holleran. He told me about attending a meditation retreat at the Dominican Retreat Centre in Dublin, on the site of the eighth-century St. Maelruain's monastery. It was a pilgrimage spot for a thousand years. There is a huge, wooded walled garden dating from the eighteenth century, with some absolutely magnificent trees. The director of the center had named an enormous 250-year-old walnut tree the "Sixth Zen Patriarch," referring to the seminal Zen master of ancient China, Hui Neng, the same master who once wrote:

> The tree of Perfect Wisdom is originally no tree.
> Nor has the bright mirror any frame.
> Buddha Nature is forever clear and pure.
> Where is there any dust?[5]

Like Hui Neng, haiku master Basho took his co-meditation inspiration from trees:

> Learn about a pine tree from a pine tree,
> and about a bamboo plant from a bamboo plant.[6]

Dogs, Not Dogma: Inter-Meditating with Animals

We can get to that inter-meditative place of "no me, no you" with animals too, such as our pets. In *The Essence of the Heart Sutra*, His Holiness the Dalai Lama writes:

> According to Buddhism, compassion is an aspiration, a state of mind, wanting others to be free from suffering. It's not passive—it's not empathy alone—but rather an empathetic altruism that actively strives to free others

from suffering. Genuine compassion must have both wisdom and loving-kindness. That is to say, one must understand the nature of the suffering from which we wish to free others (this is wisdom), and one must experience deep intimacy and empathy with other sentient beings (this is loving-kindness).[7]

This empathetic altruism is a key to inter-meditation, and I've found that sometimes it's easier to practice this with our pets or animals than with people. One of my favorite mantras is "May I be the person my dog thinks I am." Imagine if you could live up to that kind of openness and trust!

Remember heart rate variability and coherence in chapter 5? We saw that mothers and babies could sync up their heartbeats just by focused attention. The same scientist—Rollin McCraty—also applied this research to animals, too. McCraty conducted an experiment with his fifteen-year-old son, Josh, and his dog, Mabel. McCraty used two Holter (electrocardiogram) recorders, and fitted one on the dog and the other on the boy. In his paper "The Energetic Heart: Bioelectromagnetic Interactions within and between People," McCraty describes the results:

> We have also found that a type of heart rhythm entrainment or synchronization can occur in interactions between people and their pets [through] . . . an experiment looking at the heart rhythms of my son Josh (15 years old at the time of the recording) and his

May I be the person my dog thinks I am.

dog, Mabel. Here we used two Holter recorders, one
fitted on Mabel and the other on Josh. We synchronized
the recorders and placed Mabel in one of our labs. Josh
then entered the room and sat down and proceeded to
consciously feel feelings of love towards Mabel. Note the
synchronous shift to increased coherence in the heart
rhythms of both Josh and Mabel as Josh consciously feels
love for his pet.[8]

Once again, scientists have demonstrated something we know
intuitively—that there's a deep, perhaps even sacred evolutionary connection between people and their pets—a genuine
convergence well suited for inter-meditation.

Where the Wild Things Are

The "mergitating" lessons of inter-meditation aren't limited to
pets or even domesticated animals. Ever since an earthquake
destroyed Yushu, China, killing more than three thousand people,
Tibetan Buddhists have engaged in a practice of "mercy release"
by rescuing tiny shrimp from the mud near Batang River.[9] Their
inter-meditation with the shrimp and the river clears the karma for
those who have died, as well as themselves. This practice is based
on the Buddhist teachings of the centenarian Dzogchen master
Chatral Rinpoche in Nepal, a lifelong vegetarian. He writes:

Consider your own body and with this as an example,
Avoid doing anything that might bring harm to others.
Make every effort not to kill any living creature,
Birds, fish, deer, cattle, and even tiny insects,

And strive instead to save their lives,
Offering them protection from every fear.
The benefit of doing so is beyond imagining.[10]

My friend Amelia recalls Zen teacher John Daido Loori pointing to a bullfrog sitting perfectly still in the shallows near the Esopus Creek in Upstate New York. Loori told Amelia that everything she needs to know about meditation she could learn from watching that bullfrog. I don't especially love such totalizing generalizations, but perhaps something similar could be said for inter-meditation, co-meditation, and relational meditations of all kinds. "Leave it as it is, and rest your weary heart and mind," my Dzogchen master Nyoshul Khenpo taught me. Birds do it, fish do it, frogs do, too, and so can you.

As psychologist Barbara Fredrickson puts it, "communication is a single act performed by two brains." She suggests we "think about the way birds fly together or fish swim in schools. We don't like to think of ourselves as animals, but we are. And when we are really attuned to another person, we take part in this almost imperceptible dance. Like a school of fish, we're joining up and swimming along together, and this can bring a powerful sense of oneness."[11]

The Dalai Lama says something that corresponds with this perspective:

When I consider the lack of cooperation in human society, I can only conclude that it stems from ignorance of our interdependent nature. I am often moved by the example of small insects, such as bees. The laws of nature dictate that bees work together in order to survive. As a result, they possess an instinctive sense of social responsibility. They have no constitution, laws, police, religion, or moral training, but because of their nature they labor faithfully together. Occasionally they may fight, but in general the whole colony survives on the basis of cooperation. Human beings, on the other hand, have constitutions, vast legal systems, and police forces; we have religion, remarkable intelligence, and a heart with great capacity to love. But despite our many extraordinary qualities, in actual practice we lag behind those small insects; in some ways, I feel we are poorer than the bees.[12]

INTER-MEDITATION PRACTICE
Sky-Gazing

The methods of inter-meditating with nature are as myriad as bees in the breeze, stars in the heavens, microbes in the human body. One of my favorite inter-meditation practices is sky-gazing. It's a simple yet powerful technique based on one of the core Dzogchen practices. Here is my version:

> Seated with a view of sky or clouds,
> or even just water in a clean bowl,
> close your eyes.
> Inhale deeply, and exhale fully,
> letting totally go.
> Now do it again, twice more.
> (Three is the magic number.)
> Let go, let it all come and go;

let it be.
Just be,
as you are.
Rest naturally and at ease
in your body and mind, heart and soul,
and enjoy the natural state—
or whatever state you seem to be in.

Let body and mind settle in its own place,
its own way,
its own time,
as it is.
Natural breath and energy,
natural flow
let it go,
free from interference, evaluation, or manipulation . . .
and enjoy the joy
of Natural Meditation.

Don't be deceived or seduced by momentary
thoughts and experiences.
Allow all experiences to pass freely, like clouds
in a vast, open sky.
Simply Observe, Allow, and Accept.
Embrace and surrender.
Letting go means letting come and go,
letting be.
This is the essence of inner freedom
and autonomy
within interconnection.

Be still
and know
all is well.
All is as it must be, right
here, right now—
this very moment, the only moment;
this very breath, as if the only breath.
Don't let attention stray elsewhere.
Nothing to figure out, understand,
achieve, track, or remember.
No need to fabricate or contrive;
no need to even meditate.
Simply present, undistracted, at home
and at ease
in the natural state
of innate perfection,
let awareness unfurl
its myriad colors.

Hey, ho!
Buddha's not pretending.
Sitting Buddha is being
Buddha.
Standing Buddha
is Buddha too—duh!

Now slowly open your eyes.
Gently raise your gaze.
Elevate the scope of global,
three-hundred-and-sixty-degree,

sensitive, receptive awareness.
Gaze evenly into the infinite, open sky;
sky-gazing, space-mingling,
infinite-dissolving;
an exercise of natural openness and awareness,
transparency and lucidity
inseparable.
Let go and relax into the vastness of sky—
spacious, nonreactive,
fearless, and agendaless,
unencumbered—luminous.
Ahhh . . .

Space like mind has no beginning or end,
no inside or outside,
no actual form, color, size,
shape, center, or periphery.
This is the gateless gate,
opening into the infinite, magical,
buoyant way of awakefulness.

Let go and relax naturally into spacious openness
and clarity, this pristine awareness
like a transparent eyeball,
allowing thoughts and feelings
to come and go freely,
releasing all experience
into the infinitely fertile
womb of emptiness
from which it never strayed.

Resting at home and at ease
in the sky-like nature
of BuddhaMind,
everything is fine
just as it is
in the lawful unfolding of things:
let go and let be,
at home and at ease
in the natural great perfection,
the Nirvanic peace and bliss
of things left just
as they are.
Emaho!

The Five Elements

Beyond the sky, space, and the infinite openness they metaphorically represent, we can also inter-meditate with any of the five
elements, or, as the Tibetan Buddhists call them, the goddess-
like Five Pure Lights—earth, water, fire, air, and space. These
are the fundamental energies or substratum-like building blocks
of our material world and consensual reality. Each provides a
sacred way to re-connect and co-emerge Buddha nature through
inter-meditation—communing with the oneness beyond our
selfishness and sense of separateness. Co-unity and co-emergence
with the five nature elements is a path to natural mysticism, or
what I call "natural inter-meditation"—not just when we experience ourselves in nature but when we also experience nature
within ourselves. This experience alleviates craving, dissatisfaction, fear, alienation, and feelings of both scarcity and prideful

entitlement—a way to develop clear awareness and interrelate with the natural world.

> The less full of myself I am, the more room there is for another, for others.

Through this practice you can learn to see and love the beauty in the world, and develop the intuitive empathy and compassionate heart that instantly resonates with the hearts of others in mutually reciprocal cycles of connection and loving. In this way, we recognize the Buddhaness and spiritual light shining within us and within everybody around us. It's what I call pure perception and sacred outlook—a way of seeing the Buddha nature, the Divine, the light in all and everything.

Here it is, in a nutshell: *The less full of myself I am, the more room there is for another, for others.*

Some people like to inter-meditate with the fire element, perhaps with a candle or their fireplace, or even a bonfire or funeral pyre—looking, merging, blazing up, and being consumed just like the wood and the ashes. Inter-meditating with air and wind can take the form of working with your breath or practicing with the breezes. To inter-meditate with earth you could try hiking, mountain climbing, snorkeling, spelunking, or tending to a potted plant. It's all about intent. You can do it anytime; it just takes stopping, stilling your heart and mind, breathing out, and feeling a physical sensation in your body to ground and center your experience, and then re-entering the sacred, the holy now, just as it is.

The natural element that I most often inter-meditate with is water—what Tibetans call the goddess Mamaki. One recent morning I sat by a small waterfall in the woods near my house, listening to the muffled roar of water and letting my thoughts and sensations wash away. I could hardly remember my name—not that I needed it at that moment. Like a mantra or visualization or even breathing exercise, it had become redundant, for the water was meditating for me—regular as waves or cradle-rocking, untying the knots in my chakras and inner energy channels—comforting, incessant, and effortless.

As the Hindu saint Ramakrishna of Calcutta explained, "Imagine a limitless expanse of water: above and below, before and behind, right and left, everywhere there is water. In that water is placed a jar filled with water. There is water inside the jar and water outside, but the jar is still there. The 'I' is the jar."[13]

Dissolving that jar is inter-meditation.

Our practice of inter-meditation and realization that outer and inner are one and the same relates to the Tibetan Buddhist teaching of *Drala*, which means "no other" or nothing separate from the mind and its subjectivity. We don't often hear about the Drala principle these days, but Chögyam Trungpa Rinpoche—before his death in 1987—spoke regularly on this esoteric, or secret, teaching. Tibetans consider Drala as invisible yet tangible energy forces. We can personally experience these energies, ally with them, and even coerce them into higher service if we manifest an enlightened and truly selfless spiritual life. Our connection with Drala expresses itself in how we relate to the natural world, others, and ourselves—how we see them, and how we treat them: for example, by naturally practicing

Leave it as it is, and rest your weary heart and mind.

compassion, love, generosity, and empathy—all fruits of inter-meditation.

Tibetan teachings traditionally divide Drala into two parts: inner and outer. Inner refers to those inter-meditative efforts we make primarily with ourselves; outer means those we make for the benefit of others. The inner-directed goal of a spiritual life is to realize and achieve our innate purity and perfection. Through inner work we reach the truth, wisdom, clarity, and peace of mind inherent in each of us. The outer work expresses itself in how we experience and relate to others. When we inter-meditate with one soul, we inter-meditate with the whole world. This is ultimate spiritual connection.

We serve God and truth by serving each other. In time, we realize that the sacred space within us is just as vast as that which is outside of us. There is no other, only us, only this, beyond words and ideas, names and forms, including concepts. Don't just try to meditate in order to go inside or get away from it all. *We* is the new I. Easy to remember, harder to assimilate and make our own, yet not impossible. Join the we-volution!

Inter-meditation is the antidote to solipsism, selfishness, and narcissism, as well as the remedy for our fragmented and scattered lives. Cultivating an inter-meditative mindset can expand our ordinary framework until everything becomes grist for the spiritual mill and we no longer need to exclude or avoid certain experiences. Everything assumes its rightful place, proportion, size, and significance in the cosmic mandala, the great hologram of adventitious being. As we inter-meditate, we begin to see that there are no gaps in the constant flow of natural connection. We find a way of intentional spiritual presence and meaningful connection with all sentient beings—those we love, those we hate, those we don't even know, and those that haven't been born yet. Inter-meditation brings us back to the fundamental Lojong aphorism: *Join whatever you meet with awareness practice, so even the unexpected becomes the path.*

I recently read a passage in the Garrison Institute's newsletter that made a lasting impact on me: "Harold Searles, a prescient researcher in the early 1970s, found that ecological deterioration evokes unconscious anxiety, consistent with the history of an individual's ego development. What may look like general apathy is based on largely unconscious defenses against these anxieties."[14] Psychologist Renee Lertzman's recent research takes this concept even further; she notes that our response to our troubled environment resembles melancholia: "experiencing loss and mourning without a clear object."[15] It becomes increasingly difficult to make any reasonable distinction between outer and inner experience. Inter-meditation can repair our rift with the natural world; just as we connect and commingle with the people we love, so can we be *within* and not just *in* nature.

We *are* within nature, just as nature is within us. We are it and it is us. Hard to argue with that. We have an impact on our natural environment, whether through stewardship, exploitation, disregard, or destruction. Likewise, the state of our environment affects us considerably—from the cycles of the moon to hurricanes, tsunamis, plagues, pandemics, and other disasters, to being the source of our food and drink, light and energy, as well as other physical and more intangible invisible forms of sustenance. I believe strongly that we need to see beyond our small selves—beyond selfishness, short-term self-interest, and the separationist mentality—and learn to identify with our whole world. Where would we be without it?

This is not just some New Age line of reasoning. We're all indisputably interconnected in innumerable ways, and through countless lifetimes. As the early American naturalist John Muir put it, "I only went out for a walk and finally concluded to stay out till sundown, for going out, I found was really going in." Again, in the ultimate analysis, we can't differentiate between inner and outer; likewise, the distinctions between heaven and hell, great and small, superior and inferior, are merely conceptual.

Just before I was about to introduce the Dalai Lama to a stadium gathering in 2006 at my alma mater, the State University of New York at Buffalo, he took me aside and said something to me that changed my life. I immediately wrote it down to the best of my recollection; his words comprised such a striking, personal, and unusually pointed directive from him. He said:

> I only went out for a walk and finally concluded to stay out till sundown, for going out, I found was really going in.

This is not an age where mere self-growth and development or faith, meditation, and prayer are sufficient for any individual, but those must inevitably be balanced by active social engagement and compassionate actions. No one can do it alone; we need each other to become enlightened, to develop the loving-kindness and compassion implied in that spiritual realization. You should be more active on campuses and in corporate settings and not just in

spiritual centers, churches, and retreats. I see secular
ethics and contemplative education as a crucial part of
the future if this is to become a century of dialogue rather
than, like the past century, one of violence and bloodshed.

Being a long-time meditator and meditation teacher, too, these
words came as a real eye-opener for me, especially coming from
the Dalai Lama of Tibet, master meditator, philosopher, peace-
maker, human rights activist, and visionary. I took his message
of dialogue and social-divine activism to heart and embarked on
a new mission: to share the spiritual possibilities of meditating
with others—not just alone, but with everyone and everything
through inter-meditation. That's why I wrote this book: to foster
intentional spiritual presence, collective awakening, and meaningful connection to all sentient beings—ones we love, ones we
hate, and ones who haven't been born yet. I did it to encourage
awakening together and communing with, and to present inter-
meditation as a powerful means of doing all of this and more
integrating of enlightened awareness into daily life.

Inter-meditation manifests in this heart-to-heart, soulful
interconnection that transcends description. As we've seen, it's
an experience of the Divine in its natural habitat, not only in
some holy house of worship, monastery, ashram, or retreat center. This integral and well-rounded process includes all people
and animals, trees and flowers, birds and fish, bugs and bar-
nacles, as well as the (so-called) inanimate universe. As a tantric
Tibetan text sings, "The whole universe is my body, all beings
my mind." That phrase struck me so profoundly in my late
teens that I enrolled in the Bodhisattva's quest for altruistic
enlightenment—leading me to my teachers and my life as a

lama and practical mystic. I believe that countless other people have encountered some sort of similar epiphany—and if they haven't, it's waiting there for them, kind of like Dorothy's ruby slippers in *The Wizard of Oz*, just waiting to be clicked together at the heels. The Higher Power, the greater power, the awesome and world-shaking true inner power is always there. *None are deficient in inner wisdom and truth though not everyone seems compelled to connect to it.* We can all fan that inner spark into a flame that burns away all veils of delusion, existential angst, suffering, and confusion. This is the promise of enlightened and liberating, transformative spirituality.

Milarepa, Tibet's greatest yogi and poet, sings:

> When I am in retreat in my mountain cave,
> in the high Himalayan wilderness above the snowline,
> clad only in pure white Indian cotton robes
> and samaya vows,
> warm with the heat of samadhi,
> my Father-guru Marpa the Translator
> and all the root and lineage gurus,
> Buddhas and Bodhisattvas are with me.
> In spiritual practice this mountain meditator
> is never alone.[16]

Some Buddhist scriptures say that it takes countless eons for a Bodhisattva to reach enlightenment, but that's just one way of telling the story. Many have awakened in one lifetime; Milarepa is an example. The truth is, it only takes one moment of awakening—as the Zen Buddhists say, one moment of *satori*—to obliterate the darkness of eons. It's just like switching on the

Appendix I

Surya's Byte-Sized Buddhas

Thirty-Three Potent Aphorisms

1. Inter-meditation is shared spirituality beyond the polarities and dichotomies of self and other.

2. Fools seek from afar; the wise find truth beneath their feet.

3. When me, myself, and I get together in inter-meditation, no one and no thing is excluded.

4. I think you have to love first and see second.

5. Don't just let go, let come and go: let be.

6. The size of our heart directly correlates to the scope of our attention, receptivity, and intentions.

7. If you are not here now, you won't be there then.

8. Take a breath; you deserve it.

9. It's all about the *we*-ness, not just the penis or the vagina.

10. Don't overlook the profundity of ordinary people and everyday experiences and relationships.

11. It is always now. It's now or never, as always.

12. Life is chronic, but death is not necessarily final or even fatal.

13. To understand both the Big Self and the small self is to see beyond the limits of our egos and recognize that there is no separation between us and the rest of the cosmos.

14. Everything is subjective.

15. Just simply be lucidly aware, mindful rather than mindless.

16. Nowness-awareness is the authentic and unfabricated Buddha within.

17. One moment of brilliant illumination dispels the darkness of centuries.

18. Nobody can do it alone. Believe me, I've tried!

19. We need others to help get enlightened, for developing empathic compassion is as necessary and wise as wisdom itself.

20. Practice is perfect, and we just do it, just as practice *does* us, in the tides of spiritual activity.

21. We are like the mystics and holy ones, gods and goddesses walking on this altar of the earth—we're the ones we've been waiting for, so let's not waste time. Let's usher in the Kingdom of Heaven now.

22. We're all going to die, eventually; but who is going to truly *live?*

23. In this mysterious world, knowing takes second place to trusting, allowing, and flowing.

24. There definitely comes a time when we have to take it off the cushion or yoga mat, out of the therapist's office, home from the church, temple, or classroom, and into the real world where it truly counts. This is where the rubber meets the road on the spiritual path.

25. Fear of the dark can keep us from the light.

26. Essentially, we need to learn to love more genuinely, unselfishly, soulfully, and with warm compassion in our hearts—for that is why we're here.

27. We serve God and truth by serving each other. In time, we realize that the sacred space within us is just as vast as that which is outside of us.

28. Here it is, in a nutshell: The less full of myself I am, the more room there is for another, for others.

29. *We* is the new I. Easy to remember, harder to assimilate and make our own, yet not impossible. Join the we-volution!

30. Remember that our karma is not determined by what happens to us, but by what we do *with* what happens.

31. Things are not what they seem; nor are they otherwise.

32. Pain is inevitable; suffering is optional.

33. The world awaits; let's light it up.

The Fifty-Nine Lojong Aphorisms

Mind/Heart Transformation
Translated by Lama Surya Das

The Seven-Point Training in the Awakening Mind (Bodhichitta)
as taught by Atisha Dipankara in Tibet, eleventh-century C.E.

Part I: Foundational Practice
The Basis for Training in the Awakening Mind

First train in the foundations of the path, the four Mind-Changers:

- Cherishing the precious opportunity of healthy and free human life
- Mortality and impermanence
- The vicious cycle of karmic patterning and conditioning
- The suffering struggle of delusion, self-importance, and ego-separatist clinging

Part II: Main Practice
Training in the Absolute Mind of Awakening
(the non-conceptual five points)

1. Sense all that appears as like a dream.
2. Examine the insubstantial nature of unborn awareness.

3. Let even the thought of emptiness (*sunyata*, as antidote to reification) release itself.

4. Rest in the natural state, the ground of all, the essence of being.

5. In post-meditation, be like a wizard playing with magical illusions.

Training in the Relative Mind of Awakening (conceptual five points)

6. Train in giving and taking alternately (sending and receiving).

7. Breathe out the giving; breathe in the taking. Ride the breath. (This is Tonglen.)

8. Three objects, three poisons, three sources of virtue.

9. Use reminders to make everything you do into practice, train your heart/mind, and refine your attitude.

10. Send goodness and assume/receive difficulties gradually, starting with your own.

Part III: Converting Difficulties into the Path of Awakening

11. Since unwholesome thoughts and harmful actions are everywhere, integrate them into the path of transformation leading to enlightenment.

Relative Practice

12. Drive all blames into one(self).

13. Be grateful to all; cultivate appreciation, respect, and cherishment.

Absolute Practice

14. Emptiness is the best protection: recognize all this confusion as the four-fold Buddha-being (*kayas*).
15. The best way is to maintain four practices:
    - Accumulation of merit and making generous offerings
    - Purification of negativities
    - Offering to worldly spirits and allies
    - Offering to Dharma protectors, guardians, benefactors, and dakinis
16. Join whatever you meet with awareness practice, so even the unexpected becomes the path.

Part IV: Essentializing the Practice for an Entire Lifetime

17. The essentialized heart teaching is to train in five powers:
    - The power of resolve and utmost determination
    - The power of familiarization and re-habituation
    - The power of virtuous cultivation
    - The power of utterly disowning the cause of suffering—negative seeds and karmic imprints
    - The power of prayer, dedication, and elevated aspiration
18. Those five powers, with related key practices (*phowa*), are the Bodhisattva's way to release the mind at death and recognize the Clear Light of reality.

Part V: Measures of Proficiency in Mind-Heart Training

19. Everything unites in one purpose; all Dharmas agree on the point of lessening self-absorption and egotism.

20. So, of the two witnesses, hold to the principal one—your conscience, your authentic self.

21. Only a joyful, open mind and attitude, always sustaining you (or, always maintain a joyous open mind).

22. If you can practice even when distracted, you are well trained. Use difficulties to help you progress.

Part VI: Commitments of Mind-Heart Training

23. Always avoid inconsistency, impatience, pretentiousness, and partiality.

24. Change and refine your attitude, but remain natural and authentic.

25. Don't speak of others' faults or push their buttons.

26. Don't judge others.

27. Purify your strongest obscuring delusion first; strive to overcome your strongest obstacles.

28. Give up all hopes for results.

29. Give up poisonous words and actions.

30. Don't be rigid; why hold grudges, resentments, or indulge in obsessive thoughts.

31. Don't meet insult with abuse; don't malign others, including your critics.

32. Don't wait in ambush or take advantage.

33. Don't strike where it hurts most, humiliate others, or bring things to a painful point.

34. Don't pass the buck; don't transfer the ox's load to a cow. Take responsibility for yourself.

35. Don't be a spiritual competitor.

36. Don't reduce positive deeds and spiritual practice to a mere self-serving device.

37. Don't make the Dharma into an evil or fodder for pride; don't make gods into demons.

38. Don't seek happiness by rejoicing in others' difficulties or failures.

Part VII: Guidelines for Mind-Heart Training

39. All activities should be done with altruistic intention.

40. Overcome all misfortunes in one way (with one intention).

41. First thing in the morning, last thing at night, do something positive and helpful.

42. Whether high or low, win or lose, strive to be steadfast, patient, resilient, and content.

43. Protect both behavior and attitude, even at the risk of your life.

44. Train yourself in the three difficulties and remember the antidotes; overcome the inner afflictions; eradicate the continuum of the kleshas (obscuring defilements).

45. Cleave close to three essentials: your teachers, their instruction, and the requisites for practice: the enlightened Buddha, liberating Dharma, and supportive Sangha.

46. Cultivate three things that must not weaken: reverence, enthusiasm for the Dharma, and commitment to right action, correct conduct, and Bodhichitta attitude.

47. Keep body, speech, and mind inseparable from goodness and virtuous activity.

48. Take everything into practice, without discrimination. It is critical to train in all areas of life, extensively, thoroughly, and deeply.

49. Always meditate on those closely connected to you, especially whatever provokes resentment or irritation.

50. Don't depend on circumstances or be easily swayed from your convictions.

51. This time do what matters; put others first, practice Dharma on all levels, develop genuine compassion and selfless altruism.

52. Don't confuse the worldly for the spiritual, or misinterpret signs and feedback.

53. Don't be erratic, don't hesitate or vacillate; practice continuously.

54. Train decisively and wholeheartedly, without holding back.

55. Find freedom through candid inward investigation and analytical outward examination.

56. Don't make a big deal out of your practice, and don't wallow in self-pity.

57. Don't be reactive, jealous, hypersensitive, or ill-tempered.

58. Don't be unstable, fickle, or frivolous.

59. Don't expect gratitude or applause for virtuous deeds, spiritual practice, or good character; don't show off.

Notes

Introduction

1. Jelaluddin Rumi, *Rumi: Fragments, Ecstasies*, trans. Daniel Liebert (New Lebanon, NY: Omega Publications, 1999).

Chapter 2

1. George Plimpton, *When We Were Kings*, DVD, interview in film, directed by Leon Gast (Los Angeles, CA: PolyGram Filmed Entertainment/Gramercy Pictures, 1997).
2. Phillip Kapleau, *Three Pillars of Zen* (New York: Anchor Books, 2000).
3. Carol Clark, "Compassion Meditation May Boost Neural Basis of Empathy," *eScience Commons* (blog), October 1, 2012, esciencecommons.blogspot.com/2012/10/the-idea-behind-compassion-based.html.
4. Christopher Bergland, "Mindfulness Training and the Compassionate Brain," *The Athlete's Way* (blog), *Psychology Today*, December 18, 2012, psychologytoday.com/blog/the-athletes-way/201212/mindfulness-training-and-the-compassionate-brain.
5. David DiSalvo, "Study: To the Human Brain, Me Is We," *Forbes*, August 22, 2013, forbes.com/sites/daviddisalvo/2013/08/22/study-to-the-human-brain-me-is-we/.
6. Ibid.

7. Carolyn Atkinson, *A Light in the Mind: Living Your Life Just as It Is* (Santa Cruz, CA: Everyday Dharma Zen Center, 2010).

8. Mary Catherine Bateson, *With a Daughter's Eye: A Memoir of Margaret Mead and Gregory Bateson* (New York: HarperCollins, 1994).

Chapter 3

1. Saad Shaikh and James Leonard-Amodeo, "The Deviating Eyes of Michelangelo's David," *Journal of the Royal Society of Medicine* 98, no. 2 (February 2005): 75–76, ncbi.nlm.nih.gov/pmc/articles/PMC1079389/.

2. *Ram Dass, Fierce Grace*, DVD, directed by Mickey Lemle (New York: Zeitgeist Films, 2001).

3. Gyalwang Drukpa, "Blessings Like Honey," interview by Lama Surya Das, May 3, 2011, surya.org/blessings-like-honey/.

4. Chögyam Trungpa, *Meditation in Action* (Boston: Shambhala Publications, 2010).

5. Frances H. Cook, *Hua-yen Buddhism: The Jewel Net of Indra* (University Park, PA: Pennsylvania State University Press, 2010).

Chapter 4

1. Georg Feuerstein, *Tantra: The Path of Ecstasy* (Boston: Shambhala Publications, 1998).

2. Chuang Tzu, *Wandering on the Way: Early Taoist Tales and Parables of Chuang Tzu*, trans. Victor H. Mair (Honolulu: University of Hawaii Press, 1998).

3. David Steindl-Rast, *Gratefulness, the Heart of Prayer: An Approach to Life in Fullness* (Mahwah, NJ: Paulist Press, 1984).

Chapter 5

1. Daisetz T. Suzuki, *The Awakening of Zen* (Boston: Shambhala Publications, 2005).

2. Hillary Mayell, "Genghis Khan a Prolific Lover, DNA Data Implies," *National Geographic News*, February 14, 2003, news.nationalgeographic.com/news/2003/02/0214_030214_genghis.html.

3. Richard Colwell, ed., *Handbook of Research on Music Teaching and Learning: A Project of the Music Educators National Conference* (New York: Schirmer Books, 1992).

4. "Finding Social and Global Coherence," *Institute of HeartMath Newsletter,* Summer 2012, heartmath.org/templates/ihm/e-newsletter/publication/2012/summer/social-and-global-coherence.php.

5. Paul Tough, *How Children Succeed: Grit, Curiosity, and the Hidden Power of Character* (New York: Houghton Mifflin Harcourt, 2012).

6. Nicholas D. Kristof, "A Poverty Solution that Starts with a Hug," *New York Times*, January 8, 2012, SR11, nytimes.com/2012/01/08/opinion/sunday/kristof-a-poverty-solution-that-starts-with-a-hug.html.

7. Rebecca Kessler, "Hugs Follow a 3-Second Rule," *Science*, American Association for the Advancement of Science, January 28, 2011, news.sciencemag.org/social-sciences/2011/01/hugs-follow-3-second-rule.

8. Claire Bates, "How Hugging Can Lower Your Blood Pressure and Improve Your Memory," *Daily Mail*, January 22, 2013, dailymail.co.uk/health/article-2266373/Hugging-lower-blood-pressure-boost-memory.html.

9. Stephani Sutherland, "Ritual Science," *Spirituality & Health*, September-October 2012, spiritualityhealth.com/articles/ritual-science.

10. Barbara Oakley et al., eds., *Pathological Altruism* (New York: Oxford University Press, 2012).

Chapter 6

1. Emma Seppala and Maaheem Akhtar, "Compassion Behind Bars," *The Huffington Post*, September 11, 2012, huffingtonpost.com/project-compassion-stanford/prisoners-compassion_b_1865013.html.

2. Ibid.

3. Greg Boyle, "The Calling of Delight: Gangs, Service, and Kinship," interview by Krista Tippett, *On Being*, February 26, 2013, onbeing.org/program/father-greg-boyle-on-the-calling-of-delight/5053.

4. Eliza Ahmed et al., eds., *Shame Management through Reintegration*, Cambridge Criminology Series (Cambridge: Cambridge University Press, 2001).

5. "Research Shows How Emotional Similarity Reduces Stress," *News Medical*, January 29, 2014, news-medical.net/news/20140129/Research-shows-how-emotional-similarity-reduces-stress.aspx.

6. Katja U. Likowski et al., "Facial Mimicry and the Mirror Neuron System: Simultaneous Acquisition of Facial Electromyography and Functional Magnetic Resonance Imaging," *Frontiers in Human Neuroscience* 6, no. 1 (July 2012), connection.ebscohost.com/c/articles/88959107/facial-mimicry-mirror-neuron-system-simultaneous-acquisition-facial-electromyography-functional-magnetic-resonance-imaging.

7. Bhadantācariya Buddhaghosa, *Visuddhimagga (The Path Of Purification): The Classic Manual of Buddhist Doctrine and Meditation*, trans. Bhikkhu Ñāṇamoli (Sri Lanka: Buddhist Publication Society, 2011), sites.google.com/site/chewdhamma/PathofPurification2011.PDF.

8. The Dalai Lama, Tenzin Gyatso, *The Dalai Lama at Harvard: Lectures on the Buddhist Path to Peace*, trans. and ed. Jeffrey Hopkins (Ithaca, NY: Snow Lion Publications, 1988).

Chapter 7

1. Jamgon Kongtrul, *The Great Path of Awakening: The Classic Guide to Lojong, a Tibetan Buddhist Practice for Cultivating the Heart of Compassion*, trans. Ken McLeod (Boston: Shambhala Publications, 2005).
2. Thich Nhat Hanh, *Moments of Mindfulness: Daily Inspiration* (Berkeley, CA: Parallax Press, 2013).
3. Gyalwang Drukpa, "Celebrate Equality in a Practical Way," May 30, 2014, drukpa.org/index.php/en/news-updates/news-in-2014/352-celebrate-equality-in-a-practical-way.
4. Helen Keller, *Optimism* (Boston: The Merrymount Press, 1903).
5. Gavin Harrison, *In the Lap of the Buddha* (Boston: Shambhala Publications, 1994).
6. Kristin Neff, "Self-Compassion: An Alternative Conceptualization of a Healthy Attitude Toward Oneself," *Self and Identity* 2 (2003): 85–101.
7. Elisabeth Kübler-Ross, *On Death and Dying: What the Dying Have to Teach Doctors, Nurses, Clergy, and Their Own Families* (New York: Simon & Schuster, 1969).
8. Abraham Lincoln, "Address before the Wisconsin State Agricultural Society," September 30, 1859, in *Abraham Lincoln: Speeches and Writings (1859–1865)* (New York: Digireads.com Publishing, 2014), books.google.com/books?id=RMygAwAAQBAJ&printsec=frontcover&source=gbs_ge_summary_r&cad=0-v=onepage&q&f=false.
9. Tara Brach, interview in Sounds True catalog no. 1, 2001.

Chapter 8

1. Tulku Urgyen Rinpoche, *Repeating the Words of the Buddha* (Hong Kong: Rangjung Yeshe Publications, 2006).
2. Graham M. Schweig, *Bhagavad Gita: The Beloved Lord's Secret Love Song* (New York: HarperOne, 2007).
3. Kunkhyen Longchen Rabjampa, "Now That I Come to Die," trans. Herbert V. Guenther, in *Lineage of Diamond*

Light: Crystal Mirror Series, vol. 5 (Dharma Publishing, 1977), reworked and edited in undumbara.wordpress. com/2009/05/29/now-that-i-come-to-die-longchenpa/.

4. Ira Byock, "Contemplating Mortality," interview by Krista Tippett, *On Being,* November 7, 2013, onbeing.org/program/transcript/4655.

5. Graham Coleman and Thupten Jinpa, eds., *The Tibetan Book of the Dead,* trans. Gyurme Dorje (New York: Viking Books, 2006).

6. Eben Alexander, "Proof of Heaven: A Doctor's Experience with the Afterlife," *Newsweek,* October 8, 2012, newsweek.com/proof-heaven-doctors-experience-afterlife-65327.

7. Ralph Waldo Emerson, *Nature* (Boston and Cambridge: James Munroe and Company, 1849).

8. Tim O'Brien, *The Things They Carried* (New York: Penguin, 1991).

9. Lama Surya Das, *Awakening the Buddhist Heart* (New York: Broadway Books, 2000).

10. John Muir, *The Wilderness World of John Muir,* ed. Edwin Way Teale (New York: First Mariner Books, 2001).

Chapter 9

1. Thich Nhat Hanh, "The Next Buddha May Be a Sangha," *Inquiring Mind* 10, no. 2 (Spring 1994), ibiblio.org/pub/academic/religious_studies/Buddhism/DEFA/Journals/Inquiring_Mind/im_v10n2.nws.

2. Christopher Titmuss, *Spirit of Change: Voices of Hope for a Better World* (London: Hunter House, 1993).

3. Claude Anshin Thomas, *At Hell's Gate: A Soldier's Journey from War to Peace* (Boston: Shambhala Publications, 2004).

4. Joseph Campbell, Bill Moyers, *The Power of Myth* (New York: Knopf, 2011).

5. Warren G. Bennis, *On Becoming a Leader* (Reading, MA: Addison-Wesley, 1989).

6. Václav Havel, "Peace: The View From Prague," *New York Review of Books* 32, no. 18 (November 21, 1985).

Chapter 10

1. Henry David Thoreau, *Walking* (Rockville, MD: Arc Manor, 2007).

2. Taina Repo, "Taking the Well-Being Trail to France," University of Tampere, Finland, newsletter, April 10, 2013, uta. fi/english/news/research/item.html?id=88286.

3. Barbara Oakley, *A Mind for Numbers: How to Excel at Math and Science (Even If You Flunked Algebra)* (New York: Jeremy P. Tarcher, 2014).

4. Gretchen Reynolds, "Easing Brain Fatigue with a Walk in the Park," *New York Times*, March 27, 2013, D5.

5. Lucien Stryk, ed., *World of the Buddha: An Introduction to Buddhist Literature* (New York: Grove Press, 1994).

6. Shinkichi Takahashi, *Triumph of the Sparrow: Zen Poems of Shinkichi Takahashi*, trans. Lucien Stryk (New York: Grove Press, 1986).

7. The Dalai Lama, Tenzin Gyatso, *The Essence of the Heart Sutra* (Somerville, MA: Wisdom Publications, 2005).

8. Rollin McCraty, *The Energetic Heart: Bioelectromagnetic Interactions Within and Between People* (Boulder Creek, CA: Institute of HeartMath, 2003).

9. Andrew Jacobs, "In Scarred Chinese Tibetan City, Devotion to Sanctity of Life," *New York Times*, July 26, 2014, A4, nytimes. com/2014/07/26/world/asia/in-scarred-chinese-tibetan-city-of-yushu-devotion-to-sanctity-of-life-even-a-tiny-river-shrimp. html?_r=2&gwh=4C10F30EF4577B890C0A47608355C5C5 &gwt=pay&assetType=nyt_now.

10. Chatral Rinpoche, "The Benefits of Saving Lives," trans. Adam Pearcey (Rigpa Translations, 2005), lotsawahouse.org/ tibetan-masters/chatral-rinpoche/saving-lives.

11. Angela Winter, "The One You're With: Barbara Fredrickson On Why We Should Rethink Love," *The Sun,* July 2014, thesunmagazine.org/issues/463/the_one_youre_with.

12. Lucien F. Cosijns, *Dialogue among the Faith Communities* (Lanham, MD: Hamilton Books, 2008).

13. Mahendranath Gupta ("M"), *The Gospel of Sri Ramakrishna*, trans. Swami Nikhilananda (New York: Ramakrishna-Vivekananda Center, 1942). Reproduced from the webpage of Ramakrishna Math and Ramakrishna Mission, belurmath.org/gospel/index.htm.

14. Karen Ehrhardt-Martinez, "People-Centered Climate Solutions: Insights from the Climate, Mind and Behavior Program," *Garrison Institute Newsletter,* Spring 2012, garrisoninstitute.org/people-centered-climate-solutions.

15. Ibid.

16. Lama Surya Das, translation of part of a longer extemporaneous song.

Acknowledgments

I wish to heartily thank Alice Peck, Susan Lee Cohen, Janet Nima Taylor, Dzogchen Center, and my Dharma friends at Sounds True for all their help and assistance in bringing this book to fruition, as well as for continuing to lobby for enlightenment. It takes a village.

About the Author

Lama Surya Das is one of the foremost Western Buddhist meditation teachers and scholars, one of the main interpreters of Tibetan Buddhism in the West, and a leading spokesperson for the emerging American Buddhism and contemporary spirituality. He was the first person to lead Dzogchen meditation retreats in America, the practice renowned as "the innate natural great perfection." The Dalai Lama affectionately calls him "The Western Lama."

Lama Surya has spent forty-five years studying Zen, vipassana, yoga, and Tibetan Buddhism with the great masters of Asia, including the Dalai Lama's own teachers, and has twice completed the traditional three-year meditation cloistered retreat at his teacher's Tibetan monastery. He is an authorized lama and lineage holder in the Nyingmapa School of Tibetan Buddhism, and a disciple of the leading grand lamas of that tradition. He is the founder of the Dzogchen Center in Cambridge, Massachusetts, and its branch centers. Over the years, Lama Surya has brought many Tibetan lamas to America to teach and start centers and retreats. As founder of the Western Buddhist Teachers Network with the Dalai Lama in 1993, he regularly helps organize its international Buddhist Teachers Conferences. He is also active in interfaith dialogue and charitable projects in the Third World. In recent years, Lama Surya has turned his efforts and focus toward youth and contemplative education initiatives, what he calls "true higher education and wisdom-for-life training."

He is a prolific author, translator, poet, chant master, and spiritual activist. His popular books, translated into fourteen languages, include *Awakening the Buddha Within: Tibetan Wisdom for the Western World* as well as more than a dozen other books. He has written for numerous publications, including *Tricycle* magazine, Beliefnet, and *The Huffington Post*.

For Lama Surya's teaching schedule visit: surya.org. He can also be found on Facebook and Twitter.

About Dzogchen Center

Awakening the Buddha Within

Lama Surya Das founded Dzogchen Center in 1991 to further the transmission of authentic Buddhist contemplative practices and ethical values to Western audiences and the transformation of these teachings into effective forms that help to alleviate suffering and create a civilization based on wisdom, justice, and compassion.

The Dzogchen Center website, Dzogchen.org, is a regularly updated resource for Dzogchen Center information, retreat schedules, local meditation groups, podcasts and words of wisdom, and online meditation retreat registration.

DZOGCHEN CENTER
PO Box 400734
Cambridge, MA
Phone: 781-316-0113
Email: Surya@Surya.org

About Sounds True

Sounds True is a multimedia publisher whose mission is to inspire and support personal transformation and spiritual awakening. Founded in 1985 and located in Boulder, Colorado, we work with many of the leading spiritual teachers, thinkers, healers, and visionary artists of our time. We strive with every title to preserve the essential "living wisdom" of the author or artist. It is our goal to create products that not only provide information to a reader or listener, but that also embody the quality of a wisdom transmission.

For those seeking genuine transformation, Sounds True is your trusted partner. At SoundsTrue.com you will find a wealth of free resources to support your journey, including exclusive weekly audio interviews, free downloads, interactive learning tools, and other special savings on all our titles.

To learn more, please visit SoundsTrue.com/freegifts or call us toll-free at 800-333-9185.